Constructions of Intersubjectivity

Constructions of Intersubjectivity

Discourse, Syntax, and Cognition

ARIE VERHAGEN

OXFORD
UNIVERSITY PRESS

Great Clarendon Street, Oxford OX2 6DP

Oxford University Press is a department of the University of Oxford.
If furthers the University's objective of excellence in research, scholarship,
and education by publishing worldwide in

Oxford New York

Auckland Cape Town Dar es Salaam Hong Kong Karachi
Kuala Lumpur Madrid Melbourne Mexico City Nairobi
New Delhi Shanghai Taipei Toronto

With offices in

Argentina Austria Brazil Chile Czech Republic France Greece
Guatemala Hungary Italy Japan Poland Portugal Singapore
South Korea Switzerland Thailand Turkey Ukraine Vietnam

Oxford is a registered trade mark of Oxford University Press
in the UK and in certain other countries

Published in the United States
by Oxford University Press Inc., New York

© Arie Verhagen 2005

The moral rights of the author have been asserted
Database right Oxford University Press (maker)

First published 2005
First published in paperback 2007

All rights reserved. No part of this publication may be reproduced,
stored in a retrieval system, or transmitted, in any form or by any means,
without the prior permission in writing of Oxford University Press,
or as expressly permitted by law, or under terms agreed with the appropriate
reprographics rights organization. Enquiries concerning reproduction
outside the scope of the above should be sent to the Rights Department,
Oxford University Press, at the address above

You must not circulate this book in any other binding or cover
and you must impose the same condition on any acquirer

British Library Cataloguing in Publication Data

Data available

Library of Congress Cataloging-in-Publication Data

Verhagen, Arie.
  Constructions of intersubjectivity : discourse, syntax, and cognition / Arie Verhagen.
    p. cm.
  Includes bibliographical references and indexes.
  ISBN 0-19-927384-7 (alk. paper)
  1. Grammar, Comparative and general. 2. Semantics. 3. Pragmatics. I. Title.
  P151.V47 2005
  415–dc22
                                                                                 2004030591

Typeset by SPI Publisher Services, Pondicherry, India
Printed in Great Britain on acid-free paper by
Ashford Colour Press, UK

ISBN 978-0-19-927384-3 (Hbk.)
     978-0-19-922670-2 (Pbk.)

Contents

Acknowledgments	ix
Figures	xiii
Tables	xv

1 Intersubjectivity—mutual management of cognitive states	1
1.1 Small grammatical puzzles	1
1.2 Big theoretical issues	2
1.2.1 A human specialization	2
1.2.2 Common ground and the construal configuration	4
1.2.3 Human and animal communication, and the theory of argumentativity	8
Argumentation and information	9
Connected discourse	12
1.3 Variation in the balance between objectivity and intersubjectivity	16
1.3.1 Introduction	16
1.3.2 An initial illustration: a range of promises	19
Argumentation and auxiliary syntax	23
1.4 Prospects	24
1.4.1 The usage-based approach and empirical data	24
1.4.2 Preview	26
2 Negation and virtual argumentation	28
2.1 Introduction	28
2.2 Negation and perspectives	29
2.2.1 Mental spaces	29
2.2.2 Sentential vs. morphological negation	32
2.3 Conventional linguistic constraints on intersubjective coordination	35
2.3.1 The *let alone* construction: some unsolved problems	35
Fillmore, Kay, and O'Connor (1988)	35
Problem: non-semantic negative polarity?	38
Problem: pragmatic point in first conjunct?	39
Problem: what did the meaning of *let alone* develop from?	39

	2.3.2 Barely is not almost, let alone pretty much completely	41
	Argumentative orientation as linguistic meaning	41
	Argumentative direction and argumentative strength	44
	Barely and *almost* as argumentative operators	45
	Argumentative orientation constraining coreference	50
	2.3.3 The negation system for intersubjective coordination	55
	2.3.4 *Let alone* and argumentation	60
	Solution: making syntactic and semantic negative polarity coincide	60
	Solution: aligning semantics and pragmatics	61
	Solution: understanding the historical development of *let alone*	66
2.4	'Double' negation revisited: why *not impossible* does not equal *possible*	70
2.5	Conclusion	76
3	Finite complements—putting conceptualizers on stage	78
3.1	Introduction: two ways of looking at complements	78
3.2	Problems with clauses as constituents	81
	3.2.1 Introduction	81
	3.2.2 Some issues of grammatical analysis	83
	Direct object or oblique object?	83
	Subject or predicate?	87
	3.2.3 Some issues of discourse analysis and language acquisition	90
	Development	92
3.3	Use and structure of complementation constructions	94
	3.3.1 The special role of complementation in discourse structure	94
	Recursion	98
	3.3.2 A template and its meaning	100
	Productivity	102
	Type and token frequency	102
	'Exceptions' are regular	104
	3.3.3 Third-person conceptualizers and degrees of directness in intersubjective coordination	104
	Complementation and argumentativity	105
	Performativity	107
	Developing a network of complementation constructions	110

	3.3.4 Manipulating the relation between Ground and onstage conceptualizers	113
	3.3.5 *Wh*-extraction 'in the wild'	119
	Clausal constituents again	119
	The specific nature of complementation questions in the construal configuration	120
	Type and token frequencies	124
	Frequency and subjectivity	129
	3.3.6 Impersonal intersubjectivity and the irrelevance of syntactic relations	131
	Impersonal complementation constructions—extensions from the prototype	132
	Type and token frequencies, and an extended network	136
	Against syntactic relations in complementation	137
	3.3.7 Perspectival and causal connections	141
	3.3.8 Clauses as discourse segments revisited	149
	Complementation and topic continuity	151
3.4	Conclusion	154
4 Discourse connections—managing inferences across perspectives		156
4.1	Introduction	156
4.2	Concession	162
	4.2.1 Two paradoxes	162
	Duality	162
	Domain theory	164
	4.2.2 Background assumptions and mental spaces	167
	4.2.3 The double link between epistemic concessives and epistemic causals	174
	Epistemic causality and perspectives: what concessions and arguments have in common	175
	Epistemic inferences in the background	180
	Recursion again	182
	4.2.4 Concessivity and negated causality	184
	Negation of causality and the source of scope-phenomena	184
	Negation of concession produces contradiction	187
4.3	Arguing, reasoning, and construing causes	190
	4.3.1 Causal connectives imposing constraints on perspectives	190
	Dutch *want* and *omdat* (and *aangezien*)	191
	4.3.2 Causal connectives and the structure of the construal configuration	197
	Inferential and non-inferential causal relations	202

4.4 Conclusion	208
5 Concluding Remarks	210
5.1 Not everything is intersubjectivity (though intersubjectivity is widespread)	210
5.2 Grammar provides systematic instruments for mutual management—of a special kind	212
5.2.1 Looking ahead	212
5.2.2 Looking back	214
Further Reading	217
References	220
Index	231

Acknowledgments

Almost ten years ago it occurred to me that the work I was doing on subjectivity had something in common with that on the *let alone* construction, and that the similarity might be sufficiently important and interesting to turn it into a book. In the years that followed I often wondered if it would ever materialize. But then I had the opportunity, somewhat unexpectedly, to spend the academic year 2002–3 at the Netherlands Institute for Advanced Study in the Humanities and Social Sciences, and the idea started to look like a goal that might, in the end, actually be realized. For this, I am very grateful to NIAS and its directorate.

In Wassenaar, the management and staff of NIAS provided an excellent environment, in all possible respects. Wouter Hugenholtz and Jos Hooghuis helped considerably, together with Sander Bos from the Leiden Faculty of Arts and Humanities, to make it possible to exchange Leiden University for the Wassenaar villa at such short notice. Petry Kievit-Tyson and Kathy van Vliet-Leigh provided very valuable editorial support, especially in finding ways to represent Dutch text fragments in idiomatic English. Especial thanks are due to Wim Blockmans for assisting in paving the way to NIAS for me, even before he became Rector of the Institute. From the wonderful group of fellows in my NIAS year I particularly want to thank Rudy Andeweg, Jana Chamonikolasová, Ronald Giere, Jay Ginn, Koenraad Kuiper, Mary Lindemann, Esther-Mirjam Sent, Jacques Thomassen, and Jeroen van de Weijer for discussions in areas of mutual interest, and for making me explain and clarify. Ron helped to boost the feeling that what I had to say might really have some relevance beyond linguistics *sensu stricto*, and Kon put his finger on numerous unnecessary hedges and parenthetical clauses in the first drafts of Chapters 2 and 3—if there are still too many instances of *actually*, it is not his fault!

I thank Mira Ariel, Ronny Boogaart, Peter Harder, Michael Israel, Ted Sanders, and Joost Schilperoord for commenting, long ago, on pieces of work that were to become part of this book, and for stimulating me to go on. Ted had a significant influence by helping me to get a clearer picture of how to relate cognitive analyses of clause structure and of discourse. This book is not primarily about our common fascination with causation, but I trust he will nevertheless recognize a number of topics and ideas that we discussed when they were still in an embryonic stage. Joost provided data and insights from his work on language production that I remember as turning points in the development of the theory of complementation expounded in Chapter 3.

Acknowledgments

I am very grateful for the interest in my work shown over the years and the feedback by Angeliki Athanasiadou, Willem Botha, Melissa Bowerman, Jack DuBois, Ad Foolen, Cliff Goddard, Adele Goldberg, Matthias Hüning, Theo Janssen, Rudi Keller, Suzanne Kemmer, Bob Kirsner, Eliza Kitis, Frits Kortlandt, Ron Langacker, June Luchjenbroers, Chris Sinha, Dan Slobin, Sandy Thompson, Mike Tomasello, and Elizabeth Traugott. It has been inspirational support, and an incentive to finish the work. I thank Adele, Dan, and Mike for strengthening this incentive by adding enquiries about the progress of the project over the last two years. At the International Cognitive Linguistics Conference in Logroño, Spain, in 2003, Ron made me rethink some features of the way in which I connected grammatical and discourse-structural aspects of complementation constructions; I flatter myself with the thought that the baby and the bathwater have now been properly separated.

Very inspiring was the enthusiasm of graduate students in Amsterdam, Utrecht, Leiden, and elsewhere—Christine van Baalen, Louise Cornelis, Bert Cornillie, Jacqueline Evers-Vermeul, Márti Faragó, Mike Huiskes, Gerhard van Huyssteen, Frank Landsbergen, Judith Loewenthal, Niels van der Mast, Justine Pardoen, Mirna Pit, Ninke Stukker, Rada Trnavac—and of the participants in classes at the 1998 Australian Linguistic Institute in Brisbane, the 2000 Winter School of the Dutch Graduate School of Linguistics (LOT) in Leiden, the 2000 Postgraduate Conference in Linguistics in Pavía, Italy, and a number of classes in the Advanced Masters Programme in Leiden. Substantial parts of the material covered in this book were presented on these occasions, and they have undergone major and minor changes because of them. I have to apologize to all of you that it took longer to fulfill the promise that it would all appear in print than I anticipated...

However, a definite advantage of the length of the project has been that it allowed me to explore the conceptual connection between an argumentative, rhetorical approach to linguistic meaning and grammatical knowledge on the one hand, and the nature of communication as conceived in present-day approaches to animal behaviour on the other. It was Carel ten Cate who directed me to the ethological literature discussed in Chapter 1, after I had explained to him what the basic idea of my 'NIAS project' was. I hope the chapter testifies to the astonishing adequacy of this response.

I want to thank the leadership of the cognitive-linguistic community, as well as Anke Beck from Mouton de Gruyter, for their moral support during a brief period of difficulties in the last few years, when the prospect of finishing this project seemed more unlikely than ever. I certainly will never forget the long talk I had with George Lakoff, while sailing on the Pacific Ocean near

Santa Barbara in 2001, about theoretical linguistics, its recent past and our expectations for the future—and not only because we got to see flying fish.

Working with Oxford University Press has been a real pleasure. It was a very special experience, having submitted the first draft of some chapters, to engage in 'long-distance' but in-depth discussions on both foundations and details of the approach. I learned a lot, and the comments have contributed greatly to both the structure and the explicitness of the presentation. I especially thank the linguistics editor, John Davey, and Jane Wheare for their help in producing this result. I will not claim that it will be easy reading throughout—readers may be required to engage in a 'Gestalt switch' on more than one occasion—but without their help the book would have been considerably less transparent (or more opaque—though these expressions are not equivalent: see Chapter 1).

A special word of thanks also for Ariane van Santen, long-time tutor in oecumenical linguistic attitudes as well as in word-based grammar, and a colleague and friend for a number of years now. She also played a valuable role in creating the conditions that allowed me to spend the year at NIAS, and to dot the i's in the year after.

Personal thanks are also due to Ewold and Lennart (I am still not sure how to feel about the fact that some of their earliest memories involve linguistics), but, in the end, my deepest gratitude goes to Anneke.

Figures

1.1	The viewing arrangement	5
1.2	The construal configuration and its basic elements	7
1.3	Construal configuration in maximally 'objective' expressions	17
1.4	Construal configuration in maximally 'subjective' expressions	18
2.1	Two mental spaces evoked by sentential negation	30
2.2	'On the contrary' relates to evoked mental space	32
2.3	*Barely/almost half full*	48
2.4	Conventional function of 'argumentative operators' located in dimension of intersubjective coordination	50
2.5	Negation and *barely* share orientation for intersubjective coordination	57
3.1	Construal configuration for non-perspectivized utterance	106
3.2	Construal configuration for first-person perspective	106
3.3	Construal configuration for third-person perspective	106
3.4	Partial network for 'object' complementation constructions in Dutch	111
3.5	Construal configuration for second-person perspective in questions	121
3.6	'*Wh*-extraction' in the complementation-construction network	127
3.7	Construal configuration for 'subject' (impersonal) complementation constructions	134
3.8	Partial general network for complementation constructions in Dutch	138
3.9	Two patterns of thematic cohesion	151
4.1	Construal configuration for connecting O-situations in discourse	158
4.2	Theoretical configuration for 'objective' connection between segments	159
4.3	Theoretical configuration for 'subjective' connection between segments	159
4.4	Mental-space configuration for *He failed his exams although he worked hard*	169
4.5	Mental-space configuration for *He did not pass his exams although he worked hard*	172
4.6	Mental-space configuration for *He passed his exams although he did not work hard*	172

4.7	Mental-space configuration in abductive reasoning (*He worked hard, because he passed his exams*)	176
4.8	Mental-space configuration for epistemic concessivity (*He didn't work hard, although he passed his exams*)	182
4.9	Common mental-space configuration for negated causality and epistemic concessivity	184
4.10	Mental-space configuration for *The house is no less comfortable because it dispenses with air-conditioning*	185
4.11	Mental-space configuration for *The house is no less comfortable, although it dispenses with air-conditioning*	187
4.12	Mental-space configuration associated with Dutch *want*	192
4.13	Mental-space configuration associated with Dutch *dus*	200
4.14	Conventional function of concession and of argumentative causal connectives: includes operation on intersubjective coordination	202
4.15	Conventional function of (some) non-argumentative causal connectives: no constraints on structure at level S	203
4.16	Conventional function of *because* not specifically tied to one level	203
4.17	Conventional function of *daardoor* ('as a result') in dimension of object of conceptualization	207

Tables

2.1	Argumentative orientation and strength of α-*chance*	45
2.2	Argumentative orientation and strength of α-*passed*	46
3.1	CT-predicates used with 'object' complements in the first 2,000 sentences in the Eindhoven Corpus (Dutch newspaper fragments)	103
3.2	CT-predicates used with '*Wh*-extraction' in *de Volkskrant* (1995)	124
3.3	'Matrix' subjects used with '*Wh*-extraction' in *de Volkskrant* (1995)	124
3.4	Comparative frequencies of CT-verbs in '*Wh*-extraction'	125
3.5	Comparative frequencies of 'matrix' subjects in '*Wh*-extraction'	126
3.6	CT-predicates used with impersonal complementation sentences in the first 2,000 sentences in the Eindhoven Corpus (Dutch newspaper fragments)	137
3.7	Causal CT-predicates in the first 2,000 sentences in the Eindhoven Corpus (Dutch newspaper fragments)	141
3.8	From perspectival to causal-predicates	143
4.1	Correlation of morphological and sentential negation with *omdat* and *want* in Eindhoven Corpus (Dutch)	194
4.2	Correlation of morphological and sentential negation with *en* and *maar* in Eindhoven Corpus (Dutch)	194

1

Intersubjectivity—mutual management of cognitive states

1.1 Small grammatical puzzles

The issues addressed in this study may be assigned to a number of rather different levels of scientific inquiry. On the one hand, they involve some highly specific puzzles of semantic and grammatical analysis. Some of these are:

(i) The expressions *It is not impossible* and *It is possible* mutually entail one another. Yet they are not functionally equivalent in language use.
(ii) A sentence like *The danger is that depleted uranium is poisonous* does not look very complicated. Yet grammarians have not been able to agree, for more than a century now, whether the embedded clause (*that depleted uranium is poisonous*) is the subject or the predicate of the sentence.
(iii) Concessive conjunctions (*although*) look like the negative counterpart of causal ones (*because*). Yet negation of a causal relation can produce a concessive reading (*John is not the best candidate because he happens to have a Ph.D.* can mean that despite his Ph.D., John is not the best candidate), but negation of a concessive relation does not even seem to be possible (*John is not the best candidate although he happens to have a Ph.D.* can never mean that John's having a Ph.D. is a reason why he is not considered the best candidate).

Such observations give rise to the question 'Why?', the question of curiosity about causes and effects that drives any scientific investigation. In the course of this book I will propose answers to these 'Why' questions and a number of related ones.

On the other hand, I will argue that solving these puzzles involves some fundamental decisions on basic assumptions about human language and especially meaning. These decisions concern our conceptualization of relations between language and the world, and more importantly, between language and its users. So the specific and general goals of this work are intertwined: the fact that a particular *general* view makes it possible to solve a number of more and less classic *specific* grammatical problems constitutes evidence for the usefulness of this general view. In the remainder of this chapter I want to introduce and explain the general idea involved; the specific linguistic problems will be addressed in the chapters that follow.

1.2 Big theoretical issues

1.2.1 *A human specialization*

A major dimension in which cognition in humans differs from that in other animals (including other primates) is our ability to 'take another's perspective'. According to Tomasello (1999) this is the only crucial biologically determined factor distinguishing humans from other primates, in the cognitive realm.[1] Tomasello's identification of this factor also provides a succinct description of its essential content:

There is just one major difference, and that is the fact that human beings 'identify' with conspecifics more deeply than do other primates. This identification is not something mysterious, but simply the process by which the human child understands that other persons are beings like herself [...] and so she sometimes tries to understand things from their point of view. During early ontogeny [...] the child comes to experience herself as an intentional agent—that is, a being whose behavioral and attentional strategies are organized by goals—and so she automatically sees other beings with whom she identifies in these same terms. Later in ontogeny, the child comes to experience herself as a mental agent—that is, a being with thoughts and beliefs that may differ from those of other people as well as from reality—and so from that time on she will see conspecifics in these new terms. For purposes of exposition I refer to this process generally as 'understanding others as intentional (or mental) agents (like the self).' (ibid. 14–15.)

Thus Tomasello describes two stages in the developmental process. A human child understands others as beings like herself. First, the child comes to understand herself as an intentional agent, and so she automatically starts to see others as intentional agents as well. Later, she comes to understand herself as a mental agent (as having her own beliefs and thoughts that need not be generally shared or valid), and so she, again automatically, starts to see others as mental agents as well.

---

[1] In recent work Tomasello refines his position, emphasizing the need to stop thinking 'in terms of a monolithic "theory of mind" that species either do or do not have' (Tomasello et al. 2003*b*: 204) if there is to be progress in understanding the evolution and ontogeny of social cognition (see also Tomasello 2003*a*). So he is now explicitly endorsing a gradual view that is perhaps only implicit in the 1999 book (see the phrase 'more deeply' in the quotation above).

As a consequence humans are able to learn about the world 'through' others, and not only via their personal interaction with the environment (including conspecifics), so that human cognition as we now know it has, on this biological basis, a cultural origin. Tomasello's theoretical program consists of, among other things, a demonstration that other kinds of typically human cognitive abilities and products emerge from the exploitation of this one basic and distinctively human capacity to see others both as intentional and as mental agents like oneself. These abilities, traditions, and artifacts are not transmitted from one generation to another via genetic mechanisms of reproduction as such, but culturally.[2]

Human languages—whether they have some hard-wired structural features (as generative linguists tend to believe) or not—are very basic systems of conventions: all words (links of sound and meaning) are conventional, and at least a substantial part of patterns of usage is conventional as well. Conventions are mutually shared rules—your behaving in a particular way (driving on a specific side of the road, making a specific sound in order to produce a specific effect) is conventional because its motivation only consists in your expectation that others will do the same in similar circumstances, and for exactly the same reason, namely that they expect others to do so (see Lewis 1969; Keller 1998: 130–40). Therefore, knowledge of language is indeed mutually shared, and cannot be transmitted otherwise than by social learning.[3]

The basic conventional system of a human language in turn provides 'scaffolding' for the development of other cognitive abilities, greatly enhancing the possibilities for an individual to learn 'through' others (Tomasello). For example, evidence has been accumulating over the last few years that the

---

[2] There is considerable room for construing this notion 'cultural' more or less widely, as evidenced by Rendell and Whitehead (2001) and the accompanying commentaries, and by Byrne et al. (2004). The strategy advocated by Byrne et al. is not to cling to a desire for a binary distinction (animals either have culture—and then in all the richness of human culture—or they don't—, and then they have nothing that even remotely resembles human culture), but rather to decompose the notion 'culture' in relevant dimensions, some of which may to some degree also be found in other species (not necessarily jointly). To me, this seems the only sensible way to proceed, if we want to maintain the idea that human language and culture must ultimately be understandable as products of evolutionary processes of natural (and sexual) selection.

[3] At least to a very large extent (allowing for the possibility of some hard-wired features that are transmitted genetically). The emphasis in modern linguistics on syntax sometimes seems to make scholars forget that this is only one facet of human language, and not even the only special one, and that it is simply unavoidable for any theorist to assume that learning is at least a very large part of language acquisition (Hauser, Chomsky, and Fitch 2002; Tomasello and Abbot-Smith 2002; Pinker and Jackendoff, 2005). Theoretically, sounds, meanings, and links between them could also be hard-wired, of course, but such a communication system would have such different structural and functional properties from human languages as we know them, that I doubt we would still categorize it as one.

linguistic conventions of the culture in which a person develops can 'warp' an individual's conceptual space in as elementary a domain as that of spatial cognition (see Majid et al. 2004, and the refs. cited there). And in communities of autonomous adaptive agents (robots interacting with each other) the categories which the individual agents develop for handling the environment (colored objects) turn out to be much more dissimilar (despite the identity of the environment and their own 'bodies') when there is no shared lexicon than when there is (Steels 2003: 133–5).

Thus there is a strong connection between language and humans' ability to identify deeply with conspecifics and its potential benefits. However, in the view presented above, this link only consists in one being a kind of prerequisite for (full development of) the other. But if 'understanding others as like oneself' is fundamental for human life and human culture in general, then we should also expect that it has repercussions for the *content* that is systematically coded in linguistic symbols (words and constructions). That is, an important part of the *semantics* of basic linguistic units should specifically involve the cognitive handling of people's understanding of their own and other 'selves', precisely because that is what symbolic communication boils down to: coordination of the content of distinct minds (to be sure, for all kinds of different purposes). Put differently: if grammars encode best what speakers do most (Du Bois 1985: 363), and if coordinating cognitively with others is so basic a component of human practices, then we should expect to see it reflected in more than one area of grammar, including basic ones.

The purpose of this book is to provide this linguistic part of the story about humans' ability to engage in deep cognitive coordination with others. For a range of linguistic phenomena which are arguably quite basic (negation and negation-related constructions, complementation, discourse connectives) it can be demonstrated that connecting, differentiating, and 'tailoring' the contents of points of view with respect to each other (rather than organizing a connection to the world) is essential for understanding their semantics and, perhaps surprisingly, their syntax.

1.2.2 *Common ground and the construal configuration*

The ability to experience oneself and view others as mental agents underlies the concept of subjectivity. This has played a role in linguistic semantics since at least Benveniste (1958), and has been revived in the last two decades, in particular in work by Traugott (in semantic change) and by Langacker (in cognitive grammar). But 'subjectivity' is a complex concept. On the one hand, it has a dimension in which the conceptualization by a subject is distinguished from the 'object' of conceptualization; in this sense it is the counterpart of 'objectivity', and embodies the idea that one's thoughts and beliefs may differ from reality. On the other hand, we sometimes consider one point of view as possibly different from other ones (rather than as possibly different from the world); in that sense, the emphasis in 'subjectivity' lies on 'personal', 'not shared' (rather than on 'not objective').[4] The development of the notion of 'construal' in the work of Langacker and others has provided a framework in which both dimensions can be handled simultaneously in an integrated way.

Langacker (1987: 487–8) defines the *construal relationship* as follows: 'The relationship between a speaker (or hearer) and a situation that he conceptualizes and portrays, involving focal adjustments and imagery.' In this definition, the construal relation basically involves an individual (speaker *or* hearer) on the one hand, and a conceived situation on the other. Thus it corresponds closely to a 'viewing arrangement' (ibid. 139). Graphically, this can be represented as in Figure 1.1, where the vertical line corresponds to the construal relation.

This configuration, being two-dimensional, makes it possible to capture 'point-of-view' phenomena involving aspects of conceptualization that are not dictated by an object of conceptualization itself. One example is construing one element as foregrounded—'figure' in terms of the psychology of perception—and another as the 'ground'. Another is conceptualizing the position of elements, or the time of events, in terms of their relationship to

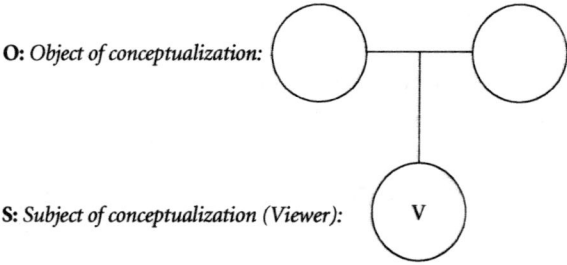

O: *Object of conceptualization:*

S: *Subject of conceptualization (Viewer):*

FIGURE 1.1. The viewing arrangement

---

[4] See Nuyts (2001a: 393–4) for discussion of these facets of the concept of subjectivity in a slightly different, but clearly related, context (different types of evidentiality). The way Nuyts, in the remainder of his paper and in Nuyts (2001b), uses the term 'intersubjectivity' is different from the way I will employ it in this book. Nuyts uses it to label a distinction *within* the dimension he calls '(Inter)-subjectivity'; namely, between evidential markers that indicate that the relevant evidence is accessible to the speaker only, or shared by a larger group. The former he calls subjective, and include, in his view, mental-state predicates such as *think*; the latter are called intersubjective, and include epistemic adjectives such as *probable*. For a somewhat different treatment of related distinctions in the present framework see Ch. 3, esp. Sect. 3.3.6.

the viewer (e.g. *here* vs. *there*, and past-tense marking). These are kinds of construal that impose structure on the object of conceptualization, represented at the horizontal level O, and/or establish a relation to the viewer (deixis, viewpoint), involving the vertical dimension. The theoretical significance of these phenomena has been recognized since the early days of structural linguistics, and they have been the object of several important studies since then (Bühler 1934; Jakobson 1957/71; Lyons 1982, to mention but a few). It has especially been the last years of the twentieth century, when the *process* of subjectification received more and more attention (Traugott 1989; Langacker 1990; Stein and Wright 1995; Traugott and Dasher 2002), that have witnessed the development of concepts which in principle make it possible to integrate different manifestations of subjectivity into a coherent theoretical framework.

In subsequent work Langacker identified the lower half of Figure 1.1 with what he calls the 'Ground'[5] (Langacker 1987: 126; 1990: 9); that is, the ensemble of the communicative event, its participants, and its immediate circumstances. Notice the mention of participants—plural—rather than a singular 'viewer'. Moreover, the configuration in Figure 1.1 provides opportunities for accommodating many cognitive abilities with respect to an object of conceptualization, but not for the special human capacity discussed above; namely, to take into account *other minds* (in relation to an object of conceptualization). In this perspective Langacker's original way of construing the construal relationship may be treated as a special case of the somewhat more complex configuration represented in Figure 1.2.[6]

The Ground of any linguistic usage event comprises two conceptualizers, the first performing the role of being responsible for the utterance, the second that of interpreting it in a particular way. In prototypical face-to-face conversations these roles are fulfilled by the speaker and the addressee, respectively, but the roles as such are given with anything that is taken as an instance of language use, even if no referents for the first and second role are known.[7]

---

[5] For clarity I will capitalize the word when it denotes this particular aspect of the construal configuration. Notice, for one thing, that 'Ground' in this sense is something completely different from the ground in a perceptual figure-ground construal.

[6] In practice many actual instances of construal configurations in the literature exhibit this structure, as in Langacker (1990), Van Hoek (2003).

[7] Especially for the case of concrete interpersonal discourse, this configuration resembles proposals by M. A. K. Halliday (1978, 1985), who distinguishes between three basic 'metafunctions' of language: ideational (cf. object of conceptualization), interpersonal (cf. coordinating subjects of conceptualization), and textual (concerned with the organization of discourse, e.g. given/new). In my view, the textual function comprises straightforward instantiations of the (vertical) construal relationship. Halliday also seems to want to restrict the interpersonal function to situations of concrete persons managing their actual social relationship. No doubt these are central to the use of language, and

O: *Object of conceptualization:*

S: *Subject of conceptualization (Ground):*

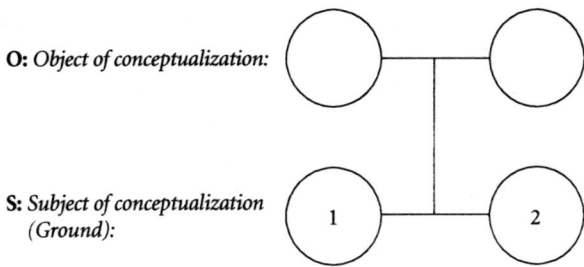

FIGURE 1.2. The construal configuration and its basic elements

These subjects of conceptualization engage in cognitive coordination by means of the utterance, with respect to some object of conceptualization. The Ground furthermore contains the knowledge that conceptualizers 1 and 2 mutually share, including models of each other and of the discourse situation. Thus, in this conception, the Ground is essentially 'common ground' (cf. Clark 1996; see Sinha 1999 for further general considerations motivating this construal of 'ground'). The point of a linguistic utterance, in broad terms, is that the first conceptualizer invites the second to jointly attend to an object of conceptualization in some specific way, and to update the common ground by doing so (this will be elaborated and modified in Section 1.2.3). The coordination relationship between the two conceptualizers is indicated by the lower horizontal line in Figure 1.2, the relation of joint attention between the conceptualizers and the object of conceptualization by the vertical line.

Even in the absence of an actual speaker, an addressee (for example, the reader of an ancient text) always takes a linguistic utterance as having been intentionally produced as an instrument of communication by another being with the same basic cognitive capacities as the addressee; otherwise it would not be justified to call the material being interpreted a 'linguistic utterance'.[8] Thus the addressee is always engaging in cognitive coordination with *some* subject of conceptualization 1, who is held responsible for the production of the utterance. Similarly, even in the absence of an actual addressee, a speaker (for example, one making a note in a personal diary) is committed to the assumption that her utterance is in principle interpretable by someone else

foundational in (at least) ontogenetic development. But since, in my view, all of *cognitive* coordination must be treated at level S as well, and also when there is no 'live' interaction (see also Sect. 1.2.3, on argumentativity), I prefer the presentation as given in the text. Still, that these proposals are in the same spirit should be obvious.

[8] This view may also be said to underlie Grice's construction (1957) of the notion of non-natural meaning ('meaning$_{NN}$'). A clear exposition of the concept of linguistic communication as influencing another person's cognition by displaying the intention to do so may be found in Keller (1998: 136 ff.).

sharing the knowledge of certain conventions. The idea that some utterance could *in principle* only be interpretable for a single individual makes the idea that it is an instance of language void. Thus the conceptual structure of Figure 1.2 is inherent in any linguistic usage event, even if not all of its features are formally marked in the utterance itself. As such, it provides a good framework for an integrated treatment of phenomena of perspectivization (see Verhagen, forthcoming).

1.2.3 *Human and animal communication, and the theory of argumentativity*

Recognizing the construal configuration as a general property of language use implements the view that language use is intimately tied to the fundamental human ability to coordinate cognitively with others. It has the additional advantage that it allows for a view of human linguistic communication as sharing basic properties with communication in other species, rather than as an evolutionary miracle. A few years ago a book on animal vocal communication appeared (Owings and Morton 1998) with the subtitle *A New Approach*. The authors state quite explicitly what they mean by this, as follows:

This book provides a discussion of animal vocal communication that avoids human-centered concepts and approaches, and instead links communication to fundamental biological processes. It offers a new conceptual framework [...] that allows for the integration of detailed proximate studies of communication with an understanding of evolutionary perspectives [...]. Animals use signals in self-interested efforts to manage the behavior of other individuals, and they do so by exploiting the active assessment processes of other individuals. [...] Communication reflects the fundamental processes of regulating and assessing the behavior of others, not of exchanging information. (ibid., i.)

As an example, consider a young animal producing a certain call upon encountering an exemplar of a specific species of predator. Even if the call is species-specific, there is no reason to say that its meaning consists of reference to the predator (the individual, or the category). The meaning of the call is to get, say, the young's mother (who has an interest in its survival) to act in a way that is most effective for the young's own interest, by exploiting the mother's capacity to assess the situation and the young's behavior. Behavioral biologists may to some extent differ on the question of whether a notion of 'information' has any role at all to play in explaining animal communication, but such differences are relatively marginal. Thus although Bradbury and Vehrencamp (2000) do not agree entirely with Owings and Morton, their initial statement also reads: 'It is widely agreed that animal signals modulate decision making by receivers of the signals' (Bradbury and Vehrencamp 2000: 259, citing a multitude of authors, going back to the seminal work of Dawkins and Krebs 1978).

Apparently, Owings and Morton consider exchange of information a human-centered concept, and so they would perhaps not object to the idea that human communication *might* primarily be a matter of exchanging information about the world. Indeed, this is both a common-sense view and one that dominates most modern semantic theories. It is nicely summarized (and documented) in chapter 10 of Jackendoff (2002):[9]

> Common sense tells us that linguistic expressions say things about the world. [...] The predominant traditions in Anglo-American semantics and philosophy of language take for granted this common sense position. They therefore consider it the task of semantic/pragmatic theory to explain how linguistic expressions say things about the world and have truth values based on their relation to the world. (ibid. 294.)

This is an accurate picture. This common-sense view of linguistic meaning is indeed quite far removed from the 'management-and-assessment' perspective of Owings and Morton, or the 'decision-modulation' view of Bradbury and Vehrencamp. But what if human language is also fundamentally a matter of regulating and assessing others, with exchange of information perhaps being secondary? There can be little doubt that the descriptive power of human languages far exceeds that of animal communication systems (as far as we know), but that does not imply that linguistic meaning consists in descriptive information and that regulatory effects are derivative. It could in principle just as well be the other way around. Precisely this position has been advocated consistently in the work of the French linguists Anscombre and Ducrot.[10] It is from this approach that I will adopt some fundamental ideas, as instruments for showing that (and how) grammatical elements and syntactic constructions have systematic, conventional functions in the dimension of intersubjective coordination.

Argumentation and information

Language use is in systematic ways always more than focusing on the same object of conceptualization in the same way. It is also inducing (and engaging in) inferential reasoning. Normal language use is never just informative, but

---

[9] An older, but still powerful, criticism of this objectivist kind of semantics, cited by Jackendoff, is Lakoff (1987). In the philosophy of language the work of the 'later Wittgenstein' has already, since 1953, seriously undermined this view. Nevertheless, Jackendoff's diagnosis of the situation in semantic/pragmatic theory at the beginning of the twenty-first century is still valid.

[10] Some early works are Ducrot (1980) and Anscombre and Ducrot (1983). In Anscombre and Ducrot (1989), a translation of a paper originally written in French, the originators give their own interpretation of the development of the theory so far. In 1995 a special issue of the *Journal of Pragmatics* was devoted to the theory (Raccah 1995). Ducrot (1996), a French text with parallel translation into English, provides an overview of the theory and relates it to some other approaches in linguistics, especially pragmatics.

always 'argumentative', in the terminology of Anscombre and Ducrot (e.g. 1989). In terms of the concept of the construal configuration developed above: engaging in cognitive coordination comes down to, for the speaker/writer, an attempt to *influence* someone else's thoughts, attitudes, or even immediate behavior. For the addressee it involves finding out what kind of influence it is that the speaker/writer is trying to exert, and deciding to go along with it or not.

In itself this is not incompatible with an 'information' view of linguistic meaning. Conceivably, the constant, conventional function of ordinary words and constructions could consist in the information they provide, with rhetorical effects coming 'on top' of that, depending on the context, and thus being variable. However, Anscombre and Ducrot argue for the opposite position, which is therefore sometimes characterized as a theory of argumentativity *in* the language system. The default condition for ordinary expressions is that they provide an argument for some conclusion, and this argumentative orientation is what is constant in the function of the expression, while its information value is more variable.[11]

For example, in a commentary on the Dutch national budget for the year 2001—the most favorable one in many years—government officials from the Ministry of Finance wrote that there was a prospect of a 'negative deficit', implying thereby that—in spite of that year's successes—there were more reasons than ever to control the budget.[12] A semantic theory should be able to explain why these words were chosen, and what causes their effect on addressees to be systematically different from that of the expression 'surplus', despite the fact that this is truth-functionally equivalent. The point is that the word *deficit* is conventionally associated with warning, that is, counts as an argument to cut spending. The use of the word *negative* does not reverse this argumentative status. On the contrary, it strengthens the point because it adds its own rhetorical force, which points in the same direction as *deficit* (that of 'warning'). As with *deficit*, this must be considered an inherent, obligatory part of the meaning of the word. It is the conventional meanings of these words that allowed the writers of this text to use them in attempting to regulate the attitudes of their readership in a way that was in their interests. If this effect were something that comes 'on top of' the informational value of the utterance—inferred by readers in context, after having computed the information—it is unclear why there should be a systematic difference in signal value between 'negative deficit' and 'surplus'; the information value is not different, so readers should be able to make the same inferences in both

---

[11] Much systematic evidence for this view concerns the way negation and related expressions work in natural languages; this is part of the topic of Chapter 2.

[12] Observation reported by Luuk Lagerwerf, *Tijdschrift voor taalbeheersing*, 22 (2000), 75.

cases. But what we actually see is that the information value of the term 'deficit' is relatively variable—in combination with a term such as 'negative' it is compatible with situations that can also be described as 'surplus'. What remains constant in such contexts is the argumentative value of the signal, its 'management potential', so to speak.

Or consider a simple sentence as in (1), for example, in case one wonders whether words like *deficit* and *negative* are sufficiently representative of normal language use in the relevant respects. This sentence looks as descriptive as one can get (Ducrot 1996: 42):

(1) There are seats in this room.

What are the properties of situations in which the utterance of (1) is appropriate? As long as one only looks at situations at level O for answers to this question, the argumentative character of (1) need not come to light, and it may appear to be 'purely descriptive'; understanding the utterance just consists of knowing how to check it against reality: are there actually seats in the room or not? Notice that as long as one thinks of meaning as residing in a relation between the words and the (or some) world, this is the only thing that one will look at. One will not have the idea of looking at relations between this utterance and adjacent ones—after all, since meaning is in the truth conditions, what difference could other utterances possibly make? However, if meaning may also reside in the intersubjective-coordination relation at level S of the construal configuration, such relations might provide just the evidence needed.

Consider what happens when the next utterance is something like *They are uncomfortable*. How should this be connected to the utterance of (1)? The appropriate way of doing that would be to use a contrastive conjunction like *But*. Something like *And moreover* would be highly incongruous. Schematically ('#' indicating lack of coherence):

(2) There are seats in this room.
   (a) But they are uncomfortable.
   (b) #And moreover, they are uncomfortable.

The reverse is the case if the next utterance is *They are comfortable*:

(3) There are seats in this room.
   (a) #But they are comfortable.
   (b) And moreover, they are comfortable.

What (2) shows is that (1) as such induces an addressee to make positive inferences about (among other things) the degree of comfort provided in this room. This is apparent from the need to use the contrastive conjunction *but* when the next utterance cancels this inference, from the strangeness of the additive connective in (2b), and from the mirror image in (3): when the inference induced by (1) is reinforced, the additive connective is appropriate ((3*b*)), and the contrastive one ((3*a*)) is not.

In other words, an addressee has to take the utterance of (1) as an attempt by the speaker to induce inferences of a specific kind; that is, as an operation in dimension S of the construal configuration. Moreover, this is part of the conventional function of the expression in (1). One simply does not know the meaning of *seat* if one can only distinguish objects as belonging to the class or not, but does not know that it licenses this kind of inference. In view of this, we may say that the meaning of the word is its contribution to the argumentative value of utterances in which it occurs.

Connected discourse
The inferential load of utterances is crucially involved in the way they relate to each other in connected discourse. Discourse consists of chains of inferential steps, including the possibility of rejecting one or more steps and 'changing course'. Consider the exchange in (4):

(4) A: Do you think our son will pass his courses this term?
    B: Well, he passed them in the autumn term.

Why can this be a coherent discourse? After all, B's utterance could be said not to address the question posed by A. The explanation is that every utterance is taken as orienting the addressee towards certain conclusions by invoking some shared model in which the object of conceptualization figures, a 'topos' in Anscombre and Ducrot's terminology. In our culture it is a rule, mutually known to the members of the culture, that passing some test normally licenses the inference that one will be able to pass other tests as well; in other words, the topos is that if someone passed a test, it is more likely that he will be able to pass other tests than that he will not. Notice the use of terms like 'normally' and 'more likely' in the formulation of this rule—it is a kind of 'default rule', not a universally valid one. We will see later that this is a critical aspect of the notion 'topos' if it is to do its work properly (Ch. 2, Sect. 2.3.3 and Ch. 4, Sect. 4.3).

Given such a topos, it is a valid inference from the statement 'He passed his courses' that he is probably capable of successfully performing certain tasks, like taking courses of this kind. In this way B's utterance can count as a coherent, in principle positive, answer to A's question. Again, an addressee takes an utterance not primarily as an instruction to construe an object of conceptualization in a particular way, but as an instruction to engage in a reasoning process, and to draw certain conclusions; it is typically not just attending to the same object, but understanding what the speaker/writer is 'getting at' (what she wants you to infer), that counts as successful communication. The latter establishes a direct relationship between the coordinating minds: the one indicated by the horizontal line of level S in the construal configuration.

The predicative use of ordinary adjectives, for example about size or quantity, also provides good illustrations (see also Pander Maat, 2006). Saying that someone is tall, in this view, does not primarily provide information about that person's length, but counts as a recommendation of some kind (depending on the topos being activated), for example to select him for the basketball team, or not to select him as a jockey. Notice that a person being called 'tall' in the jockey-selection situation may be shorter than a person rejected for the basketball team because he was 'short'. (Consider the problems this fact raises for truth-conditional treatments of the semantics of the simple sentences *John is tall* and *John is short*.) Again, the constant value of the terms is in their argumentative orientation, not (just) in their information value.

Of course, we are also able to get some information about the world from the utterances, just as we are able to get information out of the expression *negative deficit*. In this case, knowing what the relevant topos is (e.g. the taller someone is, the better the chance that he will make a good basketball player), and knowing something about the average length of persons in general and basketball players in particular, we can make certain guesses about the range of possible actual sizes for the person involved. But that is not *primary* in the conventional knowledge activated by the word *tall*. Activation of a scale of length that allows inferences about a person's actual height is dependent on knowledge of the relevant argumentative scale, not the other way around.

On the other hand, this does not necessarily mean that such an informational component has to be so indirect for all words in a language; that is, that it could never be conventional—languages are more flexible than that. For example, Anscombre and Ducrot (1989) propose the interesting hypothesis that numerical expressions in natural languages should be considered a special device, a kind of operator to remove the default-argumentative orientation of ordinary expressions. Saying that someone's height is 1.75 meters does not inherently display the argumentative orientation of saying that someone is tall or short. Still, even such expressions are not entirely devoid of rhetorical strength, as the following example shows. IBM notebook computers have a shock-protection mechanism; in an advertisement it is compared to the airbag system in cars, and then the following claim is made:

(5) Within 500 milliseconds of detecting any sudden acceleration in the notebook's movement, IBM's active-protection system will trigger the temporary parking of the head on the notebook's 60 GB hard-disk drive.

The use of the word *milliseconds* licenses inferences of speed and security. But in a time-frame of half a second an object dropped covers a distance of 1.22 meters, which is considerably more than the average height of laps and tables. (Notice that my use of *meter* here may contribute to the reader being induced to feel uneasy.)

In any case, using precise numerical specifications is obviously more artificial and elaborate than using words like *tall, short, fast, slow*, etc., which testifies to the default condition of the linguistic meaning of everyday expressions being inherently argumentative.

The parallel of this view with the basic character of animal communication will by now be obvious. It concerns the fact that human linguistic communication is primarily also a matter of influencing one another, by exploiting the cognitive capacities of others. Human language may be more involved than animal communication with influencing *mental states*, with consequences for *long-term* behavior, rather than with *immediate* behavioral effects, but this is a matter of degree. First of all, this view still implies a considerably smaller gap than the one between exchanging information with conspecifics and influencing and assessing the behavior of conspecifics; it is not so hard to conceive of mechanisms, especially in a social species, that produce pressure favoring long-term predictability of behavior. Secondly, much of language use is also conventionally aimed at immediate effects.

The latter point and its significance have also been noticed by Owings and Morton (1998). Discussing relations between communication and cognition in animals, they conclude 'that animal knowledge structures are fundamentally pragmatic, i.e. about what *to do* about objects, events, and states [. . .] According to this approach, signals are not statements of fact, that can be judged to be true or false, but are efforts to produce certain effects.' (ibid. 211). The authors then notice a parallel with speech-act theory, which is also specifically concerned with utterances that cannot be judged to be true or false—the discovery of which provided the original motivation for Austin's proposals (1962). As is well known, utterances of the type 'I promise to help you with your homework', 'Take your hands off me!', 'I now pronounce you man and wife' are not to be understood as informative, they are not descriptions of states of affairs.[13] Rather, their utterance constitutes the performance of an act; they are efforts to accomplish goals. To be sure, certain systematic conditions (called 'preparatory conditions' in the speech-act literature) have to be satisfied in order for these utterances to count as a promise, a command, and a legitimate wedding. Owings and Morton notice that 'a dedicated proponent' of the information view might try to construe these as the actual meaning of the expressions:

> Are these correlates, an information advocate would ask, not the information made available by these signals? No; this question confuses time frames of causation. Such correlates *validate* the cues as useful to assessing individuals [...] but are not the immediate cause of the assessing individual's reaction to the statement. Note that [this] proposal turns the usual view of the role of information on its head. The correlates of signals ('information') are not immediate causes of the behavior of targets of signals, they are instead long-term validators of the signal's utility. (Owings and Morton 1998: 211.)

Unknowingly, and coming from the perspective of animal communication, they arrived at a similar conclusion to Anscombre and Ducrot, turning the 'received view' about the relation between information and persuasion upside down. The fact that in this way, coming from different perspectives, the 'gap' between human language and animal communication systems is reduced is a consequence to be welcomed. However, standard speech-act theory restricts its domain of application to non-assertive utterances, which simply *cannot* be understood as truth-functional. Anscombre and Ducrot's view is more comprehensive, because it also covers statements, which are in principle analyzable as truth-functional. Assertive utterances such as *There is going to be a negative deficit*, *There are seats in this room*, *John is tall*, and *Within 500 milliseconds the system triggers parking of the head* are also attempts to accomplish something, of the same type as standard speech acts (like warning, reassurance, or advice). As we will see, this possibility of generalization is crucial for understanding certain grammatical phenomena to be discussed in the chapters below (see the discussion of performativity in Ch. 3 Sect. 3.3.3). It will especially allow for a general treatment of complementation constructions; not only those expressing speech acts (of the type *I promise that...*),

---

[13] Speech acts are also one of the important phenomena adduced by Jackendoff (2002: 327 ff.) in his defense of a conceptualist rather than truth-functional view of semantics. Obviously, the view presented here is in line with Jackendoff's plea for a shift 'from the question "What makes sentences true?" to [...] the more ecologically sound question, "How do we humans understand language?"' (p. 329). However, Jackendoff does not pursue the consequences of his own position far enough, in my view. By 'pushing "the world" into the mind' (p. 303), and conceiving of linguistic meaning as built out of percepts and concepts, he is taking a step forward (along with, by the way, the founders of cognitive linguistics in the 1980s), but the crucial role of the construal configuration in understanding linguistic meaning, and the related aspects of subjectivity and intersubjectivity still remain out of sight.

but also other ones, such as those expressing mental states (of the type *The minister is convinced that...*) in Chapter 3.

Human language may certainly be said to allow for distinguishing innumerably more distinctive 'long-term validators' of rhetorical cues than known animal communication systems. It is both possible and important systematically to distinguish between meaning components at the levels O and S of the construal configuration (see also Sect. 1.3), while the usefulness of this distinction for animal communication is at least not always obvious. But that in itself does not turn human language into a system of information exchange rather than a system for mutual influencing. While O and S must be distinguished, level S is never absent.

What this approach equips us with is, first of all, a theory of the specific nature of the intersubjective-coordination relationship at level S of the construal configuration, which can be applied in the specific analyses that follow. Methodologically, it provides an instrument for testing the presence and nature of conventional meaning at level S: we can look at coherent and incoherent linguistic contexts of different pragmatic types, to determine what the argumentative character of an expression is (if any), and what a particular grammatical element or construction contributes to that. This will be a recurrent theme too.

1.3 Variation in the balance between objectivity and intersubjectivity

1.3.1 Introduction

The fact that the conceptual structure of Figure 1.2 is inherent in any linguistic usage event does not imply that all aspects of the construal configuration have to be *symbolized*; that is, marked by means of some linguistic unit. Several features of actual construal configurations may remain fully implicit. For a linguistic sign a similar point holds: it may signal something about one aspect of the construal configuration, leaving others quite unmarked. So while certain meanings explicitly put some way of construing the object of conceptualization (along the vertical axis) on stage, others may operate entirely in the dimension of the coordination between subjects of conceptualization. In other words, Figure 1.2 represents a conceptual space which can be organized in different ways in different linguistic expressions.

Extreme cases on one side are those in which the meaning of the expression does not in any respect involve an element of the Ground and which may thus be labeled maximally 'objective'. Schematically, this sort of situation may be represented as in Figure 1.3.

O: *Object of conceptualization:*

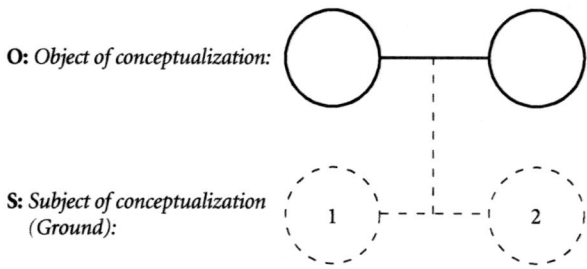

S: *Subject of conceptualization (Ground):*

FIGURE 1.3. Construal configuration in maximally 'objective' expressions

Such 'pure' cases are relatively rare, and artificial. One might think of 'common nouns and verbs considered in isolation (for example *lamp, tree*...)' (Langacker 1990: 9); the number indications mentioned in Section 1.2.3; or a name on a label. Even a noun phrase such as *the horse* or a simple-tensed sentence (*John owns a horse*) is not purely objective in this sense, as the identity of the referent or the time of the described event are accessed via the communicative situation (which is why the article and the tense marking are called 'grounding predications'). And, as we saw in Section 1.2.3, it is likely that such an assertion about ownership has certain topoi conventionally associated with it that license particular kinds of inferences (e.g. *John owns a horse, but he is actually very poor*).

The use of dotted lines in Figure 1.3 is meant to indicate that although the Ground figures in the interpretation of any utterance, it is not being signaled (in the particular case being considered) by the *conventional* meaning of any of the linguistic units used. In such cases those meanings wholly pertain to the level of the object of conceptualization, which is indicated by the use of bold lines. I will say in such cases that linguistic units 'profile' some facets of the object of conceptualization, and none at the level of the subjects of conceptualization, or of the relation between the two levels. This notation may be used to indicate differences between linguistic units in the same language, but also differences between seemingly similar elements in different languages or stages of a language (with one element conventionally marking only certain elements of the construal configuration, and the other some other, or more, elements). Thus even though in specific utterances a single common or proper noun may be used to attract an interlocutor's attention (*Wolves!*) or to invite him to respond in a particular way (*John?*), this occurrence of cognitive coordination is not due to the meaning of the nouns, so the Ground is not said to be profiled by these elements.

18   Intersubjectivity—mutual management

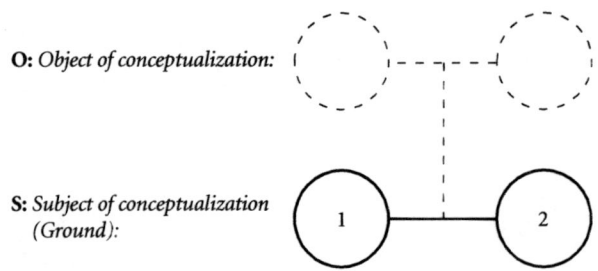

FIGURE 1.4. Construal configuration in maximally 'subjective' expressions

The extreme case on the other side is constituted by the mirror image of the situations depicted in Figure 1.3; that is, expressions which conventionally only profile elements of the Ground and/or the relationship between them, and no facet of an object of conceptualization. This is represented in Figure 1.4.

Examples of such purely subjective expressions are interjections; for example, a greeting (*Hi*), an apology (*Sorry*), or a call for attention (*Hey*). Other instances are markers of epistemic stance (*probably*), evaluative adjuncts (*unfortunately*), or particles etc. Even more simple configurations may be possible in which only one of the conceptualizers at level S is really profiled; for example, with non-interactional signs of disgust or frustration (*Yech*, *Damn*). In actual usage some facet of experience is also functioning as an object of conceptualization in these cases (such as the situation that provides the reason for the apology, or the taste of some piece of food), but none of this is indicated by the conventional meanings of these elements, which only express a subjective reaction, or organize the relationship between speaker/writer and addressee.

The fact that cases such as these and the previous ones exemplify only restricted kinds of language use demonstrates once again that the normal situation for linguistic expressions is that features of an object of conceptualization are construed in relation to one or more facets of the Ground, both of them at least partly by conventional means. Labeling objects and producing interjections constitute the opposite extremes on a continuum from maximally objective to maximally subjective expressions, and thus they are the exceptions; expressions from the middle part of this continuum constitute the rule. On the other hand, the fact that *utterances* with a purely objective or purely intersubjective nature may be quite exceptional still allows for the possibility, in terms of division of linguistic labor, that the conventional meaning of elements contributing to utterances is more or less restricted to one dimension or the other, and we will indeed encounter examples of this.

In any case, it should be kept in mind that the conceptual distinctions in the construal configuration do not always coincide with distinctions between linguistic units: one linguistic sign may very well conventionally perform functions in both dimensions, while the relative weight of each may also gradually change over time. In the next section I will illustrate the concepts involved and the considerations related to them by means of a brief analysis of different kinds of use of the Dutch verb *beloven*, meaning 'to promise'.[14]

1.3.2 *An initial illustration: a range of promises*

Consider the difference between the modern Dutch sentences (6) and (7):

(6) Het debat   belooft   spannend te worden.
    The debate promises   exciting to become
    'The debate promises to be exciting.'

(7) Hij belooft   de   grondwet   te verdedigen.
    He promises   the constitution to defend
    'He promises to defend the constitution.'

In (6) the verb *belooft* ('promises') does not describe the occurrence of someone performing an act of promising as it does in (7). Rather, in (6) it expresses a judgment on the part of the speaker of the sentence. The speaker is indicating that there is reason to have a certain expectation (here: of the debate going to be exciting), and evaluating this positively.

The use of the verb in this case may therefore be called 'epistemic'. In terms of the structure of the basic construal configuration: the use of *promise* in (6) is confined to the level of intersubjective coordination. It does not describe an aspect of the object of conceptualization itself, whereas it does so in (7); so we may label the first kind of use as 'subjective' and the second as 'objective'. This raises the question of what the relationship is between these two senses of the word. Do subjective and objective use have important features in common, or none at all? And, if they have features in common, is the distinction a sharp one, or are the boundaries between them fuzzy?

Consider the following set of sentences, each of which has *beloven* ('promise') as its finite verb and is a perfectly acceptable sentence in Dutch. (*Panorama* is the name of a weekly magazine.):

---

[14] The semantic part of the story also holds for English, but the syntactic part only has an observable basis in Dutch.

(8) De   hoofdredacteur van Panorama belooft   deze week iets
    The editor-in-chief of Panorama promises this week something
    moois   te   publiceren.
    beautiful to   publish
    'The editor-in-chief of Panorama promises to publish something nice this week.'

(9) De   hoofdredacteur van Panorama belooft   deze week iets
    The editor-in-chief of Panorama promises this week something
    moois.
    beautiful
    'The editor-in-chief of Panorama promises something nice this week.'

(10) De   redactie   van Panorama belooft   deze week iets
     The editorial-staff of Panorama promises this week something
     moois.
     beautiful
     'The editorial staff of Panorama promises something nice this week.'

(11) De   Panorama belooft   deze week iets   moois
     The Panorama promises   this week something beautiful
     (op de   voorpagina).
     on   the front page
     'Panorama promises something nice this week (on the front page).'

(12) De   Panorama van deze week belooft   iets   moois
     The Panorama of this week promises   something beautiful
     (op de   voorpagina).
     on   the front page
     'This week's Panorama promises something nice (on the front page).'

(13) De   voorpagina van de   Panorama van deze week belooft
     The front-page of the Panorama of this week promises
     iets   moois.
     something beautiful
     'The front-page of this week's Panorama promises something nice.'

(14) De   Panorama van deze week belooft   goede lectuur.
     The Panorama of this week promises   good reading
     'This week's Panorama promises good reading.'

(15) De   Panorama van deze week belooft   goede lectuur te bieden.
     The Panorama of this week promises   good reading to offer
     'This weeks Panorama promises to offer good reading.'

(16) De   Panorama van deze week belooft   goede lectuur op
     The Panorama of   this week promises good   reading PRT
     te   leveren.
     to   present
     'This week's Panorama promises to offer good reading.'

(17) De   Panorama van deze week belooft   goede lectuur te worden.
     The Panorama of   this week promises good   reading to become
     'This week's Panorama promises to be good reading.'

When one points out the difference between subjective and objective uses of *beloven* to speakers of Dutch, and then asks them to draw the boundary between the two categories in this set of examples, there is considerable variation, but also a common factor. People who start with example (8) tend to draw the line relatively close to (17)—that is, late in their series; but people who start at the other end, with example (17), do the same: they tend to draw the line close to example (8). That is, while everyone agrees that those two represent objective and subjective use, respectively, examples ranging from (9) up to (16) are considered objective by some, and subjective by others, partly depending on the order in which the sentences are evaluated. Apparently, there are instances of use that allow for either classification.

There are also theoretical reasons for allowing such dual classification in several cases. For example, in a case like (11) one can construe the magazine *Panorama* metaphorically (personification), or metonymically (a magazine is causally associated with the people producing it), in which case *beloven* ('promise') can be read as describing a speech act. Still, it is a case of figurative language, and the promising is not directly predicated of actual, identified persons, so that the notion of personal commitment in the lexical meaning of the verb is mitigated. On the other hand, one might construe *beloven* not as describing a speech act, but as itself a metonymy for 'giving rise to an expectation': promises are causally linked to future events, and thus to expectations.

More important, however, is the fact that in many cases it does not make much difference in practice which kind of construal is chosen for communication to be successful, *because the different construals share their argumentative character*; that is, their function at level S. Describing something as an act of promising counts as an argument strengthening the expectation that a desirable situation will be realized, and the contribution of fully subjective *beloven* to the meaning of (6) and (17) simply is *nothing more* than an explicit indication of this argumentative force, without referring to something in the object of conceptualization. So even if a speaker/writer had one construal in mind and the addressee construed the other, the rhetorical message would still have come across. The less the referent of the grammatical subject is associated with an intentional agent, and the more the complement evokes a non-controllable state rather than a controllable action, the harder it is to interpret *beloven* objectively.[15] But in principle there is considerable flexibility.

This is a natural ingredient of the kind of framework I am exploring here. Linguistic expressions are primarily cues for making inferences, and understanding does not primarily consist in decoding the precise content of the expressions, but in making inferences that lead to adequate next (cognitive, conversational, behavioral) moves. This 'frees' the expressions from the need to have a completely fixed conventional meaning, as long as they support the inferential purposes of speakers/writers and addressees (see Fauconnier 1994: xviii). Thus the meaning of, for example, *beloven* does not have to be considered fixed in a specific region of the construal configuration, but can be adapted to its context, shifting more to level O in certain cases, and more (or completely) to level S in others.

The boundaries of this flexibility cannot be determined theoretically, as they are conventional, and change over time. A constant element in such changes though, is that meanings typically extend from being relatively restricted to level O to being more and more applicable to level S. This is the process known as subjectification, that has occurred in the case of Dutch *beloven*, English *promise*, Spanish *prometer*, and their negative counterparts meaning 'threaten' (see, respectively, Verhagen 1995, 2000a; Traugott 1997; Cornillie 2004). The well-known general unidirectionality of this process can be immediately ascribed to a basic asymmetry inherent in the construal configuration. Even if no aspect of the Ground is explicitly marked in an utterance, its actual use is always taken as an argument for some conclusion, as an attempt to influence an addressee's cognitive system, so that it functions at level S as well. Whenever the use of some expression that is not conventionally subjective leads to successful cognitive coordination (i.e. at level S) there is a chance that the speaker/writer or addressee will reproduce the same expression for a similar goal—even without the objective conditions for its use being fully satisfied—and so the expression may get started on a path towards conventionalization of subjectivity; this is a consequence of the fact that ordinary linguistic communication is basically argumentative, not

---

[15] Thus the factors involved resemble those influencing the 'agent-oriented' vs. 'epistemic' interpretation of modal verbs (Heine 1995).

primarily informative. Thus the construal configuration and the theory of argumentativity provide a mechanism that produces pressure for meanings to develop in the direction of increased subjectivity.

Argumentation and auxiliary syntax

The same asymmetry also has interesting synchronic consequences for the syntax of these expressions (for an extensive treatment see Verhagen 1995). Notice that in fully subjective use, as in (6), *beloven* does not denote an event, and therefore does not evoke participant roles (promisor and promisee) either. This has the consequence that it cannot be used as an independent verb taking an infinitival complement clause, but must be used as a kind of auxiliary verb to another verb that provides the participant roles. In Dutch subordinate clauses this consequence is clearly observable in a restriction on possible positions of the verbs. Subjective *beloven* is only possible in a so-called verb-cluster (see (18)), while objective *beloven* is possible in the position of a verb taking a non-finite clausal complement (witness (19)):

(18) ...omdat   het debat   spannend belooft   te worden.
        because the debate exciting   promises   to become
     '...because the debate promises to be exciting.'

(19) ...als hij belooft   de grondwet   te verdedigen.
        if   he promises the constitution to defend
     '...if he promises to defend the constitution.'

The syntactic asymmetry is that subjective *beloven* is not possible in the position of objective *beloven* in (19) ((20) is unacceptable—indicated by '*'), but objective *beloven*, on the other hand, *is* possible in the position of subjective *beloven* in (18), witness (21).

(20) *...omdat   het debat   belooft   spannend te worden.
        because the debate promises exciting to become

(21) ...als hij de grondwet   belooft   te verdedigen.
        if   he the constitution promises to defend

The order of elements in (20) would make it necessary to interpret *belooft* as independently assigning roles, so that the subject (*het debat*, 'the debate') would have to be interpreted as a promisor. But this does not make sense, so the order is unacceptable. The clustering of verbs into a single complex predicate in (18) allows the subject to take the role of argument of the predicate 'be exciting', which does make sense; so the latter order is the only acceptable one.

On the other hand, objectively used *beloven* may unproblematically take the position that is specific for the auxiliary, subjective use (the same holds for the negative counterpart *dreigen*, 'threaten'). It still assigns participant roles to the relevant nominals, but it may occupy a position in the structure of the clause in which it is not *necessary* to assign such roles. This syntactic asymmetry thus straightforwardly parallels the asymmetry in the construal configuration mentioned before. All expressions that specify the object of conceptualization in one way or another always also have a function at the level of intersubjective coordination when actually used, but the reverse is not necessarily true; elements that mark aspects at level S do not have to have a correlate at level O in actual usage.

In summary, the interpretation and distribution of *beloven* in Dutch (and its counterparts in some other languages) provide a good illustration of the usefulness of the conceptual distinction between the levels of object and subject of conceptualization for semantic and syntactic analysis. At the same time, they also illustrate the point that the distinction does not at all have to coincide with a distinction of linguistic signals (see Sect. 1.3.1). Elements may in principle, within certain conventional boundaries, mark aspects of both the level of the object and that of the subject of conceptualization, though the balance between these in a particular case is also conventional and subject to change over time. All of these points will also be relevant when we come on to considering grammatical constructions specifically relating to the level of intersubjective coordination, in the chapters that follow.

1.4 Prospects

1.4.1 The usage-based approach and empirical data

It will be clear from the previous sections that the approach adopted here is essentially a usage-based one. The factors that produce the phenomena to be explained are in a very fundamental sense aspects of the *use* that human beings make of language. In addition, I will also assume that linguistic knowledge is based on usage in the sense that knowledge of words, constructions, and their meanings, as well as connections between them, is based on generalizations over usage events in the linguistic experience of speakers. This view is incorporated into most present-day versions of construction-based approaches to grammar, especially cognitive grammar (Langacker 1987, 2005) and several varieties of construction grammar (Goldberg 1995, 2003; Croft and Cruse 2004, chs. 9–11). In line with the assumptions of this approach, data from observed actual language use, both single instances and frequency data, play an important part in validating analyses and theoretical claims in this book. On the other hand, the usage-based approach is above all a theoretical position, so it does not imply that corpus data are the *only* valid kind of empirical data. When specific claims and hypotheses entail specific predictions, constructed examples and intuitions (if there is consensus about them among native speakers) can be sufficient and decisive. Especially when it is 'technically' difficult to produce corpus data that are relevant to a particular question and it is not clear that they would provide useful additional information it may be quite legitimate to restrict the empirical investigation to such intuitive data. Moreover, several parts of the discussion in the chapters that follow concern well-known problems of linguistic analysis, for which there is considerable agreement on the facts, and the claim is specifically that a good explanation requires some conceptual shift, or a new theoretical concept.

As a consequence, a mix of types of empirical data will be used in this study. Corpus observations (qualitative and quantitative ones) will be used especially when the issues involve claims about things like discourse coherence, normal (prototypical) usage, and differences in usage of apparently related constructions. A substantial part of the material will be from Dutch, mainly because it is my firm conviction that a deep understanding of details and subtleties is required to make discourse data bear on theoretical issues (see Verhagen 2000b); sometimes Dutch simply provides good opportunities to illustrate certain points (see the example of verb order in subordinate clauses at the end of Sect. 1.3.2). But English data will be used as well, and the consequences of the analyses for the analysis of other languages and for linguistic theory in general will be evident.

The adoption of a usage-based, constructional approach to grammar also implies that differences in degree of schematicity and prototypicality (entrenchment) may be relevant. In the words of Goldberg (2003: 222–3):

The construction-based framework captures linguistic generalizations within a particular language via [...] inheritance hierarchies [...] Broad generalizations are captured by constructions that are inherited by many other constructions; more limited patterns are captured by positing constructions at various midpoints of the hierarchical network. Exceptional patterns are captured by low-level constructions.

Thus a possibility to be envisaged for each of the constructional patterns under investigation is that some function may be connected to a specific, low-level pattern and not inherited by many others, or to a pattern at a higher level in the network of constructions. This will indeed turn out to be relevant in a number of cases, most specifically in connection with complementation constructions. Thus, besides an exploration of intersubjectivity in grammar, this study also contains some exercises in constructional syntax.

1.4.2 Preview

A major point of this book is that the conventional function (or simply 'meaning') of several grammatical phenomena is primarily to be located at level S and its relation to O, and that these phenomena include more than those that have long since been recognized as involving viewpoint and deixis. As a corollary, several problems in previous treatments of these phenomena must ultimately be attributed to the mistake of locating their function (too much) at level O rather than S, mostly as a consequence of a failure to distinguish sufficiently sharply between these levels and their features. To this end I will discuss negation and a number of related phenomena in Chapter 2, complementation constructions in Chapter 3, and some discourse connectives in Chapter 4. These phenomena have been chosen because their function typically is to modify or explicate the interpretation of an utterance as a whole, specifying it, for example, as a denial, as a thought, or a kind of speech act, or connecting it to other utterances in the discourse. Utterances constitute usage events, and these always count, as I argued above, as an attempt to influence an addressee's cognitive system. It is therefore especially relevant for the purposes of this study to consider grammatical elements and constructions that operate on the interpretation of complete utterances.

In the first parts of each chapter I will explore the nature of problems related to previous treatments in some detail, in an attempt to convince grammarians that a fundamentally different approach is worth pursuing, and discourse analysts that syntax may be more directly connected to their object of study than they might have thought. Thus in Chapter 2 some open questions concerning meaning and use of the *let alone* construction and its Dutch equivalent will be discussed in some detail; in Chapter 3 some inconsistencies in the analysis of complement clauses; and in Chapter 4 the difficulty in accounting for asymmetries between concessive and causal connectives.

With respect to the three 'Why' questions at the beginning of the book, I will roughly propose the following answers in the three core chapters:

(i) The difference between *It is not impossible* and *It is possible* stems from the fact that negation with *not* conventionally establishes a relation at level S rather than a relation between a subject and an object of conceptualization; this explains why there are contexts into which only one expressions fits.

(ii) The primary function of matrix clauses of complementation constructions is also located at level S. They provide specifications of perspectives rather than descriptions of events or situations, and the grammatical roles of subject, object, and predicate from simplex clauses have no straightforward application in these constructions, which have a function *sui generis*.

(iii) Concessive conjunctions always coordinate two perspectives: so again they are conventionally associated with level S, even if there is a real-world causal relation involved. Recursive application of perspective-embedding (by negating a concessive relation) does not lead to the disappearance of the conceptual perspectives; so there is no way to 'reconstruct' a causal relation from a concessive one in natural languages.

Detailed conceptual and empirical arguments for these and related claims have to wait until the relevant chapters, but this brief exposition may give a rough idea of what the general logic of the considerations will look like.

2

Negation and virtual argumentation

2.1 Introduction

In Chapter 1 (Sect. 1.2.2) I distinguished two senses of the term 'subjectivity'. One is complementary to objectivity, and consists in the recognition that the meaning of many linguistic items does not relate directly to (a model of) the world, but to a person's assessment, or construal, of a situation. The other consists in the recognition that one may have 'thoughts and beliefs that may differ from those of other people' (Tomasello 1999: 14–15). The latter in particular is the basis for intersubjectivity: the mutual coordination of cognitive systems. What I want to argue in this chapter is that the primary function of negation in natural language should be understood in terms of cognitive coordination, not in terms of the relation between language and the world, or the language user and the world. This is not to say that negation has no consequences for the relation between a language user and the world—it has. But in view of systematic aspects of its use, it belongs to a part of the linguistic system that can only be treated coherently in terms of its function in regulating relations between distinct 'mental spaces', rather than between language and the world. Following up on the discussion of the theory of argumentativity in Chapter 1 (Sect. 1.2.3), part of what I will do here is interpret (with modifications) basic insights from Ducrot (1996) and related work in cognitive terms. The goal is to construct a general framework that allows for the incorporation of other phenomena, to be discussed in this chapter and in subsequent ones. A central role in the linguistic argumentation for this framework will be played by the *let alone* construction (Fillmore et al. 1988) and its Dutch counterpart (*laat staan*, lit. 'let stand'), specifically because of a number of problems in the analysis of their semantics and pragmatics which find a natural solution in the framework proposed here. Other pieces of linguistic evidence will involve the difference between sentential and morphological negation, and the function (in discourse) of 'double negation' (litotes).

2.2 Negation and perspectives

2.2.1 *Mental spaces*

Consider the fragment in (1):

(1) This time, there was no such communication [about the plans]. It's a pity because it could have resulted in greater participation by employers.

The second sentence contains two instances of the pronoun *it*, and both are used anaphorically; that is, referring back to an antecedent in the preceding discourse. The intriguing phenomenon is that they do not have the *same* antecedent. In fact, they have contrary antecedents: the first refers to the *absence* of communication (that is, what is a pity), the second to the *presence* of communication (that is, what could have resulted in greater participation). Apparently, both the negative idea of lack of communication and its positive counterpart are sufficiently activated in the context to make them accessible for reference by means of *it*.[1] In this respect the real discourse fragment in (1) differs from the constructed one in (2), which appears incoherent (indicated by '#'): What does the second *it* refer to? Although silence about the plans implies lack of communication about them, the idea of communication is not sufficiently accessible to allow *it* to refer to it:

(2) #This time, they remained silent [about the plans]. It's a pity because it could have resulted in greater participation by employers.

Let us assume, for a start, that the presence of sentential negation (*not*, *no* (as in (1)), *nobody*, *nothing*, etc.) has the effect that the speaker/writer is taken to instruct the addressee to entertain *two* distinct cognitive representations, or two 'mental spaces' in the sense of Fauconnier (1994), and to adopt one and abandon the other. In this case the mental space to be rejected would contain the idea that there is communication, while the other one is similar to the first, except that communication is absent; the latter is the one to be adopted, at least for the time being. Then the difference between (1) and (2) can be straightforwardly analyzed, as only (1) will activate a cognitive constellation in which both absence and presence of communication are cognitively accessible. Consider Figure 2.1.

The use of a negative expression in the communicative situation by the speaker/writer (Space$_1$) 'opens' another mental space (indicated in Figure 2.1 by the line from *not* to Space$_2$), in which a thought p is valid that corresponds

---

[1] See Ariel (1990) for a general theory of anaphoric discourse reference in terms of degrees of (cognitive) accessibility. The fact that grammatically identical expressions are used for anaphoric reference is evidence that they have roughly the same degree of accessibility.

30   Negation and virtual argumentation

p = 'there was communication'

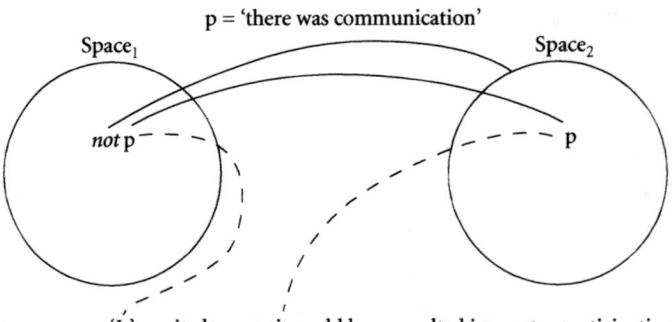

[Figure: Two circles labeled Space₁ (containing "not p") and Space₂ (containing "p"), with correspondence lines between them, and dotted lines from both to the caption below.]

'It's a pity because it could have resulted in greater participation'

FIGURE 2.1. Two mental spaces evoked by sentential negation

to the negated thought p in Space₁ (indicated by the 'correspondence line' between the ps in the two mental spaces). The pronoun *it* can take an element from either mental space as its antecedent;[2] the dotted lines indicate which interpretations are assumed for fragment (1).[3]

The spaces 1 and 2 in Figure 2.1 correspond to the conceptualizers 1 and 2 in the basic construal configuration introduced in Chapter 1 (see Fig. 1.2). However, I will continue to depict mental-space configurations as in Figure 2.1. The first reason is that this keeps the presentation in line with the conventions in the literature on mental-space theory. But there is also a reason concerning content. As mentioned in Section 2.1, one of my questions is precisely how the operation performed by *not* should be interpreted in the framework of the construal configuration: Does it primarily operate on the (vertical) construal relationship, or on the (horizontal) relation of intersubjective coordination? This question can only be answered after we have considered other negation-related expressions (see Sect. 2.3.2, especially the discussion of argumentative operators). Still, it is possible to unify the concept of Ground originally developed by Langacker, given the modification

---

[2] In other words, it does not impose a constraint on the interpretation of the discourse as to the mental space in which an antecedent should be found. In Chapter 4 (Sect. 4.3) we will encounter elements that do impose precisely such constraints on interpretation. Notice that in this sentence the modal *could* functions as an indication of which mental space is to be selected for the interpretation of *it* and possibly other elements.

[3] Perhaps this presentation suggests that it was the encounter with the example that triggered the idea of applying mental-space theory to these phenomena, but the reverse is true. I had already convinced myself of the usefulness of the approach and elaborated a considerable part of the details to be discussed in this chapter, when I decided to do a search on the Internet (using Google) for the string 'it's a pity because it'. Example (1) was one of the best instances of the kind I was looking for. (Understandably, there were more examples in which *it* refers to the same situation than examples like (1)—i.e. examples of the type 'It's a pity because it is bad'.)

O: *Object of conceptualization:*

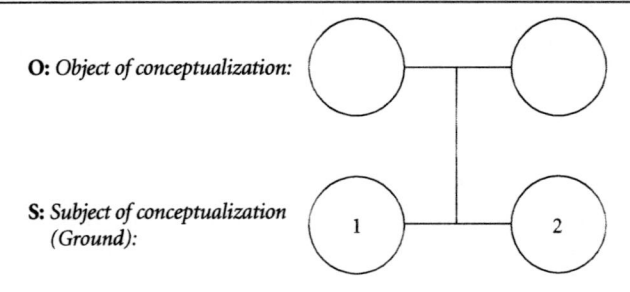

S: *Subject of conceptualization (Ground):*

FIGURE 1.2. The construal configuration and its basic elements

suggested above, with the basic mental-space concepts as originally developed by Fauconnier.

From a logical point of view a speaker who makes any assertion contradicts all potentially relevant assertions that are inconsistent with the one he has just made. One might thus wonder whether a configuration as in Figure 2.1 should not be assumed for all linguistic utterances. An immediate disadvantage would be, of course, that this would make it lose much of its attractiveness (e.g. How could one explain the difference between (1) and (2) if both evoke several mental spaces?). However, it can actually be demonstrated that such an assumption is wrong. Consider the fact that if someone is sad this implies that this person is not happy. Would this mean that saying, for example, *Mary is sad* also involves setting up an alternative mental space in which the counterpart of 'sad', namely 'happy', is predicated of Mary? That the answer to this question must be negative can be demonstrated on the basis of the behavior of the connective *on the contrary*.[4] Consider the two fragments in (3) and (4):

(3) Mary is not happy. On the contrary, she is feeling really depressed.
(4) #Mary is a bit sad. On the contrary, she is feeling really depressed.

What exactly is contrary to 'feeling depressed' in (3)? Not the opinion which the speaker has just expressed (that Mary is not happy), but its counterpart (that Mary is happy). So a sentence introduced by *On the contrary* is opposed to the position of Space$_2$ evoked by the use of a negative expression in Space$_1$, as depicted in Figure 2.2.

From the fact that fragment (4) is not coherent it can be concluded that mental spaces with different epistemic stances towards the same proposition are not activated on the basis of entailments of what is expressed explicitly. It is only the actual *use* of linguistic negation that sets up a configuration of the

---

[4] Dutch *integendeel* behaves in exactly the same way, but its Afrikaans descendant *inteendeel* does not (see Verhagen 2002: 404–9).

type represented in Figures 2.1 and 2.2. Already in this sense linguistic negation can be said to have a special function in regulating an addressee's cognitive coordination with other points of view. The addressee is invited to adopt (at least for the time being) a particular epistemic stance towards some idea, and to abandon another one that is inconsistent with it—possibly one that the addressee might entertain himself. These kinds of cognitive consequences do not necessarily follow when there is no linguistic negation. Thus linguistic negation cannot be considered as only relating language to the world, reversing the truth value of an utterance.

2.2.2 Sentential vs. morphological negation

This approach makes it possible to formulate an important difference between the function of sentential negation and that of morphological negation, with the prefix *un-*. Fragment (5), with morphological negation, is as incoherent as (4), and not as coherent as the sentential negation case in (3):

(5) #Mary is unhappy. On the contrary, she is feeling really depressed.

Just as *sad* in (4) does not project a second mental space, neither does *unhappy* in (5). Only sentential negation projects two mental spaces with different epistemic stances towards the same proposition. Morphological negation, on the other hand, is an instrument for reversing the scale associated with the adjective to which it is attached, and does not invite the addressee to consider-and-abandon the thought of applying that scale with its normal orientation. A configuration as in Figure 2.2 is not set up, so there is no alternative mental space for *on the contrary* to relate to.

This analysis provides an important step towards a solution of the 'problem' of double negation, or litotes (Horn 1989: 296–308; Van der Wouden 1996). The question is how to explain the use and effects of combinations of

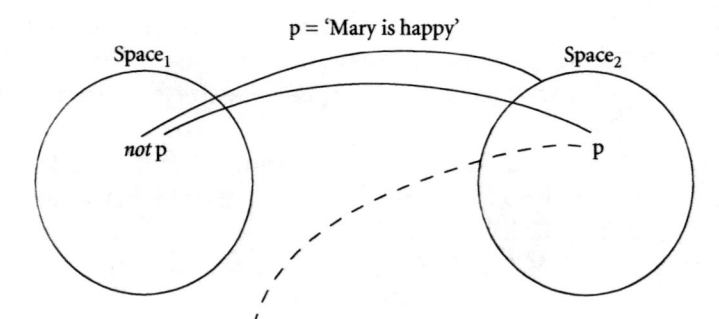

'On the contrary, she is feeling really depressed'

FIGURE 2.2. 'On the contrary' relates to evoked mental space ($\neq$ Space$_1$)

sentential and affixal negation, as in *not unhappy* and *not impossible*. For some of these, the scalar ones of the *not unhappy* type, there seems to be a special 'niche' available, the 'non-excluded middle' of someone being not unhappy but not happy either. The morphological negative form expresses something contrary to the positive form, not its contradiction. A contradiction (by means of *not*) and a contrary do not cancel each other out completely, which makes the combination applicable to a special 'neutral' zone of a scale. This is a consequence of the different semantics proposed above. While *un-* reverses the scale associated with the predicate to which it is attached, sentential negation invites one to consider-and-abandon the idea of applying that predicate, and a special case satisfying the latter instruction is to take a neutral position. But what about the non-scalar cases? Or, as Horn (1989: 298) formulates it: 'if something is *not inconceivable* or *not impossible*, what else can it be but *conceivable* or *possible*? [...] Why don't these doubly negated forms, amounting presumably to the contradictory of a contradictory, result in complete redundancy?' An actual corpus example of such an expression in Dutch is (6).[5]

(6) Het vinden van die noemer is niet onmogelijk.
    The find-INF of that denominator is not impossible
    'Finding such a common denominator is not impossible.'

Logically, if something is not impossible, it is possible. But when we take the context into consideration it turns out that the use of 'not impossible' is not just something more than tautological—it is practically obligatory. The context of (6) is given in (6'), and this whole piece is much more coherent and easier to read than the constructed 'equivalent' in (6").

(6') Mensen die verandering willen op één noemer brengen is
     People that change want on one denominator bring is
     altijd lastig omdat zij allicht verschillende soorten verandering
     always hard because they likely different types change
     willen. Maar het vinden van die noemer is niet onmogelijk.
     want But the find-INF of that denominator is not impossible
     'It is always hard to find a common denominator for uniting people who are in favor of change, because they are likely to wish for different kinds of change. But finding such a common denominator is not impossible.'

---

[5] From the Eindhoven Corpus, in the version available from the Free University in Amsterdam, and described in Uit den Boogaart (1975) and Renkema (1981).

(6″) Mensen die verandering willen op één noemer   brengen is
     People   that change   want on one denominator bring   is
     altijd lastig omdat zij   allicht verschillende soorten verandering
     always hard because they likely different   types   change
     willen. Maar het vinden van die   noemer   is mogelijk.
     want   But the find-INF of that denominator is possible
     'It is always hard to find a common denominator for uniting people
     who are in favor of change, because they are likely to wish for
     different kinds of change. But finding such a common denominator is
     possible.'

On the basis of the analysis presented above, I suggest that (6″) is less coherent because it does not explicitly evoke a consideration of two opposite epistemic stances, while such a configuration is required to connect the last sentence to the preceding discourse. In other words, part of the answer to Horn's question is that *not impossible*, just like *not happy*, evokes two mental spaces, while *possible*, just like *unhappy* (and, for that matter, *impossible*), does not. This does capture to some extent what makes (6′) easier to process. The text is understood as presenting two different mental spaces, the first with a negative attitude towards trying to unite people in favor of change, the second with a positive one. The opposition between these attitudes towards the same issue is what makes the fragment coherent, and this conceptual configuration is explicitly activated by the use of sentential negation.

Although this is a critical part of a solution to the problem of double negation, it is not the whole story. Notice that the context of the *not impossible* sentence does not contain a representation of anyone saying or thinking that finding a common denominator *would* be impossible. We cannot say that, in general, negative sentences are presuppositional in the sense that they somehow presuppose the presence of their affirmative counterpart in their context (see Horn 1989: 63–73), even though this kind of use may be prototypical in many situations (ibid. 172–5), and is possibly essential in the process of the acquisition of negation (ibid. 167–8). Thus while the presence, in the context, of a configuration as in Figure 2.2 is necessary for the use of *on the contrary* (*integendeel* in Dutch), such a dual mental-space constellation is not required for the use of sentential negation itself. It must be possible to connect the second mental space evoked by *not X* to some point of view elsewhere in the discourse, but this does not have to be the positive view that *X*. The relation between the contents of these two mental spaces is less direct than that. In the next section I turn to the question of what the nature of this relationship is. As we will see, it crucially involves the notion that using language involves cognitive coordination in the sense of mutual attempts to influence other people's minds and behavior. Section 2.4 will then take up the issue of completing the solution to the present 'problem' of double negation.[6]

2.3 Conventional linguistic constraints on intersubjective coordination

2.3.1 The let alone *construction: some unsolved problems*

Fillmore, Kay, and O'Connor (1988)

As we have seen, the English expression *on the contrary* and its Dutch equivalent *integendeel* require a negative expression in their context. They may be regarded as the lexically fixed part of a grammatical template or construction, consisting of two clauses of which the first must contain a form of sentential negation. A related expression that has explicitly been treated as a construction is *let alone*. It achieved fame as the example Fillmore, Kay, and O'Connor (1988) used to illustrate their approach to grammatical theory, now generally known as construction grammar.[7] Although I find this approach important and illuminating (see Verhagen 2002, 2003*b*), I will not be directly concerned with this part of their paper.[8] Here I will focus on the semantics of *let alone*, as it will require a view of the function of negation that is especially relevant in the present context.

---

[6] The mental-space approach suggests a parallel to another part of Ducrot's theory, namely his notion of 'polyphony' (see Ducrot 1996: 54 ff., esp. the discussion of 'enunciators', pp. 68 ff.). The concept of mental spaces and Ducrot's concept of multiple 'voices' being present in the interpretation of a single utterance may be seen as no more than different labels for what is essentially the same fundamental insight. To an important extent I believe this is true, although the topoi associated with the terms are different. The term 'mental spaces' puts more emphasis on an individual's mental capacity for entertaining different viewpoints, whereas 'multiple voices' more strongly evokes the inherent dialogic nature of verbal communication. But I do not see these views as incompatible, on the contrary. The individual's capacity is put to use in concrete linguistic communication (when the abstract mental spaces are assigned to actual people), as well as something that has emerged in the individual as a result of interaction with real other persons during childhood, which in turn has an evolutionary, biological basis (Ch. 1, Sect. 1.2.1; see also Sinha, forthcoming, for an illuminating discussion of the complementarity of individual mental life and social-cultural interaction). I will use the mental-space terminology mainly for two reasons. First, it is more widely known and used in the international linguistic literature, as far as I can see. Secondly, many people feel, I have noticed, that the notions of 'dialogue' and 'voice' have to be stretched considerably in order to make them apply to narrative and written discourse, while the management of viewpoints is an integral part of those kinds of discourse as well. In that respect, the mental-space terminology seems to be more neutral.

[7] The paper has been reprinted in Kay (1997: 1–48) and in Tomasello (2003*a*: 243–69). In the latter version some sections have been left out that are relevant to my discussion. The version I will refer to is the original one from 1988. Several aspects of the analysis of Fillmore et al. have been the subject of discussion, amendment, and revision in subsequent work, but, as far as I know, the problems with the semantics of *let alone* in connection with *barely* and *almost* have not been dealt with.

[8] Issues of construction grammar will receive more attention in Chapter 3, especially in connection with the status of so-called '*Wh*-extraction'.

Some examples of the *let alone* construction are given in (7)–(9):

(7) He doesn't like shrimps, let alone squid.
(8) I doubt if he made colonel in World War I, let alone general.
(9) I was barely awake in time for lunch, let alone for breakfast.

The idea is that *let alone* is a characteristic feature of a kind of formal schema stored in long-term memory with a range of properties associated with it (Fillmore et al. 1988: 512 ff.). These properties are therefore immediately available when the schema is activated. The schema has the form given in (10):

(10) **Schema:**
    F ⟨X A Y *let alone* B⟩

The syntactic characteristics of the construction are detailed in (11), which specifies what kind of syntagmatic relations hold among the elements of the construction, as well as other structural features:

(11) **Syntactic characteristics:**
    let alone is a kind of coordinating conjunction (exhibiting specific syntactic properties differentiating it from other coordinating conjunctions);
    let alone is a negative-polarity item;
    A and B are contrasting elements (complete constituents);
    X and Y are variables;
    the force indicator F is some 'negative-polarity trigger'.

Some instances of F are *-n't* in (7), *doubt* in (8), and *barely* in (9). The semantic characteristics are given in (12), which is related in obvious ways to the syntactic schema and its characteristics in (10) and (11):

(12) **Semantics:**
    F′ ⟨X A Y⟩ *let alone* F′ ⟨X B Y⟩
    where F′ is the speech act associated with F, and:
    the construction (directly or indirectly) expresses two negative assertions:
        ¬(X A Y), and ¬(X B Y);
    the conjuncts represent two points on the same scale;
    the proposition in the first conjunct implies the one in the second:
        ¬(X A Y) ⇒ ¬(X B Y), such that the first speech act (F′ ⟨X A Y⟩) is stronger than the second (F′ ⟨X B Y⟩).

Applied to example (8):

(i) the sentence expresses the two negative assertions 'He did not make colonel in World War I' and 'He did not make general in World War I';
(ii) 'being colonel' and 'being general' represent two points on the same scale of military ranks, and 'being general' is higher on the scale;
(iii) there is an implicational connection: 'He didn't make colonel in World War I; *a fortiori:* He didn't make general in World War I'.

The polarity property means that a negative context is required for the proper use of *let alone*. For example, the connector cannot be used in a sense resembling that of 'a fortiori' or 'in fact', with two positive statements— witness the unacceptability of (13):

(13) *He certainly made colonel in World War I, let alone general.

(14) He certainly made colonel in World War I, in fact, he even made general.

Finally, (15) gives the pragmatic characteristics, that is, a specification of what the construction is used for in communication:

(15) **Pragmatics:**
The construction as a whole allows the speaker to be *relevant*—by addressing (here: negating) a contextually relevant proposition in the second conjunct—and at the same time to be *informative*—by redirecting the addressee to a new proposition which is more informative (the one in the first conjunct).

Fillmore et al. assume that on the basis of the 'immediately preceding context' (p. 532) some specific question (e.g. whether someone became general) is 'in the air'. According to their analysis the speaker addresses this question by negating it in the *second* conjunct, and in doing so he satisfies the pragmatic principle of relevance. But at the same time he is maximally informative by producing a more informative statement in the *first* conjunct, to which the addressee is redirected. Thus, '[t]he construction [...] is pragmatically sensitive to a conflict between two Gricean maxims, the maxim of informativeness (or Quantity) and the maxim of relevance (or Relation)' (Fillmore et al. 1988: 513). What is meant here by 'more informative' is strictly that a sentence has more entailments than another one, not that the sentence would be 'more telling' for the addressee in a more vague sense.[9] When a speaker believes the

---

[9] Perhaps this is the reason why Fillmore et al. elsewhere in their paper go to the trouble of addressing 'a potential confusion'. They sometimes use the term 'stronger' and 'weaker' as a shorthand for 'more informative' and 'less informative' respectively, but they recognize that, in another sense, 'the

more informative sentence to be true, then by the maxim of Quantity that is what he should say, but if that sentence does not address the issue raised in the preceding context, the maxim of Relation requires him to say something else. The *let alone* construction, according to this analysis, allows a speaker to do both, and so to deal with such a conflict.

Problem: non-semantic negative polarity?
Fillmore et al. are the first to point to some problematic aspects of their own analysis. First of all, consider (11). This specifies negative polarity as a *syntactic* feature; it is a requirement imposed on the linguistic form of the construction. Why is it not conceived of as purely semantic, with the syntactic facts as a consequence? The reasons have to do with examples like (16) (see Fillmore et al. 1988: 528–9):

(16) *He almost reached Denver, let alone Albuquerque.

(17) 'He almost reached Denver' ⇒ 'He did not reach Denver'.

The problem is that the first conjunct of (16) entails that he did not reach Denver, as stated in (17). Despite this apparent negative character, *almost* does not count as a 'licensor' for the use of *let alone*. Therefore Fillmore et al. adopt the position that *almost* is negative semantically but not syntactically. Then (16) can be said to violate the last criterion in (11), a syntactic property of the *let alone* construction. This is clearly not a very attractive solution (and to be fair, Fillmore et al. make it clear that they would also have preferred a reduction of the syntactic constraints to semantic properties). For one thing, it re-establishes a sharp conceptual distinction between syntax and semantics, which goes against the spirit of construction grammar. With this move, syntactic and semantic properties must be conceptualized as essentially independent of each other, even if both types of information are accessed simultaneously in the use of a construction. But the solution is not only inelegant, it does not even solve all the analytic problems. Example (18) is in a way the reverse of (16). This sentence is fine, although the first conjunct entails a *positive* statement, as represented in (19).

(18) He barely passed the first statistics course, let alone the second one.
(19) 'He barely passed' ⇒ 'He passed'.

Fillmore et al. suggest that the meaning of *barely* might be decomposed as *almost not*, which contains a negation, and that one might argue that this

speaker's and hearer's attitude to the B clause can be said to be stronger in the sense that it is uttered in greater confidence, being supported by the A clause' (Fillmore et al. 1988: 532). They suggest that the latter is a consequence of the combination of a more and a less informative clause in one sentence, but I think it could also be seen as a consequence of the scalar relationship between the conjuncts (see (12)).

provides an explanation for the above observations. However, it is clear that this will not suffice:

Nonetheless, *let alone* sentences with *barely* as trigger present a problem [...] because only the negative part of the meaning of *barely* is interpreted as obtaining in the second ⟨X B Y⟩ conjunct. That is, [*He barely reached Denver let alone Chicago*] means not 118, but 119.

(118) He *barely* reached Denver; a fortiori he *barely* reached Chicago.

(119) He *barely* reached Denver; a fortiori he did NOT reach Chicago.

[...] an explanation would [...] be required why only the *not* part of this complex operator distributes semantically to the second, ⟨X B Y⟩, conjunct in *let alone* sentences. We are not at present able to offer such an explanation. (Fillmore et al. 1988: 529.)

Problem: pragmatic point in first conjunct?
Another problem, this time one that Fillmore et al. do not elaborate themselves, is that of the unnatural order of the conjuncts, given the characterization of the pragmatics of the construction. As we have seen, Fillmore et al. propose that the pragmatic function of the construction is to redirect the addressee to the new proposition in the first conjunct, since this is more informative than the second one. This implies that the new information that the addressee should focus on *precedes* other material (the less informative conjunct), and this is highly unnatural in view of what we know about the effects of word order (see Verhagen 1986, and refs. cited there).[10] This consequence would minimally require some motivation. It suggests that something is wrong with the assumed pragmatic function, and that an alternative is called for which does not have this undesirable consequence.

One reason why this problem does not surface in Fillmore et al. (1988) is that they do not consider the usage of actual *let alone* sentences in actual contexts—despite the fact that in their own formulation context is crucial. Thus they lack a significant empirical foundation to analyze the way such sentences contribute to the development of a discourse. I will try to provide an alternative, taking such empirical considerations into account.

Problem: what did the meaning of let alone *develop from?*
The third and final problem concerns the relation between the present construction and its historical source. The question is: what motivated the use of the elements *let* and *alone*, each with its own meaning, in a way that

---

[10] In a way, this observation is acknowledged by Fillmore et al. when they say that related conjunctions such as *in fact* and *if not* have 'the more "natural" order' as they 'present the stronger point second' (1988: 533).

allowed the combination to develop into the present-day construction? Of course, it is true that speakers of English at present know the phrase and its meaning as a unit, but constructions and new meanings do not come out of the blue. Rather, they evolve from previous linguistic units through repeated usage with variation (Croft 2000). Thus it must be possible to tell a story linking the present construction to, in this case, the imperative of *let* and the adverb *alone*, without abrupt breaks.

Such an explanation is also a prerequisite for explanations of why other languages sometimes employ similar elements to perform the same function, but sometimes also very different ones. For example, the German element corresponding to English *let alone* is *geschweige (denn)*, which is related to *schweigen*, 'keep, be silent' (see Pasch 2000). The Dutch one is *laat staan* (lit. 'let stand'). There is ample evidence that the latter originated from the first-person expression *Ik laat staan*, or, with enclitic pronoun, *'k laat staan*, meaning 'I let X stand', that is, 'I do not speak of X' (see *WNT*, s.v. *laten* and s.v. *staan*).

According to Traugott (1995: 37–8) the English expression was originally 'an imperative directed at an addressee (*let me/something alone*), or a participle construction' (as in *the book let alone by X*, meaning, roughly, 'the book ignored by X').[11] In present-day English it 'indirectly directs an interlocutor to act in a certain way, this time to redirect the linguistic act of construal'. While Fillmore et al. do not, as far as I can see, use the term 'construal', it is clear that Traugott accepts their characterization of the pragmatic function of the construction, and tries to link it to the original meaning of its elements, with the change seen as an instance of the general process of subjectification; the expression supposedly started as *describing* an act of redirection (someone leaving one task or thing for another), and now just marks a relation between the speech-act participants, entirely within level S of the construal configuration. Although this does not look unnatural at all, there is one major problem. The goal of the original, objective redirection was the *complement* of *let alone*, while in Fillmore et al.'s analysis it is now the clause *preceding* the connector, and there is no plausible story as to why and how such a strange shift could have occurred.

Clearly, this problem is connected to the second one, that of the proper pragmatic characterization of the present construction: what is it that the construction is used for in connected discourse? A solution to any of the three

---

[11] The OED, s.v. *let*, also states that the origin of the present construction is the imperative or a participle, but suggests the present rather than the past participle, citing an example with *letting alone X*.

problems mentioned should ideally contribute to solving the other ones as well.

2.3.2 Barely is not almost, let alone pretty much completely

In order to find a solution to these problems, and especially the first one, it is useful to step back for a while, as it were, and dwell upon some general properties of Fillmore et al.'s approach. Specifically, I want to turn to the conception of negation, which has a crucial role to play in the analysis of this construction.

Argumentative orientation as linguistic meaning
How do Fillmore et al. conceive of negation? What kind of work does it do in their view? Given their use of entailment relations to illustrate their semantic analysis, one can say that in their approach the semantics of negation is basically truth-conditional; that is, that it concerns the relation between language and the world. To say that someone did not pass an exam, for example, thus means that the proposition that he did is invalidated through a confrontation with the state of affairs in the (or some) world. In cognitive terms: it instantiates a view of linguistic meaning as concerning coordination of language users with the world. In terms of the basic construal configuration introduced in Chapter 1 (Fig. 1.2, repeated here for convenience), meaning, including the meaning of negation, operates at most on the vertical connection between a subject of conceptualization and an object of conceptualization.

O: *Object of conceptualization:*

S: *Subject of conceptualization (Ground):*

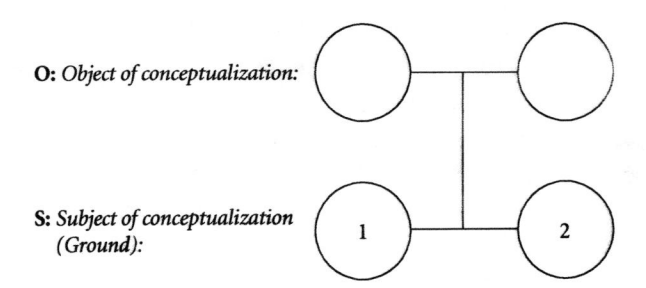

FIGURE 1.2 The construal configuration and its basic elements

However, according to the theory of argumentativity introduced in Chapter 1 (Sect. 1.2.3) language use is in systematic ways always more than construing an object of conceptualization in the same way. It always involves inducing and performing inferential reasoning, and linguistic meanings may also conventionally be associated *directly* with the level S of intersubjective coordination. As we have seen, there are good reasons to assume that the normal situation for meanings in ordinary language is to have *some* conventional relation to this level. Saying that there are seats in a room orients an addressee to positive conclusions about the degree of comfort of the room, by the conventional meaning of the words. And giving the answer B to A's question in (20) orients an addressee to certain conclusions about the son's abilities and the prospects for his study in the future.

(20) A: Do you think our son will pass his courses this term?
B: Well, he passed them in the autumn term.

A large part of the evidence that Anscombre and Ducrot (1989) and Ducrot (1996) adduce in support of their theory involves the behavior of negation and some related expressions. The claim is that several elementary linguistic units and constructions, including negation, specifically operate on the relationship of intersubjective coordination. On this view, a negative version of B's utterance in (20), that is 'He didn't pass them in the autumn term', is not an indication that the particular state of affairs mentioned does not hold in the world. The negation first and foremost invalidates the conclusions that may ordinarily be drawn from the statement (given a relevant topos). That is, this answer is interpreted as orienting the addressee towards the conclusion 'He is not going to pass'. This is also a coherent answer to A's question, but now one with an opposite orientation.

As far as this straightforward form of negation is concerned, a proponent of the informativity view could in principle still argue that the consequences of its use for inferential reasoning constitute a derived function, secondary to the descriptive nature of negation. In other words, it is in principle conceivable that the *conventional* function of a negative form (its linguistic meaning) only concerns the vertical relation between a subject and an object of conceptualization. An effect on the horizontal level of intersubjective coordination would then be seen not as part of the conventional meaning of negative forms, but as a consequence derived in contexts of use. However, starting from the insight in Chapter 1 that the primary function of language is communication, and that interaction is crucial in language learning (see Sinha 1999; Tomasello 1999, 2003a), we may expect the reverse picture to be more adequate. Operating on intersubjective coordination is then seen as the primary conventional function of negation, while operating on the relationship between subject and object of conceptualization is secondary. What I want to argue now is that the latter position is supported by the structure of grammar.

The point is that negation is a part of a *system* in language with specific properties that show that the function of intersubjective coordination is indeed primary, and that description, or coordination with the world, is secondary.

Consider, for example, the relation between the expressions *a small chance* and *little chance*. These may well refer to the same percentage of probability, for example 20 per cent, but their roles in orienting an addressee to certain conclusions are different. In their import they are exactly opposite, as can be demonstrated with (21) and (22). Suppose someone is considering whether or not to perform a surgical operation on a patient who is in a serious condition; then it is coherent for this person to say (21*a*), but not (21*b*):

(21) There is a small chance that the operation will be successful.
    (*a*) So let's give it a try.
    (*b*) So let's not take the risk.

What this shows is that saying *There is a small chance* orients an addressee to the same conclusions as the positive statement *There is a chance*. On the other hand, (22) exhibits the reverse pattern: (22*a*) is not coherent, but (22*b*) is:

(22) There is little chance that the operation will be successful.
    (*a*) So let's give it a try.
    (*b*) So let's not take the risk.

Saying *There is little chance* orients an addressee towards the same conclusions as the negative statement *There is no chance*. Notice that it makes no difference what the actual percentage of the chance of success is. Whatever turns out to be the case, *a small chance* basically orients the addressee to the same general kind of conclusions as *a chance*, while *little chance* orients him to the same sorts of conclusions as *no chance*. There does not seem much prospect, then, for deriving the difference between the intersubjective functions of these expressions from a descriptive difference without somehow introducing the argumentative orientations in the derivation—that is, in a non-circular way. Rather, the argumentative difference must itself be taken to be conventional; that is, part of the linguistic meaning of these expressions.

It is important to emphasize that the expressions do not by themselves indicate positive vs. negative *recommendations*. At the same time, this does not imply that their linguistic function is context-dependent. Suppose the context is not that of a surgeon wondering whether or not to perform an operation, but of a policeman wondering whether or not to interrogate a seriously injured victim of a shooting, who is waiting to be operated upon. In that situation it may very well be coherent to say 'There is little chance that the operation will be successful. So let's give it a try' (cf. (22*a*)), employing a topos of the kind 'The more important certain information is, the more acceptable it is to take risks in obtaining it'. In that sense, the pragmatic import of the expression *little chance* is context-dependent. But the significant point is that its effect is still the same, in this context, as that of the expression *no chance*, and the reverse of the effect of *a small chance*. In this context, it would be coherent to say 'There is a small chance that the operation will be successful. So let's not take the risk' (cf. (21a)). Thus the conventional, context-independent linguistic meaning of the construction *little X* is to reverse the orientation of the inferences associated with the predicate X (with less 'force' than *no* would have; see below), whatever topos is being employed. The equally conventional context-independent meaning of *a small X* is to maintain the orientation of the inferences associated with the predicate X, while their strength is less than with unmodified affirmation.[12]

Argumentative direction and argumentative strength
The generalization over negation and expressions like *little chance* is that their use has the function of directing the addressee to infer that certain conclusions are invalid. Straightforward negation represents the situation in which the conceptualization of a specific situation and a cultural, or at least shared, model of a type of situation are aligned. Given a certain topos, the situation in the world provides arguments for invalidating certain conclusions without any qualification. This is the locus of the difference with *little X*. The latter shares its argumentative orientation with negation, but presents it as weaker. Similarly, *a small X* shares its argumentative orientation with unmodified predication, but presents it as weaker. This is summarized in Table 2.1.[13]

Obviously, the second column does not represent a binary distinction, but a scale on which expressions can also occupy 'in-between' positions. For instance, the strength of *no chance* is arguably maximal, while that of *a chance* may easily be surpassed by that of, for example, *every chance in the world*.[14] Argumentative operators with less than maximal strength may leave some room for discussion and negotiation. We saw in Chapter 1 (Sect. 1.2.3) that a statement that cancels inferences associated with a previous one must be marked with a contrastive connective like *but*. This also applies to the cases

---

[12] The structural complexity of these interactions is one of the sources of much confusion about the relation between 'meaning' and 'context'. As the present discussion demonstrates, much also depends on the construal of 'meaning'. Construing it, as I do here, as 'guiding inferences' or 'constraints on interpretation' allows certain kinds of relations between meaning and context that would simply be inconceivable if meaning were taken as denotation, or contribution to truth conditions, for example. For some general discussion see Verhagen (1997).

[13] In view of the above remarks about context independence of meanings, it should be clear that the choice of the plus sign for the orientation of *a chance* is in principle arbitrary. But if it were to be replaced by the minus sign then all other markings would have to be reversed as well.

[14] A search for this exact expression on the Internet with Google on 7 May 2003 resulted in 624 hits.

TABLE 2.1. Argumentative orientation and strength of α-chance

	Orientation	Strength
a chance	+	high
a small chance	+	low
no chance	−	high
little chance	−	low

we are considering here; for example, (23a) produces a coherent discourse (unlike (22a)):

(23) There is little chance that the operation will be successful.
 (a) But let's give it a try.
 (b) #But let's not take the risk.

But when the strength of the negation used is maximal, there is no room for cancelling the inference that it is not worth trying; someone who utters (24) is simply inconsistent:

(24) #There is no chance that the operation will be successful. But let's give it a try.

A difference like this is a natural consequence of differences in strength and of the scales involved having definite boundaries; it does not undo the parallels in argumentative orientation. Distinguishing argumentative strength from orientation precisely allows us to formulate in a natural way what negation has in common with other expressions that at first sight do not look like negation but nevertheless behave in highly similar ways. In the next two chapters we will encounter similar situations.

Barely *and* almost *as argumentative operators*
This same idea also allows for a generalization over *not* and *barely*. Notice that the implication in (19), repeated here for convenience, means that *barely* does not negate the proposition descriptively, with respect to what is the case in the (conceived) world:

(19) 'He barely passed' ⇒ 'He passed'.

Now consider the question of how it affects the inferences towards which the addressee is oriented, for example in cases such as (25) and (26). Imagine a context similar to the one we considered before, in which someone is contemplating the prospects of her son making it through the first year of college:

(25) He passed his first statistics course. So there is hope.

(26) #He barely passed his first statistics course. So there is hope.

To say that someone passed a course orients the addressee towards the conclusion that he is capable of passing, and therefore it makes sense to present this as a basis for the conclusion in the second clause (there may be hope). But to say that he barely passed is to invalidate such a conclusion (despite the 'actual fact' that he passed), as can be seen from the fact that (26) is incoherent, given the relevant topos.

As we have seen with other expressions, it is also possible here to make (26) coherent; namely, when we are hoping for him to fail (for whatever reason). Interestingly, in such a situation it is (25) that becomes incoherent. So this confirms the point that the orientation of an utterance containing *barely* is opposite to that of the same clause without that element, and that *this* function of the element is itself context-independent. In other words, it is not possible to find a single coherent topos with which (25) and (26) have the same argumentative orientation.

In the dimension of intersubjective coordination *barely* does the same thing as negation, orienting the addressee towards negative conclusions. It is not as strong an indicator as *not*, but the direction of the argumentative orientation is the same. The distinction between orientation and strength is thus indeed systematic. The expression *little chance*, as we have seen, also shares its negative orientation with *no chance*, but it does not have the same strength.

In this dimension of intersubjective coordination *barely* can also be naturally characterized as the negative opposite of *almost* (see Lundquist and Jarvella 1994).[15] To say that someone almost passed an exam actually suggests that in principle this person has the capacity for passing, despite the fact that he actually has not achieved this so far. Consider the fact that (27) is coherent

TABLE 2.2. Argumentative orientation and strength of α-*passed*

	Orientation	Strength
passed	+	high
almost passed	+	low
didn't pass	−	high
barely passed	−	low

---

[15] Ducrot (1996: 200–12) also presents an insightful discussion of *almost*, but he does not contrast it with *barely*. Horn (2002) contains an overview of several analyses of *almost* and *barely*, in various frameworks.

(under the same topos), while (26) is not, despite the 'actual fact' that he did not pass in the situation of (27), while he did according to (26):

(27) He almost passed his first statistics course. So there is hope.

At the same time it is clear that 'almost passing' is not as strong an argument for the conclusion about hope as unqualified passing. Thus, as indicated in Table 2.2, the distinction between orientation and strength is fully applicable here as well (with the same provisos as were given above with respect to the scalar nature of the strength column).

As with the expressions in Table 2.1, the ones in Table 2.2 with a non-maximal strength may also leave room for discussion that the maximal ones lack, for example:

(28) (a) He barely passed. But he did!
(b) #He didn't pass. But he did!

While the second clause of (28a) successfully cancels the inferences associated with the first, the speaker of (28b) is simply inconsistent. Notice, incidentally, that (28a) provides additional evidence for the argumentative character of the meaning of *barely*: otherwise it would be impossible to explain why the utterance is not completely redundant (recall that *barely p* logically entails *p*).

This way of analyzing the function of constructions such as *little X*, *barely p*, and *almost p* presupposes that 'ordinary' predicates always carry some argumentative force. Otherwise these elements would have nothing to operate on. We have already encountered several pieces of evidence showing that this assumption is in fact correct. It is strikingly confirmed by a pair of examples first presented by Horn (1996; see also Horn 2002). Consider example (29):

(29) The tank is half full.

What could the kind of inferences licensed by an instance of this expression be? Many people would tend to say: 'It depends', namely, on one's assumptions. Nevertheless, there is certainly a tendency here for such an expression to count as some sort of positive assessment. Truth-conditionally it is equivalent to an utterance of (30):

(30) The tank is half empty.

But the latter is a pessimist's construal of the situation, and as such it is opposed to the optimistic construal expressed in (29). Or, to put it somewhat more concretely, if the issue is whether we should worry how far we can travel before running out of petrol, (29) counts as a reassurance, while (30) counts as advice to start looking for a filling station and stop for refueling.

In itself this provides a strong indication for the argumentative character of ordinary lexical expressions such as 'full' and 'empty'. Now recall that I mentioned in Chapter 1 (Sect. 1.2.3) that numerical expressions may be considered a special kind of operator for removing a default argumentative value. And indeed, in order to avoid an argumentative orientation in saying something about the amount of petrol one would have to say something like (31):

(31) The level of petrol in the tank is at 50 per cent.

This is an uncommon way of talking about such a situation, to be used only in very special situations (e.g. a scientific experiment), but not in everyday language.

Nevertheless, one might still attempt to analyze the argumentative difference between (29) and (30) as a secondary effect, to be derived from the primary descriptive contents. For example, one could see the basic linguistic meaning of these sentences as the same (essentially truth-conditional equivalence), and argue that since the speaker has the choice between the lexical items *full* and *empty* (and possibly a quantitative expression like (31)), his use of one rather than the other would lead to Gricean implicatures of the desired kind. I do not find this a very elegant solution to begin with, but the primacy attributed to descriptive content in this view becomes entirely untenable when we consider the effects of using *almost* and *barely* in this kind of utterance. Consider (32) and (33):

(32) The tank is almost half full.

(33) The tank is barely half full.

Observe that there is actually slightly more fuel in the tank when it is barely half full than when it is almost half full, as depicted in Figure 2.3.

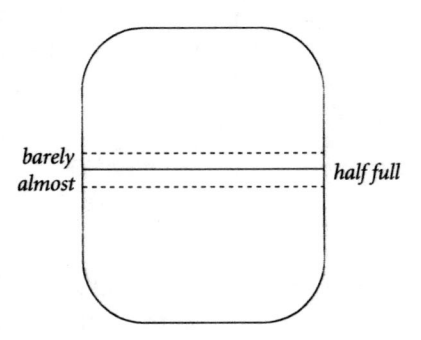

FIGURE 2.3. *Barely/almost half full*

So by any primacy of descriptive contents over allegedly derived, pragmatic, argumentative effects (32) should be more of a warning than (33). After all, in the former case there is slightly less than 50 per cent fuel in the tank, and in the latter slightly more. However, *almost half full* still counts as reassuring, a confirmation of confidence in the distance one can cover without refueling, while *barely half full* counts as a warning, advice to start looking for possibilities of refueling soon. So what we have to conclude is that such elements as *barely* and *almost* operate *directly on inferences* associated with the concepts they modify, not indirectly via the descriptive contents of the terms as such.

As in the other cases we discussed before, it is important to realize here too that *barely* does not necessarily evoke the negative idea of a warning and *almost* the positive idea of reassurance. Rather, their effect is dependent on what, in a particular instance of use, the relevant types of inferences, that is the relevant topoi, are. Suppose, for example, that we are not worrying about whether we should stop for refueling, but that we are actually busy filling the tank, with person A regulating the flow of fuel to the tank and person B keeping an eye on the progress of the process in order to signal to A when it is time to cut off the flow. The utterance of (32) (*The tank is almost half full*) may then count as a warning ('Be prepared; the moment to switch off the flow of fuel is approaching'). In the same circumstances the utterance of (33) (*The tank is barely half full*) may count as reassurance ('Take it easy; the moment to switch off the flow of fuel is still far away'). The rule is, again, this; whatever the issue associated with the concept mentioned explicitly in the utterance, the use of *almost* confirms the inferences associated with the higher end of the scale involved, whereas the use of *barely* excludes these inferences (and may therefore tend to evoke inferences associated with the lower end of the scale).

This is a rather abstract characterization of the meaning of these two rather mundane words. But it is the same kind of abstractness that is necessary in the characterization of the function of other expressions that are not exotic either, as we have seen. This abstractness is connected with the fact that these elements operate directly on the relation of intersubjective coordination, as represented by the heavy lines in Figure 2.4.

The context-independent, conventional linguistic meaning of these 'argumentative operators' is to guide the addressee in particular ways with respect to the kind of inferences to be drawn, at a particular point in a discourse. They also impose some constraints on the objects of conceptualization they are combined with (hence the continuous vertical line in Figure 2.4); but these need not comprise much more than that the object of conceptualization must

50   Negation and virtual argumentation

O: *Object of conceptualization:*

S: *Subject of conceptualization*
   (Ground):

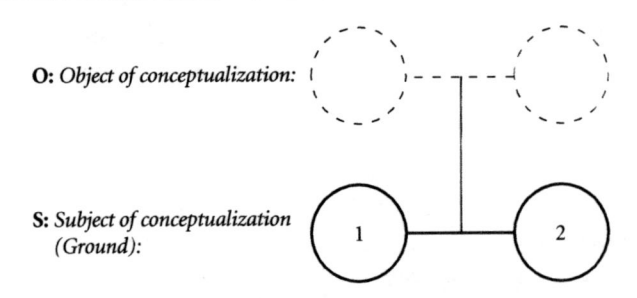

FIGURE 2.4. Conventional function of 'argumentative operators' located in dimension of intersubjective coordination

be construed in a way that will support the relevant inferences.[16] They are not sufficient for deriving their argumentative roles. The interpretive outcome of their application to some situation is largely dependent on the object of conceptualization chosen, and especially on the topoi associated with it. In other words, the context dependence of the specific inferences activated in the cases that we have observed a number of times in the discussion so far is a consequence of the fact that the conventional meaning of these elements is located in the dimension of intersubjective coordination. It is in that dimension, I argue, that the function of each element is constant.

Argumentative orientation constraining coreference
The fact that such ordinary linguistic constructions as *almost p* and *little X* have to be characterized as related only to the intersubjective dimension of the construal configuration testifies to the normality and automaticity of inferential reasoning in everyday cognition and language use. If intersubjective coordination can to some extent be linguistically managed, as this analysis entails, independently of a specific construal of an object of conceptualization, then we should expect that there are *reciprocal* connections between the two dimensions. The argument is this. People may base their inferences on their models of the world and its causal properties, so features of an object of conceptualization may constrain such inferences; but if people can also understand what a speaker/writer wants them to infer on the basis of linguistic features such as

---

[16] Thus locating the conventional meaning at level S of the construal configuration does not necessarily imply that the elements can be freely combined with exactly the same set of concepts. For example, it is perfectly normal to say *Mountain X is almost the highest one in the world*, but quite strange to say *Mountain Y is barely the highest one in the world*. The felicitous use of *barely* apparently requires some room for improvement, and if a mountain already is the highest one, that is not easy to conceive. The point is not that there are no links whatsoever between a meaning functioning at level S and features of level O; as we have already seen in Chapter 1, Section 1.3.2 (on *promise*), such connections are flexible, and changeable. In the same way, the possibilities of use of *barely* have been expanding gradually (Traugott, 2006), and have not necessarily reached an end point.

argumentative operators, then they may also adapt their understanding of an object of conceptualization to support their inferences. We have seen some examples of how another construal of an object of conceptualization can change the particulars of inferences at level S. But the marking of a particular kind of argumentative orientation may also influence the way in which elements at level O are conceived. This can be shown on the basis of results from research (including some elegant experiments) by Lundquist and Jarvella (1994). Consider example (34).[17]

(34) Our two sons, Charles and George, were playing a game. Halfway through, Charles had sixty points. So the youngest was probably going to win again.

If the addressee knows what game is being played, or which of the two boys is the youngest, he may know who is predicted to win on the basis of this (presumably shared) knowledge about the object of conceptualization, and thus successfully engage in cognitive coordination with the speaker/writer with respect to the conclusion in the last clause. It may even seem that one simply *must* know one of these things about the object of conceptualization in order to derive this inference. But argumentative operators may also guide reasoning here, even if one does not possess this kind of information. Consider (35) and (36):

(35) Our two sons Charles and George were playing a game. Halfway through, Charles had almost sixty points. So the youngest was probably going to win again.

(36) Our two sons Charles and George were playing a game. Halfway through, Charles had barely sixty points. So the youngest was probably going to win again.

Readers who had read (35) and were asked afterwards who they thought had won the game strongly agreed that it was Charles; on the other hand, readers who had read (36) and were asked the same question strongly agreed that it was George. The difference between (34) on the one hand and (35) and (36) on the other is not that the latter two contain more explicit information about the rules of the game, or the ages of the boys (they don't); it only consists in the presence of the words *almost* and *barely*. But, as I have argued, *almost* orients the addressee towards some conclusion associated with, in this case, gaining points, whereas *barely* excludes such

---

[17] The examples used in illustration are adapted from those in Lundquist and Jarvella (1994) for the purposes of the present discussion.

inferences. Therefore (35) invites the positively oriented inference that the number of points Charles has gained makes it likely that he will win; (36) invites the negative inference that this number of points makes Charles's winning *un*likely, and consequently the expression *the youngest* must be taken as referring to George.

Again, it must be emphasized that the interpretations I have just sketched, even though readers tend to agree on them to a significant degree, are not really *determined* by the use of *almost* and *barely*, respectively. As the background topos for these interpretations I have been using a cognitive model of the general type 'More is better'; in this case that the purpose of playing a game is to get as many points as possible. With that topos, the use of *almost sixty points* suggests that Charles is winning and the use of *barely sixty points* that he is losing, *despite* the fact that the actual number of points in the former case is lower than in the latter.

But suppose the rules of the game imply that the points involved are *penalty* points, so that the winner is the one with the lowest amount of points. Then, of course, the whole story is reversed. With such a background assumption, the likely winner, referred to by *the youngest*, in (35) is George, not Charles, and in (36) it is Charles, not George.[18] But whatever the specific features of different contexts, it is clear that the presence of linguistic constraints on inferences, operating in the intersubjective dimension of language use, can guide the construal of the object of conceptualization, to make it consistent with the argumentative orientation, given a topos.

In this area too it can be shown that *almost* does not function like negation, despite the fact that *almost p* entails *not p*. Consider the difference between (35) and the negative formulation in (37):

(35) Our two sons, Charles and George, were playing a game. Halfway through, Charles had almost sixty points. So the youngest was probably going to win again.

(37) Our two sons, Charles and George, were playing a game. Halfway through, Charles did not have sixty points. So the youngest was probably going to win again.

While the second sentence in (35) evokes a clear positive orientation towards winning, it definitely does not in (37). Its relevance in this context is clearly a negative one; that is, the inverse of the orientation of (35). Accordingly, there

---

[18] But this is not the default model (in our culture) for the relationship between gaining points and winning a game, which explains why there was consensus about the first interpretation mentioned in the text.

is a tendency to interpret *the youngest* in (35) as Charles, but as George in (37). So once again, in the way it contributes to connecting discourse segments, the negative formulation is actually similar to the one with *barely* (see (36)), despite the fact that having barely sixty points logically excludes not having sixty points (yet).[19]

Another class of elements besides argumentative operators that is relevant here is that of discourse connectives. I have already used one before in this chapter, namely the element *so* in the examples above. As can be seen from these examples, *so* instructs the addressee to interpret the clause it introduces as an inference licensed by the preceding discourse, given relevant topoi (and possibly 'intermediate' inferences). Thus the connective relates to the level S of intersubjective coordination already because it invokes knowledge (the topos) on the part of the addressee that is not part of the object of conceptualization. In the above cases the inference concerns an expectation about a probable future, so the relation of this clause to the previous discourse does not at all correspond to a relation in the object of conceptualization either. In this case the dimension of intersubjective coordination is the *only* level at which the relation marked by *so* exists (though the use of the word may be compatible with situations where a discourse relation reflects one in the world).

The reverse of *so* in English is *but*. Rather than marking an explicit discourse segment as an inference licensed by the previous discourse, *but* marks a discrepancy between the next segment and such inferences from the preceding discourse. Both *so* and *but* may also have effects on the construal of an object of conceptualization. For example, consider (38):

(38) Our two sons Charles and George were playing a game. Halfway through, Charles had barely sixty points. But the youngest was probably going to win again [anyway, as his brother had even fewer].

While in example (36), with *barely* and *so*, we interpreted *the youngest* as referring to George in order to make the discourse coherent, we interpret this

---

[19] People sometimes have the feeling that the amount related to the use of *barely* 60 is less than 60. In actual usage I have not so far found convincing examples where this is really the case. But it is not hard to find examples of *barely* with a number that clearly demonstrate that the number mentioned *is* a minimum, e.g. 'After barely 18 months in management,...', 'At prime time, we are regularly breaking barely 50% of the audience', 'We have...ages ranging from barely 50 to 70+' (from the Yahoo group 'overfiftywomen'). Possibly, then, it is the negative argumentative orientation of *barely* that people 'project' on to the object of conceptualization when consciously considering the question of what the actual number associated with a *barely* expression is ('*Barely* shares its argumentative orientation with *less*, so *barely* 60 must be less than 60'). As discussed in this section, there are clear cases in which it is the argumentative orientation that determines the interpretation at level O, so the occurrence of instances of language use of the above type could be expected.

nominal as referring to Charles in (38), also for reasons of coherence. In both cases the first sentence invites the inference that Charles is not likely to win, the difference being that *but* in (38) signals that inferences from the preceding discourse should be cancelled (with the additional clause providing grounds for this move). Again, we have to leave it at this rather abstract characterization, because the meaning of *but* itself does not provide information about the content of the inferences to be cancelled, nor about the specific content of the discourse that is to follow.

It is also interesting to consider the conjunction *and* in this context. While *so* explicitly marks an inference in a text, and *but* a discrepancy of inferences, we can say that *and* seems to be unmarked, or neutral, in this respect. It may be that it suggests a common background, or assumed context, to which both the preceding and the following segment relate, but in many cases it is just additive, not to be interpreted in a causal, nor in a contrastive, way:

(39) He said he was sorry, and I think he meant it.

Although *and* does not impose either a parallel or a contrastive reading, it does occur in both types of relationships in actual usage:

(40) He has been stealing, and now he has to pay for it.

(41) I have been working all my life, and I never got a word of appreciation.

Given the additive character of *and* itself, the causal use in (40) is less marked than the adversative use in (41), which sounds even more like a reproach than a formulation with *but*, but I will not go into this particular aspect further here. In any case, it is clear that a contrastive interpretation of a relationship marked with *and* is dependent on our sharing a cultural model, in this case one according to which working hard is something that should be appreciated, at least at some moments in a person's lifetime. Without such an implicit but shared cultural model, a contrastive interpretation is hard to impose on a relationship marked by *and*, witness (39), as well as the difference between (42) and (43):

(42) This house is beautiful, and it is cheap. [→ All the more reason to buy it!]

(43) This house is beautiful, but it is cheap. [→ Let's not buy it, perhaps there are hidden defects.]

The descriptive content of the clauses is the same in these cases, so any inference derivable from properties at level O should be equally available in both cases. But, as indicated in the examples, this does not seem to be the case. In particular, it is very hard to impose the interpretation 'Let's not buy it' on

(42). So it is only because of the presence of the explicit contrast marker *but* in (43) that we take the second clause as cancelling the inference that we should buy the house, and then look for a background assumption that may be invoked to justify this cancellation. One possibility is that hidden defects might explain the unexpected low price, which is a good reason not to buy the house, despite its being beautiful.[20] I will return to discourse connectives, and different ways in which they relate to the levels O and S of the construal configuration, in Chapter 4.

2.3.3 *The negation system for intersubjective coordination*

There are several other linguistic elements that can be regarded as argumentative operators like *barely* and *almost*. Consider the examples in (44) and (45):

(44) Our two sons Charles and George were playing a game. Halfway through, Charles already had sixty points. So the youngest was probably going to win again.

(45) Our two sons Charles and George were playing a game. Halfway through, Charles only had sixty points. So the youngest was probably going to win again.

These demonstrate that the function of *already* is to some extent similar to that of *almost*. *Already* also orients the reader to a positive conclusion from the information about having sixty points, whereas *only* looks more similar to *barely* in that it excludes such a positive conclusion. Other elements performing such operations on relations between different kinds of situations and inferences are *just, merely, I doubt,* and more like them.[21] Thus several elements have a function that operates directly on the inferences the addressee is supposed to draw from an utterance and that is therefore to be located at level S of the basic construal configuration.

---

[20] The argumentative status of *but* (*mais* in French) has been analyzed by Ducrot (1996: 42 ff. and several previous publications). See also Foolen (1993) for a comprehensive overview and many references, and Spooren (1989) for a corpus-based and experimental investigation of Dutch *maar*.

[21] These elements are various members of the class of semantic elements known in the literature as 'negative-polarity licensors', that is, elements that can satisfy the requirements for the felicitous use of negative-polarity items. For example, *a wink* in a phrase such as *sleep a wink* in English is a negative-polarity item, as it normally requires a negative context. 'He didn't sleep a wink last night' is fine, while it is not felicitous to say 'He slept a wink last night'. This expression can also be licensed by a few other elements, e.g. *hardly* ('I hardly slept a wink last night'), which are therefore also negative-polarity licensors. Recall that *let alone* is also characterized as a negative-polarity item (see Sects. 2.3.1 above and 2.3.4 below). There is a huge literature concerning the precise nature of these classes of elements, going back to (at least) Klima (1964). Two recent studies, with many references to other ones, are Van der Wouden (1997) and Israel (1998). These also pay attention to *positive*-polarity items and their contexts.

This is not to say that these elements are basically all synonyms (or antonyms). They are not; on the contrary. For example, the use of *already* suggests that the number of points gained is more than might normally be expected at this stage in the game, and thus also implies that the actual number of points is sixty (or perhaps more), while *almost*, as we have seen, implies that it is less than sixty. Notice, however, that while such lexical semantic properties making *already* different from other elements are important, they do not exhaust the semantics of the word. Suppose we assumed that *already* just means 'sooner than might be expected' and *barely* 'slightly more than X'. Then it should be easy to combine the two words in one clause; after all, one can very well have gained slightly more points sooner than might be expected at a certain point in a game. But such a sentence, as in (46), looks more like a contradiction than a balanced judgment, which supports the idea that the two words basically indicate opposite argumentative orientations:

(46) ??Halfway through, Charles already had barely sixty points.

As is evident from Van der Wouden (1997) and Israel (1996, 1998), the meanings of such 'polarity items' (see n. 21 above) are actually highly diverse, in ways that are not really different from the ones in which any lexical item can differ semantically from another one. Accordingly, I do not claim that the analysis presented in this section of (especially) *barely* and *almost* provides an exhaustive characterization of the semantics of these elements. Rather, the main point is that the distinctions laid out in the basic construal configuration—most specifically the two parallel dimensions O and S, connected by cultural cognitive models (topoi)—are indispensable in any semantic characterization of these and other elements. In other words, the main claim here does not concern all of the specifics of the semantics of a number of elements, but the proper characterization of the 'conceptual space' in which these words and constructions occupy points or regions: this is the dimension of intersubjective coordination in the basic construal configuration.

Furthermore, the class of elements that function primarily in this dimension includes straightforward negation. The argument for this conclusion is a linguistic one; that is, it is based on an issue of linguistic generalization. If the primary function of negation were to instruct the addressee about an object of conceptualization, then one would expect that its grammatical and discourse properties would overlap with those of elements that indicate similar aspects of an object of conceptualization. That is, it should behave more like *almost* than like *barely*, since negation and *almost* both imply lack of applicability of a predicate. But since negation behaves linguistically like *barely*, and not like *almost*, the function of negation is better seen as primarily concerning intersubjective coordination. Only in that way is there a prospect of constructing an analysis that is both general and coherent of the ways the elements involved relate to and interact with each other.

This generalization over the semantics of sentential negation and *barely* can be represented in the mental space configuration in Figure 2.5.

The use of negation as well as *barely* involves the following cognitive constellation. The speaker/writer envisages that the addressee might entertain a thought q; for example, that there is hope for his son's future in college. This is represented as '?q' in Space$_2$. She furthermore believes that she shares the knowledge of a certain cultural model with the addressee; for example, that passing a statistics course in our culture normally provides good grounds for the conclusion that one can also pass other sorts of courses. This is represented by the topos 'P → Q' in both Space$_1$ and Space$_2$. Both the use of *not p* and that of *barely p* invalidate q (given the topos), inviting the addressee to consider ¬q more justified than q, at least at this point in the discourse. All of these operations are entirely contained in the dimension of intersubjective coordination. Figure 2.5 only involves cognitive processes; that is, elements and relations between them at level S of the construal configuration. It thus turns out to be essential that the different spaces used in the analysis of negation are indeed in a strict sense *mental* spaces, and not just any kind of distinct representations, for example, distinct 'possible worlds': the linguistically most relevant properties of negation, the ones that it shares with other elements in the same paradigmatic class, are purely cognitive operations.

In Section 2.1 (Figs. 2.1 and 2.2) the utterance of a negative sentence *not p* was represented as involving the projection of a second mental space that contained the counterpart p. The representation in Figure 2.5 differs in

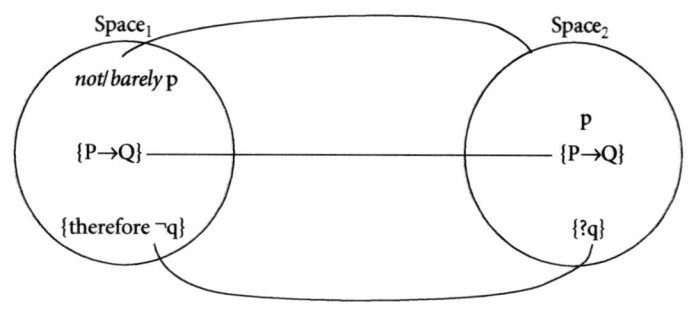

Space$_1$: not/barely p, {P→Q}, {therefore ¬q}

Space$_2$: p, {P→Q}, {?q}

p = 'He passed his first statistics course'
q = 'There is hope for his future'

FIGURE 2.5. Negation and *barely* share orientation for intersubjective coordination

particular because of the presence of general knowledge structures and inferential processes, not only of what is linguistically explicit and its direct counterparts, as in Figures 2.1 and 2.2. In principle, this is an application of a general idea of mental-space theory; namely, that conceptual content can get mapped from one mental space to another 'for free' as long as there is nothing blocking it (Fauconnier 1994, 1997). The special point here is that the activation of such structures and processes in Space$_2$ is conventionally associated with the use of an element from the negation system such as *not* or *barely*. The speaker/writer has to assume, for example, that the relevant topos P → Q can be activated in Space$_2$ to license an inference q (if p), or otherwise his utterance of *not/barely p* would not make sense.[22] This is what makes negation constructions constructions of intersubjectivity in the fullest sense.

Recall that when I introduced the notion 'topos' in Chapter 1 (Sect. 1.2.3) I noticed that it formulates a kind of default rule; not a universally valid one. In that context, this was simply a matter of descriptive adequacy: the kind of rule licensing an inference from the presence of seats to comfort can only be a defeasible one. But in the present context we must conclude that topoi *must* be default rules, laying down what is *normally* the case: otherwise there would be no way to generalize over the behavior of negation, *barely*, and other inference-cancelling operators and connectors. Thus a topos cannot be regarded as a case of material implication.[23] This is why capital letters are used to represent topoi in Figure 2.5: the propositions involved in this relationship are generalizations, not particulars—'singular statements' in terms of Popper (1972); for the latter, lower-case letters are used. The fact that a coherent account of an important subsystem of grammar requires this view of topoi is, in my view, a very telling indication of the character of much of everyday cognition.

The two mental spaces from Figure 2.5 correspond to the two conceptualizers in Figure 2.4, repeated here for convenience.

At the beginning of this chapter I raised the question: Is negation to be analyzed as primarily an operation on the relation between a conceptualizer and an object of conceptualization, or an operation on the relation between

---

[22] Notice that neither speaker/writer nor addressee has to *believe* in the (validity of the) topos; it is mutually shared *knowledge* of these rules that is required. One can use an observation to decrease the validity of a topos (e.g. *John failed his courses in winter and passed them all in spring, so one does not really predict anything about the other*), but even that does not undo the utility of a topos, as long as the knowledge that the rule is generally used in the community for deriving inferences is shared.

[23] These points have in several forms also been addressed in other contexts (see Oversteegen 1997; Lagerwerf 1998 and some refs. cited there). Ducrot (1996: 144) suggests that it might in fact be quite old: 'we do admit that there might be exceptions but that does not prevent the *topos* [e.g. that warm weather in general makes a walk pleasant] from being valid, which is the point this highly

O: *Object of conceptualization:*

S: *Subject of conceptualization (Ground):*

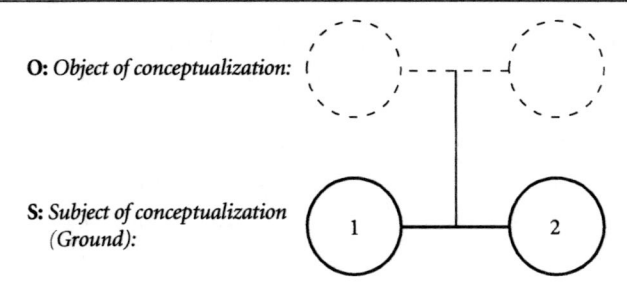

FIGURE 2.4. Conventional function of 'argumentative operators' located in dimension of intersubjective coordination

conceptualizers? The answer is obviously: the latter. The fact that the question makes sense and that the answer is linguistically relevant also testifies to the usefulness of integrating mental spaces into the construal-configuration approach, which allows us to distinguish sharply between the (vertical) construal relation and the (horizontal) intersubjective coordination relation.

Differences between *not* and *barely* precisely concern the relationship *between* level S and level O. In the former case, p is simply claimed to provide an incorrect picture of the object of conceptualization, in the latter case it is not. But this difference at level O is not sufficient, so to speak, to make them belong to two entirely different semantic classes of expression. The difference makes *barely p* a somewhat less forceful argument than *not p*, leaving some room for discussion and 'negotiation' (see the discussion of argumentative strength in Sect. 2.3.2).

In general, we can, of course, make inferences about what the world must look like on the basis of what the speaker/writer is communicating with a negative utterance, or one containing *barely* or *almost*. Such inferences about the object of conceptualization may turn out to be similar in the case of, for example, *not* and *almost*, but as far as the system of the language is concerned these kinds of inferences appear to be secondary, given the way these elements contribute to the coherence of discourse, as we saw in the previous section.[24]

famous formula attributed to Aristotle makes: "exceptions make it possible to uphold the rule in unforeseen cases" '. The ideas of 'admitting' and 'exceptions' are closely related to concessive relations, and in Chapter 4 (esp. Sects. 4.2.2 and 4.2.4) we will indeed find that a proper understanding of these issues is critical for a consistent and adequate analysis of the relations between concessive and causal connectives.

[24] And also given their similar grammatical behavior as negative-polarity licensors (see n. 21). However, as I said above, it is not my intention to provide a (re)analysis of the issue of negative polarity in terms of the present approach, although I think this would be both a promising and a challenging project. Israel (1998) goes a long way in this direction, in my view (see esp. pp. 141 ff. and ch. 6).

The primary ones concern the ways that addressees and speakers/writers engage in assessing and managing each other's cognitive states and processes.

2.3.4 *Let alone* and argumentation

Solution: making syntactic and semantic negative polarity coincide

We can now return to the problems related to the analysis of the *let alone* construction (see Sect. 2.3.1). The first problem with Fillmore et al.'s analysis of the syntax and semantics of the *let alone* construction was that they considered its apparent negative polarity as a syntactic rather than a semantic property. However, from the perspective that we have now developed we may say that their view of semantics was not formulated in terms of the construal configuration. The latter makes a crucial distinction between the level of an object of conceptualization and that of the subjects of conceptualization engaging in cognitive coordination in a linguistic usage event. Thus it is not just conceivable but actually to be expected that several linguistic elements have a conventional meaning operating only, or primarily, at the latter level. From this perspective the failure to make this distinction in the conceptual apparatus used for semantic analysis cannot but lead to a distorted view of the meaning of elements that basically operate at level S.

The first and decisive move we have to make now in order to solve the problem is to simply assume that *let alone* also functions at this level. It is an operator on the conclusions to be drawn from the conjoined clauses, rather than on their descriptive contents. Consider (18), repeated here for convenience:

(18) He barely passed the first statistics course, let alone the second one.

According to the approach developed so far, *barely* invalidates the default conclusions associated with 'He passed' (given some topos), just as negation does, so that the conclusion might be something like 'He is unable to pass statistics'. It is this conclusion that provides the basis for the stronger statement in the second conjunct, that he has definitely not passed the second course.

As another example, consider (47), from a Dutch newspaper (*de Volkskrant*, 30 August 1993):

(47) De   ruimteschaarste in Japan begint zo nijpend te worden dat
     The space-shortage in Japan begins so acute   to become that
     er   maar nauwelijks plaats is voor alle levenden   laat staan voor
     there just barely   room is for all living-PLUR let stand for
     alle doden.
     all dead-PLUR

'Lack of space in Japan is becoming so acute that there is scarcely enough room for all the living—let alone for all the dead.'

Again, the first conjunct descriptively implies that there is still enough space in Japan for the living. But the use of *maar nauwelijks* ('scarcely enough') cancels inferences associated with 'enough space (for the living)', such as that there is a fair chance of some space being available for other purposes. It thus provides good grounds for the conclusion that there is certainly no space for all the dead, as expressed in the second conjunct.

So the claim is that this approach allows us to do away with a discrepancy between syntactic and semantic features in the analysis of the *let alone* construction. The requirement of a negative context can be analyzed as a semantic one, once it is recognized that the conventional meanings of both negation, *barely*, and *let alone* operate primarily at the level of cognitive coordination between subjects of conceptualization, not at the level of coordination between a subject and an object of conceptualization. This general property of semantic structure thus also contributes to a more coherent and simpler view of linguistic knowledge, as it renders certain discrepancies between syntactic and semantic properties of constructions superfluous.

Solution: aligning semantics and pragmatics
This effect can be extended to the second problem noted in Section 2.3.1, that of the unnaturalness of the order of the conjuncts. Recall that the pragmatic characterization of the construction by Fillmore et al. (repeated below), implies that the less informative conjunct follows the more informative one, and is placed at the end of the sentence:

(15) **Pragmatics:**
The construction as a whole allows the speaker to be *relevant*—by addressing (here: negating) a contextually relevant proposition in the second conjunct—and at the same time to be *informative*—by redirecting the addressee to a new proposition which is more informative (the one in the first conjunct).

The proposal formulated in (15) makes two related predictions that can be tested relatively easily. Fillmore et al. formulated their hypothesis about the pragmatics of the *let alone* construction explicitly in terms of relations between the sentence involved and its context, but they did not check it against occurrences of *let alone* sentences in actual discourse fragments. Now if the pragmatic function of the construction is to shift attention to the first conjunct, then the first prediction we can make is that it should be easy for the text following a *let alone* sentence to relate to the contents of this first conjunct; after all, the element to which attention is redirected is a likely candidate for the topic of the next sentence. And the second, more specific, prediction is that the topic of the immediately following discourse should never be the same as the content of the *second* conjunct of a *let alone* sentence; after all, attention is supposedly shifted away from it, according to (15).

These are straightforward predictions. However, it is obvious that neither prediction is borne out. As an example, consider (47′), which gives the text following (47):

(47′) Lack of space in Japan is becoming so acute that there is scarcely enough room for all the living—let alone for all the dead. Tokyo's municipality has therefore thought up the following controversial solution: a twenty-meter-high final resting place, with several storeys, and 5200 small vaults in it. For an amount between €2000 and €3000, the surviving relatives may purchase a compartment for the ashes of the deceased.[25]

The sentence about Tokyo's plan for a skyscraper graveyard does not connect to the contents of the first clause of the *let alone* sentence, which is about lack of space for the living. If anything, it relates to the second conjunct: the lack of space for the dead. This topic provides the general background for the whole text.[26]

Would it be at all possible for the first conjunct to provide the topic for the text? The constructed text in (48) shows that this is in fact quite awkward:

(48) #Lack of space in Japan is becoming so acute that there is scarcely enough room for all the living—let alone for all the dead. Tokyo's municipality has therefore decided that from now on single-family dwellings are forbidden, and all apartment buildings must be at least twenty storeys high.

The reader is left wondering what the point is of the claim about room for the dead. So in fact it is the second conjunct that demands attention.

Moreover, the first sentence of (47) is the first sentence of the entire newspaper article, which makes it quite difficult to conceive what 'addressing a relevant proposition' with the second conjunct might involve. Fillmore et al. explicated the relation between the second conjunct and the context of a *let alone* construct as follows:

---

[25] 'De ruimteschaarste in Japan begint zo nijpend te worden dat er maar nauwelijks plaats is voor alle levenden—laat staan voor alle doden. Het gemeentebestuur van Tokyo heeft daarom de volgende, controversiële, oplossing bedacht: een meerdere verdiepingen tellende laatste rustplaats van zo'n twintig meter hoog, met daarin 5200 kastjes. Voor de somma van 4500 tot 6000 gulden kunnen de nabestaanden zich een bergplaats aanschaffen voor de as van de overledene.'

[26] The title of the article was 'Even for its dead, Tokyo has no space' ('Zelfs voor zijn doden heeft Tokyo geen plek').

By way of the raising of what we may call the CONTEXT PROPOSITION, the immediately preceding context has created conditions under which a speech act represented by the weaker B clause is an appropriate or relevant response (Fillmore et al. 1988: 532).

But example (47) does not have any preceding context. Nevertheless, it functions perfectly well in its context.

In other words, the example shows that Fillmore et al.'s idea that the function of *let alone* is to allow the speaker/writer to resolve a conflict between the Gricean maxims of relevance and informativeness is misguided; *let alone* does not necessarily redirect attention to the first conjunct, and does not require that the issue addressed in the second conjunct should have been raised in the preceding context either.

In 4 of the 8 instances of *laat staan* in the Dutch Eindhoven Corpus (see n. 5) the text immediately following the construction is concerned with aspects of the second conjunct only, and these are completely normal text fragments, like (47). Furthermore, none of the other 4 cases is followed by text that is concerned with aspects of the first conjunct only. So both predictions derived from Fillmore et al.'s analysis of the pragmatics of the construction are problematic.

It seems appropriate then to reconsider the pragmatic function of *let alone* in discourse. A good starting point is to look more closely at the instances in which the second conjunct provides the topic for the subsequent text, and consider *how* this text is connected to the *let alone* sentence. First of all, the next sentence may be introduced by the contrastive conjunction *but*. As this marks the cancellation of inferences licensed by the previous discourse (see the discussion at the end of Sect. 2.3.2), it provides a good instrument for finding out what the argumentative orientation of a *let alone* construct is. Thus, consider fragment (49):

(49) All this fussing in and around the dressing rooms of the Rotterdam Doelen [Concert Hall] seemed to indicate that one cannot be sure about anything with a 'grande vedette'—not about a performance, not about a rehearsal, let alone about an interview. But exactly at five she slipped in through the stage door, wearing a beige raincoat. Perfectly inconspicuous, completely unassuming. Obviously tired—but immediately willing to have a conversation in her dressing room.[27]

---

[27] 'Heel dat nerveuze gedoe in en om de kleedkamers van de Rotterdamse Doelen leek erop te wijzen dat je met een 'grande vedette' nergens zeker van bent—niet van een optreden, niet van een repetitie, laat staan van een interview. Maar klokslag 5 uur glipte ze in een beige regenjas naar binnen door de artiesteningang. Volmaakt onopvallend, volkomen pretentieloos. Duidelijk moe—maar meteen bereid tot een gesprek in haar kleedkamer.'

In the first sentence the journalist evokes the picture that getting an interview with some famous star is highly unlikely. The nervous behavior of people in and near the dressing rooms indicates that she might not even perform or rehearse, so an interview, being higher on the scale of 'non-obligations', seems completely out of the question. However, as the subsequent piece of text, starting with *but*, states, the interview did take place. So what appears to be going on here is that the speaker/writer makes the addressee entertain the thought that the interview will not take place; this is the inference that is subsequently canceled. In (49) the use of *let alone* can be seen as a rhetorical device, contributing to the strength of the contrast. First the reader is invited to identify with a state of mind in which an interview is the last thing to be expected,[28] *but* then he learns that it actually did take place. This should clearly add to the reader's admiration for the artist.

Secondly, there are topic continuations without a contrastive connection. But notice that with a contrastive connection the topic that is continued in the subsequent text is the positive counterpart of the second conjunct of the *let alone* sentence, not the negative version expressed in that sentence itself. Without a contrast it is only the negative version itself that can be the continued topic of the subsequent text. An example is (47): the topic of the text is the *lack* of room for the dead, so the negative import of the *let alone* sentence is included. Taking the positive version ('there is room for the dead') as the topic of the text produces incoherence:

(50) #Lack of space in Japan is becoming so acute that there is scarcely enough room for all the living—let alone for all the dead. Tokyo's municipality has now approved a proposal that allows relatives of the city's inhabitants a final resting place next to their loved ones.

Only the addition of a contrast marker (*but, however, still...*) to the second sentence in (50) can make such a text coherent.[29] Similarly, changing the contrastive relation of (49) into a parallel one, while preserving the positive version of the topic, leads to incoherence:

(51) # one cannot be sure about anything with a 'grande vedette'—not about a performance, not about a rehearsal, let alone about an interview. And

---

[28] Notice that this state of mind is represented explicitly in the text, in the form of the complementation construction *seemed to indicate that.* The next chapter is devoted completely to an analysis of such constructions as devices for instructing an addressee about how to engage in cognitive coordination.

[29] Notice that this 'strategy' does not work in (48), i.e. when the subsequent text takes the first conjunct as providing the topic. This is an additional indication that the pragmatic function of the *let alone* construction is not to redirect attention to this conjunct.

indeed, exactly at five she slipped in through the stage door [...] willing to have a conversation in her dressing room.

These phenomena are related. When the content of the second conjunct of a sentence of the type *A let alone B* is continued in the subsequent discourse, this can only happen in one of two ways: the discourse proceeds about B with a contrastive connective, or the discourse proceeds about not-B without a contrastive connective.

Finally, the third possibility is that the topic of the entire *let alone* sentence is simply dropped. An example is (52), about a Dutchman who is visiting a restaurant in France, where he gets into a conversation with members of the local population:

(52) 'German?'—Because his French is so good?—'No, Dutch'. It then becomes quiet in a friendly kind of way, because not everyone in Reims knows what a Dutchman is, let alone where he comes from. In the commercial domain, friendliness is reduced considerably when I want to pay with traveler's checks made out in dollars. The fact is that these things have two advantages for a tourist [...]^[30]

At the beginning of this fragment the nationality of the main character is a candidate topic. The reader is then made to think, in the *let alone* sentence, that it will be so no longer, and then indeed nothing else is said about it. Attention is clearly not shifted to the first conjunct (whether people know what a Dutchman is). Rather, the function of the *let alone* sentence appears to be to 'close' the topic associated with the whole scale involved in the interpretation of the sentence, everything having to do with being Dutch. It allows the discourse to move on to a different subject.

Thus we see three types of connection between a construct of the type *A let alone B*, a discontinuous one and two continuous ones:

(i) the discourse moves on to a totally different topic (the whole issue of *A let alone B* is dropped, A as well as B: Example (52));
(ii) the discourse proceeds about B, after a contrastive conjunction (*but*, etc.: Example (49));
(iii) the discourse proceeds about 'not B' (e.g. its consequences, what to do about it), without a contrastive conjunction (Example (47)).

---

[30] '"Duitser?"—Wegens zijn goede Frans?—"Nee Nederlander". Het wordt dan vriendelijk stil, want niet iedereen in Reims weet wat een Nederlander is, laat staan waar hij thuis hoort. Op zakelijk gebied wordt de charme aanmerkelijk getemperd als ik met traveller cheques in dollars wil betalen. Die dingen hebben nl. voor de toerist twee voordelen'.

The generalization is that *let alone B* evokes the inference that at this point in the discourse there are good reasons to drop the idea B. If the idea B *is* taken up again, this can only happen after a contrastive conjunction.

So the discourse function of *let alone* seems to be not to shift attention to the first conjunct but to evoke the idea that the positive content of the second conjunct B ('room for the dead'; 'where a Dutchman comes from'; 'an interview with a star') is not worth considering any further, for very good reasons provided in the first conjunct. This constrains the possibilities for coherent continuations, without, of course, reducing them to only one type. Subsequently, the counterpart of B may be considered in the rest of the text, a strong contrast may be constructed (contrary to expectation, B *is* being considered), or the idea may indeed be dropped.[31]

This analysis establishes a strong relation between the semantics of the *let alone* construction, as analyzed in Sections 2.3.1 and 2.3.4 (based on Fillmore et al.'s analysis in (12)), and its pragmatic function. The former, in the argumentative analysis, comes down to the following:

(53) X_{negative} *let alone* Y means:
inferences associated with X must be cancelled;
X is lower on some relevant scale than Y;
therefore, cancellation of inferences associated with Y is strongly supported.

The pragmatic function, as we have now reanalyzed it on the basis of relations between *let alone* sentences and their subsequent contexts, is: 'Y is not a topic worthy of further attention'. It is clear that this pragmatic function is closely connected to the semantics, and in any case much more directly so than in Fillmore et al.'s original analysis. All in all, this analysis gives a more coherent, integrated picture of different aspects of the construction than was originally possible.

Solution: understanding the historical development of let alone
The analysis developed in the previous sections also allows us to explain why, in English, the elements *let* and *alone* were suitable for use in this pattern. According to Traugott (1995) these elements originally constituted an imperative not to pay attention any more to some concrete or abstract object. We may assume that they must often have constituted an instruction for the

---

[31] As mentioned above, half of the instances of *laat staan* in the Eindhoven Corpus (85 per cent of which is written text) were of the discontinuous type. In the Corpus of Spoken Dutch as it is presently available (5th release, 2003) this even seems to be the function in a clear majority of cases, but further research on the completed corpus is necessary to determine whether this is a significant difference.

addressee to leave a topic for what it is, on its own (and thus indirectly to proceed with other topics that *are* worth thinking and talking about); with increasing frequency and/or salience, this has ultimately become conventionalized as the function of the construction. Notice that the present analysis of the modern construction, focusing on its effects in intersubjective coordination, allows for a more straightforward connection between its historical source and its present function than Fillmore et al.'s analysis did (see Sect. 2.3.1). As in several other cases of subjectification (Verhagen 1995, 2000*a*; Langacker 1998), the change involved a loss of objective content, without much or any change in the structure of the subjective construal involved (in this case, the speaker/writer's instruction to the addressee).

The Dutch equivalent of *let alone* (*laat staan*, lit. 'let stand') originates in a first-person expression, 'I let stand' (see sect. 2.3.1). This differs in two respects from its English counterpart: the complement (a verb meaning 'stand' rather than an adjective meaning 'alone') and the use of first person rather than an imperative (implicit second person). However, the effects of its use in discourse, and especially when applied to topics being evaluated for consideration, are very similar. My saying at a particular point in a discourse that I 'leave' some idea 'standing'—that is, leave it where it is and do not try to 'move' it any more—is inviting the addressee to do the same; that is, to abandon the idea. This has become the conventional function of the construction, with a concomitant change in form, namely the loss of the first-person marker *ik* (or, perhaps more likely, the reduced variant '*k*).

Thus the fact that different elements in different languages ('let alone' in English, 'let stand' in Dutch) at present play a very similar, if not identical, role, can be explained, but only if we adopt the analysis of the constructions as operating in the dimension of cognitive coordination between subjects of conceptualization that I have developed in this chapter. Something parallel can be claimed for the fact that the modern English expression *let alone* translates into German as *geschweige* (*denn*), which, being related to *schweigen* ('keep silent'), has probably always been applicable to 'possible topics for consideration' only; it also accounts for the fact that in modern English *let alone* is considered synonymous with the expression *not to mention* (see OED, s.v. *let*).

Again, the general point of this approach is to consider *let alone* primarily as an operator on the conclusions to be drawn from a statement, not on the descriptive contents of the statement. The negative nature of the whole construction—the strong instruction that some idea is not worth pursuing—makes it understandable that there is a condition of negativity for the first conjunct; negating a premiss in an obvious inferential scheme (given a mutually shared model) is a good way to invalidate a conclusion.[32] At the same time, it makes it understandable that we sometimes find instances of a *let alone* construction in which the first conjunct lacks a conventional negative element: such cases have the special property that they allow, in a more or less straightforward way, for a negative inference that can be used as the basis for the instruction to abandon some idea in the second conjunct. A corpus example from Dutch is (54):

(54) Above, in the passages on the 'social relevance' of art, it was noted that freedom is an essential feature of art. This holds true even for the artist. Let alone that the government may presume anything in this area.[33]

The first sentence introduces freedom as an essential feature of art. This is not in itself negative, but apparently it was, for the writer, a kind of starting point for a chain of inferences leading to a strong negative conclusion, one that can be paraphrased as 'It is crucial for art to be free, so no one should try to control art, not even artists themselves, let alone the government'. It is true that several readers do not consider this a very well composed text, but it is an advantage of the present analysis that it provides a way to understand why it can be spontaneously produced. Given the context about freedom being essential for art, there is a conceptually negative pragmatic interpretation for the first conjunct which 'licenses' the use of *let alone*, along the lines indicated in (54'):

(54') [...] This holds true even for artists [→ *Even artists should not try to impose policy or guidelines for art.*] Let alone that [...]

---

[32] Data from Pasch (2000), as well as examples of older uses provided in the *OED* and the *WNT*, suggest that this condition did not hold originally in any of the three languages mentioned, and only developed later as the constructions came to be used purely at the level of intersubjective coordination, devoid of descriptive content. Once the use of some form of negation in the first conjunct has become obligatory, it is conceivable that some speakers attribute the negative character of the whole construction to this explicit negative element and not to the element *let alone*. It is then in principle possible to interpret the latter as only a marker of some scalar ordering, that may also be employed in non-negative contexts (a form of reanalysis). Perhaps this is the explanation of the occurrence of some 'purely positive' uses (that cannot even be read as 'implicitly negative', as the ones discussed in the text below) noticed already in Fillmore et al. (1988); see Verhagen and Foolen (2003) for some parallel observations on modern Dutch usage. More detailed diachronic research is required before conclusions can be drawn about possible past and present developments of the negation components in form and meaning of the construction.

[33] 'Hiervóór, in de passages over de "maatschappelijke relevantie" van de kunst werd reeds opgemerkt, dat de vrijheid een wezenskenmerk van de kunst is. Dat is het zelfs voor de kunstenaar. Laat staan dat de overheid zich hier iets mag aanmatigen.'

This kind of usage appears to be produced rather easily. Browsing other corpora, one soon encounters similar cases. An example from the Corpus of Spoken Dutch is (55), and one from *de Volkskrant* from 1995 is (56):

(55) je   hebt al   zoveel   moeite met tweepersoonstenten
     you   have already   so much   trouble with two-person-tents
     kopen / dus laat   staan dat 'k met driepersoonstenten aan moet
     buy-INF so   let   stand that I with three-person-tents PRT must
     komen.
     come
     'you already have such a problem with buying two-person tents / let alone that I should propose three person tents then.'

(56) Je   moet   gestoord zijn om daar   vlakbij te gaan staan, laat
     You   must   disturbed be   for there nearby to go   stand let
     staan om te dansen.
     stand for to dance
     'You must be out of your mind to go and stand close to that [= an island of loudspeakers], let alone to dance.'

In (55) the addressee's having 'trouble' with buying two-person tents suggests that he does *not* want to buy them, which licenses the invalidation of the conclusion that he might want to consider buying three-person ones, and thus the use of *let alone*. Similarly, the statement in (56) that one must be out of one's mind to go and stand close to the loudspeakers conveys that one should *not* stand there, licensing the invalidation, with *let alone*, of the conclusion that one might consider dancing there.

The proposed intersubjective function of *let alone* (semantics and pragmatics) is to make the addressee cancel relevant inferences associated with the concept mentioned in the second conjunct, and make him recognize that this concept and associated ones may thus not be worthy of further consideration. This provides a way of unifying these different cases, which is another point in its favor. More generally, it supports the claim that the dimension of intersubjectivity is crucial for the proper characterization of several conventional linguistic meanings, including grammatical ones. We can thus add this to the previous conclusion about the nature of the conceptual basis for the linguistic generalization over negation and elements like *barely*, as opposed to elements like *almost*; they must be recognized as conventional linguistic constraints on operations in the dimension of intersubjectivity rather than as contributing (primarily) to the conceptualization of some object.

2.4 'Double' negation revisited: why *not impossible* does not equal *possible*

Before concluding this chapter there is one remaining issue to be addressed. At the end of Section 2.2.2 I mentioned the problem of double negation, quoting Horn (1989: 298): 'if something is *not inconceivable* or *not impossible*, what else can it be but *conceivable* or *possible*? [...] Why don't these doubly negated forms, amounting presumably to the contradictory of a contradictory, result in complete redundancy?' I proposed that the presence of two mental spaces evoked by sentential negation, one contradicting the other, made *not impossible* crucially different from *possible*; but I had to admit at that point that this could not be the whole story. It could have been the whole story if it were true that the mental space contradicted by *not impossible* had to be linguistically expressed in the preceding context, but that is not the case. Negation is not presuppositional in that way (unlike, for example, *on the contrary* in English, or *integendeel* in Dutch). If a dual-mental-space configuration can be imposed on the interpretation of the text if that is required for the interpretation of *not impossible*, then the question is why something similar is not possible if it is required for the interpretation of *possible*.

I believe the answer to that question can be derived from the analysis of negation and *barely* vs. *almost* in Section 2.3.2. But before presenting that argument it is useful to point out that the problem, and thus also the need for a solution, is even bigger than suggested at the end of Section 2.2.2. As we saw there, Horn used precisely the words *conceivable* and *possible* in the examples in his question, as they do not have a 'zone of indifference' like the one between 'happy' and 'unhappy' which can be described by means of 'not unhappy' and nothing else. Thus he suggests that the problem of double negation is at least less urgent, if not non-existent, for negation of a contrary concept than for negation of a contradictory one. However, in actual usage many if not most of the non-contradictory *un*-forms are not at all meant to evoke the 'zone of indifference'. Most of the time the use of expressions of the type *not unhappy* implies that the person involved is happy (etc.). An example from Dutch is (57), from an interview printed in *de Volkskrant* in 1995:

(57) Ik ben bepaald niet ongelukkig met de uitspraken van Wim Kok.
I am definitely not unhappy with the remarks of Wim Kok
'I am not at all displeased at Wim Kok's remarks.'

The presence of 'definitely' in this sentence already suggests that the speaker is actually quite happy with what Wim Kok has said, and the next sentence makes this especially clear: 'It is good that things that have been general practice for a long time are being said openly.'[34] Notice that 'It is good' does not add a new evaluation, but simply explains the speaker's previous statement. This situation is quite normal; 8 out of the 10 instances of *niet ongelukkig zijn* ('be not unhappy') in *de Volkskrant* of 1995 were of this type, and only 2 were used to indicate Horn's 'zone of indifference'. So the question remains for *not un-X* expressions that are not logically equivalent to *X* too: Why do people use them at all?

Horn seeks the solution in the application of (Gricean) pragmatic principles, with implicatures being derived precisely from the fact that the speaker undertakes the effort of formulating his message elaborately: 'the use of a longer, marked expression in lieu of a shorter expression involving less effort on the part of the speaker signals that the speaker was not in a position to employ the simpler version felicitously'. The simple expressions are used for stereotypical situations, the longer ones for 'situations outside the stereotype, for which the unmarked expression could not have been used appropriately' (Horn 1989: 304), and Horn mentions a number of special stylistic effects of *not un-X* expressions that can be explained in this way. While I do not want to deny the usefulness of this perspective, it does not really account for the ordinariness of their actual use in many instances, such as (57), where it is quite hard to see a special rhetorical effect of saying 'not unhappy' instead of 'happy'.

What is more, the question of what motivates the use of *not un-X* expressions is a special case of a more general question that cannot be answered in the same way as Horn suggests for *not un-X*. This general question is: What motivates the use of an apparently less informative expression when a more informative one would be appropriate? Strictly speaking, *X is not unhappy* does not entail *X is happy* (because *unhappy* is the contrary of *happy*, not its contradiction). By the same token, *X is not happy* does not entail *X is unhappy*. But *X is unhappy* does entail *X is not happy*. *X is unhappy* is thus more informative than *X is not happy*, as the former asymmetrically entails the latter. But that raises the question: Why do people say *not happy* in situations where it is evidently not false to say *unhappy*, such as (58) (from a book review in the *Volkskrant* corpus mentioned above)? It looks as if this kind of use does not conform to Grice's 'Maxim of Quantity' (1975).[35]

(58) Maar toch: Passmore is niet gelukkig. Hij lijdt aan onverklaarbare
     But still Passmore is not happy.   He suffers at inexplicable

---

[34] 'Het is goed dat dingen gezegd worden die in sterke mate al lang praktijk zijn.'
[35] See Fillmore et al. (1988: 532), as well as the discussion of the pragmatics of *let alone* in Section 2.3.1, and n. 9.

pijnen in zijn knie, die ondanks een operatie niet verdwijnen.
pains in his knee that despite an operation not disappear
'But still: Passmore is not happy. He suffers from inexplicable pains, which do not go away, despite an operation.'

Clearly, the general question about the motivation for the use of sentential negation where another (readily available) expression would be more informative subsumes the question about the motivation of *not un-X* expressions (that is, the 'problem' of litotes) as a special case. But there seems to be little prospect of a purely pragmatic answer to this more general question, to be based on a difference between using a longer expression in lieu of a shorter one. I suggest that the answer is rather to be sought in the following combination of specific semantic properties of sentential negation: (1) the construction of two mental spaces representing distinct epistemic stances towards the same idea (see Sect. 2.2.2); (2) the function of invalidating *inferences* associated with this idea (rather than the idea itself; see Sect. 2.3.3).

The paragraph preceding (58) lists several features of the life of Laurence Passmore (hero of the novel *Therapy* by David Lodge): he is the author of a successful TV series, has an attractive wife and an intelligent mistress, a fine house in his home town and a fancy apartment in London, and a great car. All of this is, of course, evidence for concluding that Passmore has little to worry about, little to wish for, little reason to try to change his life, etcetera (given a few well-known cultural models in western society). It is at that point in the text that (58) occurs. The reader is invited to consider-and-abandon (notice the contrastive marking *But still*) a positive epistemic stance towards such, presumably obvious, *conclusions* from the previous discourse, not to abandon a positive stance towards the descriptive contents of these passages themselves.

Notice that this is precisely the configuration depicted in Figure 2.5 in Section 2.3.3. According to this configuration, a negative expression of the form *not/barely p* may evoke a background mental space from which the positive statement *p* is absent. The reason for this proposal lies in the need to capture some linguistic generalizations. The primary function of linguistic negation is to instruct the addressee to perform certain cognitive operations, namely, to invalidate conclusions that are inferrable from the information available at that point in the discourse, and not primarily to tell the addressee about a discrepancy between the object of conceptualization and the world. What we can see now is that this also lays down the *conditions of use* for sentential negation. Upon encountering a case of sentential negation, it must be possible for the addressee to 'empathize' with Space$_2$; that is, he must be able to recognize that some thought q may be justified at that point in the discourse, and he must be able to construe *not p* as canceling the validity of q (Space₁), but he does not have to have entertained *p* as an object of conceptualization itself.

Under this analysis, the use of sentential negation in (58) is appropriate, and differs crucially from the use of 'unhappy'. The use of 'not happy' acknowledges something that the use of morphological negation would not acknowledge; namely, a reader's inferences based on the immediately preceding context. There are good reasons at this point in the text to adopt another epistemic stance than the one the author is proposing now (in the present, negative, utterance); it is this cognitive state of a reader, induced by the text, that the new sentence directly operates on, confirming (for the reader) that he has understood the text correctly so far. This is not to say that it would be impossible to use 'unhappy', but that would amount to having the reader do more inferential work himself, which could make the text look less coherent, whereas the use of sentential negation immediately provides an appropriate cognitive configuration, because it is its conventional function to evoke that configuration.

The 'not unhappy' case in (57), then, is quite similar. Example (57) is the first sentence of an interviewee's answer to a question which was formulated in the printed interview as in (59):

(59) According to Wim Kok, the Labor Party has shaken off its 'ideological feathers'. Losing the socialist ideology is 'in certain respects a liberating experience', he said last Monday. What do members of the Old Guard think of that?[36]

Both readers and interviewee understand that the whole point of asking the question is to envisage the possibility, if not expectation, that elderly social democrats might disagree with Kok. That possible attitude is described with the term *ongelukkig* ('displeased'), and it is the epistemic stance towards that idea that the speaker of (57) considers-and-abandons. So he is using a *not un-X* expression quite appropriately, but without special stylistic effects. This is not to say that the latter never occur. In the proper circumstances they may very well arise, in the ways mentioned by Horn (1989: 304). But the facts of usage show that such expressions are frequently used for cases *within* the range of the stereotype, so it is an advantage of the present approach that such stylistic effects are not considered necessary.

---

[36] 'Volgens Wim Kok heeft de PvdA haar "ideologische veren" afgeschud. Het verlies van de socialistische ideologie is "in bepaalde opzichten een bevrijdende ervaring", zei hij maandag. Wat vindt de oude garde daarvan?'

The same analysis applies straightforwardly to other cases, such as (60):

(60) De uitvallen van de Enschedeërs waren beslist niet
 The charges of the Enschede-PERSON-PLUR were certainly not
 ongevaarlijk.
 un-dangerous
 'The charges by the Enschede players were certainly not harmless.'

The presence of 'certainly' already suggests that the concept the author is entertaining is that of the presence of danger, not of its absence; that is, not some 'neutral zone' between danger and harmlessness. And without any transition the sentence following (60) gives two examples of obviously dangerous situations: the goalkeeper of the other team barely stopping an Enschede forward, and a back making a save on the line.[37] The point of the use of negation is, again, to cancel an inference from the preceding text, as can be seen in (60'):

(60') Al stond Twente dan met de rug tegen de muur, de
 Although stood Twente then with the back against the wall the
 enkele uitvallen van de Enschedeërs waren beslist niet
 few charges of the Enschede-PERSON-PLUR were certainly not
 ongevaarlijk.
 un-dangerous
 'Even though Twenty had its back to the wall, the few charges by the Enschede players were certainly not harmless.'

The content of the first clause licenses the inference that the *Twente* team (= Enschede players) did not pose any threat to their opponents, and it is this inference (expressed as *ongevaarlijk*, 'harmless') that the addressee is invited to consider and abandon. The latter point is what motivates the use of sentential negation. In this case, the fact that the first clause is concessive is also a linguistic cue to the presence of a dual-mental-space configuration (see Ch. 4). Without the negation in the main clause, as in (60"), the whole sentence is far less easy to process, despite the fact that, as we have seen, the intended denotation of *niet ongevaarlijk* is 'dangerous'.

(60") ?Al stond Twente dan met de rug tegen de muur, de
 Although stood Twente then with the back against the wall the

---

[37] 'Zo kon doelman Tie met moeite de doorgebroken Jeuking afstoppen en haalde De Zoete een door Naga ingeschoten bal nog net van de doellijn.'

enkele uitvallen van de Enschedeërs waren beslist
few charges of the Enschede-PERSON-PLUR were certainly
gevaarlijk.
dangerous
'Even though Twenty had its back to the wall, the few charges by the Enschede players were certainly dangerous.'

Finally, let us now turn to *not impossible*, which is logically equivalent to *possible*—the intriguing case of 'contradiction of contradictories', where two negations seem to *have* to cancel each other out. Consider once again the actual example, with its context, given in (6').

(6') Mensen die verandering willen op één noemer brengen is
People that change want on one denominator bring is
altijd lastig omdat zij allicht verschillende soorten verandering
always hard because they likely different types change
willen. Maar het vinden van die noemer is niet onmogelijk.
want But the find-INF of that denominator is not impossible
'It is always hard to find a common denominator for uniting people who are in favor of change, because they are likely to wish for different kinds of change. But finding such a common denominator is not impossible.'

The content of the first sentence ('Finding a common denominator is hard') provides a basis for the conclusion that it is not worth trying. In terms of practical consequences, it can be read as advice not to bother. It is this conclusion that the addressee can empathize with when encountering the negative expression *not impossible*, which obviously counts as an invitation to cancel the inferred advice not to bother. In the end, the position that the writer tries to convey here is that it *is* worth trying, and it is to that end, in this context, that the use of *not impossible* is entirely appropriate and not equivalent to *possible*; recall the observation from Section 2.2.2 that (6''), in which *not impossible* was replaced by *possible*, was a less coherent piece of text. Again, the point is that the primary conventional function of a negation is to cancel inferences, as represented in Figure 2.5—guiding the addressee's cognitive processes—not to report something about the world.

The short answer to Horn's question 'Why don't these doubly negated forms [...] result in complete redundancy?' (quoted above) is, then: Because sentential negation operates primarily in the dimension of intersubjective coordination, level S of the construal configuration in Figure 1.2, while morphological negation operates primarily at level O.

2.5 Conclusion

The point of departure of this book is that all language, when actually put to use, involves the coordination of one cognitive system with another, and especially that the proper characterization of several important linguistic phenomena has to be undertaken with respect to that dimension of intersubjective coordination rather than with respect to relations between language and the world—or, in a more sophisticated version, between individual language users and some world. Inspired by theoretical work from Ducrot (1996) in particular, and using analytic and theoretical notions from other cognitive and pragmatic research traditions, this chapter has elaborated that basic idea for the phenomenon of negation and related expressions. In view of properties that negation shares with other expressions in the same linguistic paradigm, and of the way it interacts with some other operators and connectives, a central linguistic subsystem primarily operates in the dimension of intersubjective coordination (see Fig. 2.4). It consists of instructions to perform inferential operations of a certain type, independently of the 'objective' content of the utterances. The accessibility of certain cultural models (topoi) to provide material for these inferential processes is presupposed, but nothing about their content is itself coded in the conventional meaning of the elements of the system. Elements in this system, besides sentential negation itself, are operators like *barely* and *almost*, connectives like *so* and *but*, and the grammatical construction characterized by the elements *let alone* (in English); but morphological negation (*un-*, *in-* as prefixes for adjectives) is not a part of this system, and does not profile the intersubjective coordination relation.

The primacy of the dimension of intersubjectivity in the way this system works has been demonstrated in particular by showing that it provides a natural and coherent solution to a number of problems in other accounts that do not incorporate a (sharp) distinction between, on the one hand, cognitive coordination with another subject of conceptualization and, on the other, construal of an object of conceptualization. As part of this demonstration it has been necessary at a number of points to take several 'steps back', and consider underlying assumptions about linguistic meaning and language use, and to develop and validate alternative assumptions; ultimately they allow for the conclusion that the key to the solution of these problems lies precisely in this distinction. The phenomena involved occur at several levels:

(1) sentence-internal grammar, e.g. the fact that *almost* cannot occur in the first conjunct of the *let alone* construction although *almost p* entails *not p*;

(2) discourse structure, e.g. the fact that the interpretation of antecedents of discourse anaphors can be influenced by argumentative operators and connectives and their interaction;
(3) a variety of 'context effects', e.g. the fact that combinations of sentential and morphological negation can lend greater coherence to a text, making it easier to process than superficially simpler expressions with the same informative content.

Precisely the fact that the approach adopted here helps to unify our understanding of the linguistic elements involved across such levels as syntax, semantics, and discourse pragmatics lends it considerable support.

3

Finite complements—putting conceptualizers on stage

3.1 Introduction: two ways of looking at complements

One of the most explicit and straightforward ways to attribute something to a particular mind is the use of a verb of perception, cognition, or communication, as in (1):

(1) (*a*) George saw that his opponent was closing in.
   (*b*) George knew that his opponent was closing in.
   (*c*) George said that his opponent was closing in.

Uttering such a sentence in each case explicitly involves attributing to George the thought that his opponent is closing in. In this way a generalization is made over these three examples which divides each of them into two parts: one expressing the relevant perspective, and one expressing the thought involved. The structural aspect of this distinction involves the complementation structure of the sentences: the perspective is what is indicated in the matrix clause; the thought being perspectivized is contained in the embedded clause.

However, instead of saying that such sentences attribute thoughts to some person's mind, one might say that they constitute descriptions of events (in a somewhat extended sense) of seeing, knowing, and saying, respectively. In that case one views them as analogous to the sentences in (2):

(2) (*a*) George saw something.
   (*b*) George knew something.
   (*c*) George said something.

The structural side of viewing the sentences in (1) as descriptions of events is that they are essentially classified as instantiations of transitive structures, like the simplex sentences in (2). The subordinate clauses in (1) supposedly fill the direct-object slot associated with the verbs *see*, *know*, and *say*, which happens to be occupied by the nominal *something* in (2). The fact that the sentences in (1) exhibit a complementation structure does not make their overall structure crucially different from simplex transitive clauses; complements are simply clausal constituents of larger structures that are defined totally independently. It is this view that has been dominant in most of linguistic practice in (at least) the last two centuries.

At first sight it might seem as if these two views could be perfectly compatible—different construals of the same phenomenon, but not mutually exclusive. However, I will be claiming that the two approaches differ in crucial respects, leading to incompatible analyses of their grammatical structure. The view that complementation sentences express events of seeing, knowing, saying, etc. just as simplex sentences with such verbs mostly do construes the content of the matrix clause as an object of conceptualization. Instead, I will propose that the matrix clause of a complementation sentence invites an addressee to identify with a particular perspective on an object of conceptualization that is itself represented in the embedded clause. The matrix clause functions in the intersubjective dimension of the construal configuration; that is, at level S rather than O. From that perspective, several persistent problems—some quite old, some more recent—in the analysis of complementation phenomena turn out to have their ultimate source in the mistake of viewing such sentences as primarily describing events. The analysis in terms of intersubjectivity does not provide the solution to these problems; rather, it does something better: it makes them disappear.

Regarding complementation sentences as having essentially the same function and structure as simplex clauses also instantiates the view that the properties of special cases can and should be reduced to general rules. All sentences are analyzed with the same limited set of grammatical notions (especially 'subject' and 'object'); when an object happens to have the form of a clause—resulting in the whole sentence being a case of complementation—rather than a noun phrase, any difference between the complete sentences should be derivable from the difference between clauses and noun phrases. On the other hand, viewing complementation as specifically devoted to operating in the domain of intersubjective coordination implies that it has at least *some* properties that are not derivable from general principles that hold for all sentences. As a consequence, complementation constitutes a prototypical construction in the sense of construction grammar (Goldberg 1995, 2003): a template that has irreducible properties of form and meaning, and which must therefore be assumed to be stored as an independent unit in people's long-term memories. So in the case of complementation the exploration of the idea that it has a special function in the dimension of intersubjective coordination and exploration of issues of grammatical organization are closely intertwined.

Moreover, there is also a close connection with issues of discourse and usage. First of all, discourse phenomena will play an important role in motivating the intersubjectivity view of complementation, because differences between coherent and incoherent texts can expose the argumentative character of words and constructions (see Ch. 1, Sect. 1.2.3). Secondly, there are complementation sentences which are used to describe events, but these cases are not prototypical. This means that the category of complementation constructions is considered to be a network of related subconstructions, with some members being more central than others. This internal structure will have to be motivated, and the nature of the extensions from central to less central members has to be explored; this is another area where discourse and actual-usage data have an important role to play.

I will begin by expanding on the persistent problems mentioned above. As with the problems related to the *let alone* construction in Chapter 2, this will be done in some detail. The reason is that I want to expose the fact that the view of complement clauses as basically just another type of constituents really leads to deep contradictions. Problems in syntax will be discussed in Section 3.2.2 and problems in discourse analysis in Section 3.2.3, which also considers some issues concerning acquisition.

The point of departure for developing the intersubjectivity view of complementation constructions will be the way they contribute to the structure of discourse (Sect. 3.3.1). Section 3.3.2 will give the first formulation of the form and meaning of the prototypical complementation construction, based on semantic considerations and frequency data from corpora. In Section 3.3.3 the question of the function of the construction is elaborated further. The specific question is: Do *third*-person matrix clauses as in (1) really operate on the intersubjective dimension of coordination between speaker/writer and addressee, and if so, how precisely does this work? Starting from a discourse perspective again, it is shown both that the answer is positive, and that the mechanisms can be formulated well in terms of the theory of argumentativity that was also crucial in Chapter 2, especially the distinction between direction and strength of an argumentative orientation. On this basis a first version of a network of complementation constructions is presented. Section 3.3.4 introduces the idea that the role of the lexical content, especially the verbs, of the matrix clause in complementation constructs functions as an operator on the relation between the conceptualizers, allowing the speaker/writer to suggest various degrees of identification with the perspective that is 'put on stage'.

In Section 3.3.5 the concepts developed so far are applied to the special phenomenon that is known in the syntactic literature as 'long-distance *Wh*-movement' or '*Wh*-extraction'. The way this is normally understood presupposes the constituent view of complement clauses, so it merits special attention. Using corpus data, I argue that such sentences conform to a standardized formula, belonging to the low-level prototypical 'core' of the network of complementation constructions, in which the degree of distinctness between the Ground and the onstage perspective is minimal. Usage data show that the idea of 'movement' of a constituent over a clause boundary does not apply to such cases.

Sections 3.3.6 and 3.3.7 are devoted to two types of extensions of complementation constructions. The first concerns the position of 'impersonal' perspectivization (e.g. *It is obvious that...*) in the network; this comprises a treatment of what many traditional approaches call 'subject clauses'. It is here in particular that the grammatical relations of 'subject' and 'object' can be shown to be irrelevant for describing the structure of complementation constructions; this has the interesting consequences that these notions are not generally relevant in the structure of sentences, not even in a single language. The second is about a special, and relatively rare, set of complementation sentences that are used to indicate causal relations rather than (straightforward) perspectives. In Section 3.3.8, finally, it is shown how assigning matrix and complement clauses to the intersubjective and objective level, respectively, also helps to improve our understanding of the way linear cohesion works in relations between antecedents and anaphors in discourse.

This is quite a program. So let's get started.

3.2 Problems with clauses as constituents

3.2.1 Introduction

In many grammatical traditions of recent centuries, going back to at least 'traditional grammar' as it arose and developed in the nineteenth century, complement clauses are primarily characterized in structural and abstract grammatical terms; namely, as a specific, clausal instead of nominal, type of filler for a position in the syntactic structure of a clause, in this case an argument position of a verb. In the examples in (1), for instance, the complement clauses are characterized as (direct) objects of the verbs; in example (3), the complement clause is analyzed as the subject of the predicate *be obvious*:

(3) That his opponent was closing in, was obvious to George.

So just as the sentences in (1) are considered to have the same overall structure as the ones in (2), sentence (3) is supposed to have the same structure as *Something was obvious to George*. And, taking the analogies a step further, the complement clause in (4) is also considered to be the subject of the entire sentence, because its role looks the same as in (3), even though there can be no nominal subject in the position of the clause in (4):

(4) It was obvious to George that his opponent was closing in.

So this view of complement clauses emphasizes similarities between the matrix clauses of complex sentences and simplex clauses. A simplex clause denotes a state of affairs, primarily determined by the main verb, with its participants (one or more). A complex sentence is also seen, in this conception, as expressing a situation determined by the matrix verb, the only difference being that one of the participants in this situation happens to be expressed by a clause, not a noun phrase as in the simplex sentence. This view presumes, as I suggested above, that generalizing over nominal and clausal constituents in a syntactic structure is a desirable goal. This is a manifestation of the preference for abstractness in grammatical analysis, maximizing the role of similarity and viewing differences as superficial, secondary.

A consequence of this tendency is also that complement clauses are treated as a special case of the even more abstract category of 'subordinate' clauses, which comprises adverbial and relative clauses besides complements (subject and object clauses). These are all viewed as clausal manifestations of constituents (adjuncts, modifiers, arguments) of abstract syntactic structures.

This view of complementation constructions is 'top-down'. From the point of view of the whole structure, it is observed that its constituents sometimes take the shape of a nominal, sometimes that of a clause. This perspective 'from wholes to parts' is intertwined with, and in turn reinforces, the view of matrix clauses of complements as describing events, which I claim is responsible for a number of persistent problems to be discussed shortly.

The alternative is a 'bottom-up' view. One starts with simplex clauses, and observes that they are sometimes combined into larger wholes, called complex sentences. There have been proposals in some functionalist traditions in modern linguistics that are steps in this direction, specifically in discourse-oriented approaches (Halliday 1985, ch. 7; Matthiessen and Thompson 1988; and other papers in Haiman and Thompson 1988). In principle, I think these initiatives are on the right track, although they are not totally without problems. I will propose here that grammatical combinations of clauses comprise an autonomous set of related constructions which should not be reduced to other patterns; that is, which should not be analyzed as clausal instantiations of abstract constituents.

3.2.2 *Some issues of grammatical analysis*

If complements are clausal constituents filling a syntactic argument position, then a major prediction should be that in all positions in which a clause can appear as an argument of a verb, a noun phrase should also be possible.[1] However, there are a number of problems with this prediction, and these problems already have a considerable history.

Direct object or oblique object?

First, complement clauses can occur in environments in which a noun phrase is impossible:

(5) (a) Hij was bang dat hij het niet zou halen.
    He was afraid that he it not would manage
    'He was afraid that he was not going to make it.'

  (b) *Hij was een nederlaag bang.
    He was a defeat afraid
    *'He was afraid defeat.'

---

[1] Strictly speaking, the reverse might also be expected, that is, that clauses would be normal in positions of argument noun phrases (as suggested by the phrase structure rule NP → S in the 'traditional' generative theory). There are a few verbs that seem to conform to this expectation, but the pattern is actually very rare. For example, the most prototypical kinds of direct objects in particular can only be nominal, not clausal:

(i) (a) He made an apple pie.
    (b) *He made that an apple pie came into being.
(ii) (a) She gave John enough money.
    (b) *She gave John that he would have enough money.
    (c) *She gave that John would have enough money.
(iii) (a) The missile destroyed the factory.
    (b) *The missile destroyed that nothing remained of the factory.

One may object that this does not require some special explanation, since the kind of semantic object denoted by a clause (say, a proposition) is not the kind of thing that can be made, given, or destroyed. But if this really were the whole explanation for the unacceptable sentences in (i), (ii), and (iii), then it actually becomes unclear why, for example, a sentence such as (iv) is perfectly acceptable, despite the fact that the proposition 'that he would have enough money' is produced, and transferred to John (notice that (ii) and (iv) are both typical ditransitive constructions). Minimally, a further specification is required as to the difference between the sort of transfer involved in promising and that involved in giving that would account for the difference in acceptability.

(iv) She promised John that he would have enough money.

Moreover, a new explanation is then also required for the acceptability of the cases where both a nominal and a clausal object are possible, as with *promise* (e.g. *She promised John some money*) or *know* (e.g. *He knew the Archbishop, He knew that John had become Archbishop*). But such explanations are not inconceivable. So although considerations such as these may already cast doubt on the idea of clauses as grammatical arguments, they are not as problematic as the ones discussed in the text.

84   Finite complements

  (c) *Hij was dat bang.
      He was that afraid.
      *'He was afraid this.'

(6) (a) Experts waarschuwden dat de winst lager zou uitvallen.
       Experts warned   that the profit lower would turn-out
       'Experts warned that the profit would turn out to be lower.'

   (b) *Experts waarschuwden een lagere winst.
       Experts warned   a   lower profit
       *'Experts warned a lower profit.'

   (c) *Experts waarschuwden dit.
       Experts warned   this
       *'Experts warned this.'

There are more examples of restrictions on the kind of noun phrases that can occur as objects of complement-taking verbs. Thus, verbs like *think* and *say* (as well as their Dutch counterparts *denken* and *zeggen*) cannot take nominal objects with a lexical head (**He thought/said an idea*), while they can take pronominal objects (such as *What* in *What do you think?*, and *something* in *He said something funny*). But the cases in (5) and (6) demonstrate *absolute* restrictions. Not only lexical nominals are excluded where a clause is possible, but so are pronominal ones, as the unacceptability of the c-sentences illustrates.[2] In (5) there is a grammatical generalization that prohibits calling the complement clause a direct object: *being afraid* is a copular construction (with *afraid* as the nominal predicate) and these, being intransitive, never take a direct object. Instead of 'direct-object clause', the Dutch grammatical tradition (the most influential representative being Den Hertog 1973 (1904)) classifies the complement of (5a) as a 'prepositional object clause', even though there is no preposition. The reason is that *bang zijn* ('to be afraid') can take a nominal argument in the shape of a prepositional phrase (*ergens*

---

[2] Jackendoff (2002: 140–1) also notices discrepancies between possible environments for clausal and nominal constituents, citing such examples as in (i):

(i) (a) John expressed { his innocence
                       { *that he was innocent
    (b) John objected   { *his innocence
                       { that he was innocent

In the end such examples may very well also illustrate that noun phrases and clauses are not simply two different ways of filling an object slot, but Jackendoff suggests that these cases can be handled by stipulations about the kinds of argument that verbs take (so-called subcategorization frames) which do not undermine the overall framework, and may be necessary anyway. Because such solutions are not inconceivable for certain cases (see n. 1), I decided to focus on the kind of phenomena discussed in the text; these not only have a long-standing reputation of being serious problems, they can also be shown to lead to contradictions, as I argue in this section.

bang voor zijn, cf. English 'to be afraid *of* something'), and that a 'dummy' prepositional phrase can be added to a sentence such as (5a). Indeed, the examples in (7) are all acceptable:

(7) (a) Hij was er   bang voor dat hij het niet zou   halen.
        He was there afraid for that he it not would manage
        'He was afraid that he was not going to make it.'

   (b) Hij was bang voor een nederlaag
       He was afraid for a   defeat
       'He was afraid of defeat.'

   (c) Hij was daar bang voor.
       He was there afraid for
       'He was afraid of this.'

The idea is, then, that the 'dummy' prepositional phrase is deleted in cases like (5a). But first of all there is an important asymmetry between (7a) on the one hand and the *b*- and *c*-cases on the other. While the latter are the only acceptable ways of formulating these messages, the former is highly unusual. For example, in all the issues of the daily newspaper *de Volkskrant* from 1995, only 2 instances can be found of *bang zijn dat*...with such a 'dummy' prepositional phrase, against 605 cases without one. The only reason to maintain that such an unusual pattern underlies the much more normal one is that this 'saves' the possibility of generalizing over clausal and nominal arguments in terms of their grammatical function as constituents of a larger structure—clearly a forced analysis. Furthermore, the pursuit of generalization over clausal and nominal constituents leads to the loss of another generalization, namely that pertaining to similarities between complements of different matrix predicates. There is an obvious similarity between (5a) and a sentence like *He feared that he was not going to make it*; in this sentence the complement clause *is* considered to be a direct object, so calling it a prepositional object in (5a) makes it impossible to capture this similarity in the grammatical analysis.

Example (6a) is also analyzed as not containing a direct object, but a prepositional one. It is true that a prepositional 'dummy' phrase can be added to (6a) (cf. (8a)), and that (8b) and (8c) are fully acceptable as opposed to (6b) and (6c):

(8) (a) Experts waarschuwden ervoor   dat de winst lager zou   uitvallen.
        Experts warned   there-for that the profit lower would turn-out
        'Experts warned that the profit would turn out to be lower.'

(b) Experts waarschuwden voor een lagere winst.
   Experts warned   for a   lower profit
   'Experts warned about a lower profit.'

(c) Experts waarschuwden hiervoor.
   Experts warned   here-for
   'Experts warned about this.'

An additional argument for refusing to call the complement clause a direct object is that it is possible to add a participant to (6a) which cannot be anything other than a direct object; witness (9a).

(9) (a) Experts waarschuwden ons dat de winst lager zou uitvallen.
       Experts warned   us that the profit lower would turn-out
       'Experts warned us that the profit would turn out to be lower.'

That this nominal participant fills a direct-object role is confirmed by the fact that (9b) is the passive counterpart of (9a), and the rule that in Dutch the grammatical subject of a passive always corresponds to a direct object:[3]

(9) (b) We werden gewaarschuwd dat de winst lager zou uitvallen.
       We were   warned   that the profit lower would turn-out
       'We were warned that the profit would turn out to be lower.'

Since this nominal participant and the complement can jointly occur in a single sentence, the complement clause cannot be assumed to fill the object role.

The counter-arguments adduced in the case of *bang zijn dat...* ('be afraid that...') apply here as well. The use without the dummy prepositional phrase is much more normal than with it (in this case: 234 cases without, 22 cases with the 'dummy' phrase, in the same corpus). The preference for generalizing over (6a) and (9a–c) leads to the loss of a generalization over the structural and semantic similarity between (6a) and a sentence like *Experts said that the profit would turn out to be lower*. In this case this runs even more counter to the intuition of language users, as *waarschuwen*, like its English counterpart *warn*, is a lexical (transitive) verb, not a copular expression.[4]

---

[3] Only direct objects 'passivize' in Dutch; see Haeseryn et al. (1997: 1404–5). Some indirect objects of a specific class of verbs can appear as the grammatical subject of a construction characterized by the use of the verb *krijgen* ('to get', 'to receive'), which Haeseryn et al. call 'semi-passive' (ibid. 963, 1420–1). But in (9b), the standard passive auxiliary *worden* (lit. 'to become') is used.

[4] This intuition is so strong that it is almost impossible to convince students in grammar classes that they should not call the complement in (6a) a direct object. And when they learn some 'trick' to avoid it, the feeling that this move is artificial remains. This is one of the situations that contribute to the bad reputation of grammar as a bag of tricks that has little to do with the reality of language.

What appears to be going on is the following. A grammarian wonders about the structure of an apparently complex expression, say *They promised that it was going to rain*. He perceives a similarity between this expression and another one that has a different, simpler surface structure: *They promised rain*. He uses this similarity between structurally different expressions as a basis for the answer about the structure of the complex case. So for the purpose of grammatical analysis he (implicitly or explicitly) attaches more value to such similarities than to similarity of surface structure itself; that is, the similarity between *They promised that it was going to rain* and *They warned that it was going to rain*. This is a specific manifestation of the general priority given to alternations over similarity of surface structure as a basis for grammatical analysis (for a general critique of this priority of alternations see Goldberg 2002). The specific force motivating this priority in this particular case is the view of matrix clauses as descriptions of events and the concomitant 'from-whole-to-part' approach in the characterization of complex sentences.

Subject or predicate?
The same attitude is the background of another long-standing problem; namely, the analysis of complement clauses in copular constructions of the following type:

(10) Het gevaar is dat de middenklasse zich vervreemd voelt van
     The danger is that the middle-class REFL alienated feels from
     de politiek.
     the politics
     'The danger is that the middle class feels alienated from politics.'

(11) Het probleem is dat er   te weinig leraren zijn.
     The problem is that there too few teachers are
     'The problem is that there are too few teachers.'

The question is: Are the complement clauses the subjects or the predicates in such sentences? In the history of nineteenth- and twentieth-century syntax both answers have been defended. The most influential Dutch grammarian of the nineteenth century (Den Hertog) argued for an analysis of the complement clauses as subjects (Den Hertog 1973: 62–3), and this position was also adopted in the twentieth century, in the framework of the then current version of generative linguistics, by Blom and Daalder (1977). But Den Hertog's conclusion did not remain unchallenged in the nineteenth century (see Elffers 1979: 101 ff.), and following up on that Elffers (ibid.) argued that the clauses should be analyzed as predicates in a twentieth-century framework as well. Without going into too much detail, it can be demonstrated that *both* positions involve argumentation based on the *same* kind of observations;

namely, once again, similarities between superficially different expressions. The fact that the same sort of evidence can lead to totally incompatible analyses provides a good reason, in my view, to start wondering about the relevance of this kind of evidence for syntactic analysis at all.

Consider the pair of examples (12) and (13). The first is a case where the assignment of grammatical functions is unproblematic, as *reëel* ('real') is an adjective; so the noun phrase *Het gevaar* ('The danger') must be the subject. The question is whether (13) has the same structure; that is, whether the grammatical role of *reëel* ('real') in (12) is performed by the noun phrase *Het gevaar* ('The danger') or the complement clause in (13):[5]

(12) Het gevaar van escalatie is reëel.
 The danger of escalation is real
 'The danger of escalation is real.'

(13) Het gevaar is dat de zaak escaleert.
 The danger is that the matter escalates.
 'The danger is that things will escalate.'

Now observe that the predicate of the copular sentence in (12) allows for fronting in a pseudo-cleft construction, but the subject does not:

(14) Wat reëel is, is het gevaar van escalatie.
 What real is is the danger of escalation
 'What is real, is the danger of escalation.'

(15) ?? Wat het gevaar van escalatie is, is reëel.
 What the danger of escalation is is real.
 ?? 'What is the danger of escalation, is real.'

Even if (15) is not totally unacceptable, it is in any case not a pseudo-cleft construction, since it lacks the characteristic property of being a 'specifying sentence', in which a relatively vague concept denoted by the leftmost constituent is given a more detailed specification by the rightmost constituent (Akmajian 1970; cf. Blom and Daalder 1977).[6] So the possibility of being

---

[5] Notice the presupposition that either one *must* be the case.

[6] Thus the following example, formally similar to (15), is a normal copular sentence, not a pseudo-cleft sentence:

(i) Wat het gevaar is, is wel duidelijk
 What the danger is is PRT clear
 'What the danger is, is clear.'

What this sentence expresses is that the answer to the question 'What is the danger?' is clear. It is not a paraphrase of the sentence *The danger is clear*; the pseudo-cleft sentence corresponding to that would be *What is clear, is the danger.*

fronted in a pseudo-cleft construction may be construed as a test for predicatehood. Now observe the parallel between (14)/(15) on the one hand and (16)/(17) on the other:

(16) Wat   het gevaar is, is dat de   zaak escaleert.
     What the danger is is that the case escalates
     'What the danger is, is that things will escalate.'

(17) *Wat dat de zaak   escaleert is, is het gevaar.
     What that the matter escalates is is the danger
     *'What that things will escalate is, is the danger.'

A nominal predicate as in (12) may be split off in such a construction, witness (14). The fact that the noun phrase *Het gevaar* ('The danger') in (13) passes this test—witness (16)—and that the complement does not—witness (17)—is an argument for assigning the noun phrase the status of predicate in (13), and assigning the complement clause the status of subject. This entails that the nominal predicate has been fronted, or 'topicalized', in (13). This analysis seems to be confirmed by parallels such as the following:

(18) Ècht gevaarlijk is dat verarmd uranium giftig   is.
     Really dangerous is that depleted uranium poisonous is
     'What is *really* dangerous, is that depleted uranium is poisonous.'

(19) Het èchte gevaar is dat verarmd uranium giftig   is.
     The real   danger is that depleted uranium poisonous is
     'The *real* danger is that depleted uranium is poisonous.'

The first constituent of (18) is an adjective phrase, which therefore has to be the (topicalized) predicate phrase, so that the complement clause must be the subject. Since the semantic relationship in (19) is the same as in (18), the complement clause is the subject here as well, and the initial noun phrase (*Het echte gevaar,* 'The real danger') must also be a topicalized predicate phrase.

Notice that these arguments are, again, entirely based on perceived parallelisms between sentences with different surface structures. The problem is that similar arguments can be adduced for the opposite conclusion. Compare (13) with (20) and (21):

(20) Het gevaar bestaat dat de zaak   escaleert
     The danger exists   that the matter escalates.
     'The danger exists that things will escalate.'

(21) Het gevaar is levensgroot aanwezig dat de zaak escaleert.
     The danger is life-sized present that the case escalates
     'The danger is looming large that things will escalate.'

In these two sentences there seems to be no way of escaping the conclusion that the initial noun phrase is the subject. Sentence (20) does not even contain a copula; it has an ordinary main verb ('exist'). The complement clause would probably be analyzed as an extraposed complement to the noun *gevaar* ('danger'); that is, as derived from essentially 'The danger that things will escalate exists'. Sentence (21) does contain a copular construction, but here the predicate must be *is aanwezig* ('is present'), *aanwezig* being an adjective; hence the initial noun phrase can only be the subject (with the complement clause again analyzed as extraposed from this noun phrase). But these two sentences also exhibit semantic parallels to (13), which would lead to the conclusion that the initial noun phrase in (13) must also be the subject.

Thus we end up in an insoluble dilemma: analyzing the complement clause in (13) as a nominal predicate makes us miss some generalizations (e.g. with sentences with preposed nominal predicates like (18)), but analyzing it as a subject makes us miss other ones (as illustrated by (20) and (21)). This situation makes it understandable that the issue has never been satisfactorily resolved since the nineteenth century; at the same time, it suggests that something is wrong with the underlying assumption that it must be possible to characterize the grammatical structure of these complex sentences as that of a simplex clause with another clause as one of its constituents.

3.2.3 *Some issues of discourse analysis and language acquisition*

The view of complements as constituents emphasizes similarities not only between complex and simplex sentences but also between complement and adjunct clauses. In fact, both are often treated as subcases of a general phenomenon called 'subordination'. This generalization has been challenged in some functionally oriented linguistic frameworks, especially by scholars investigating relationships between grammar and discourse structure. Consider examples (22) and (23):

(22) He left early because he wanted to be on time.

(23) He promised that he would be on time.

In the constituent view of clauses both sentences contain one matrix and one subordinated clause. In (22), the *because*-clause fills the position and the role of an adjunct phrase (cf. 'He left early *for that reason*'), and in (23) the *that*-clause fills the position and role of an object (cf. 'He promised *this*'). In discourse analysis the consequence of this view is that the sentences also have an equivalent status; as sentences they are seen as *units* of a larger stretch of discourse. Thus discourse relationships should hold *between* such units and not play a role internal to them. However, from the point of view of discourse the latter position is unattractive, because it misses a generalization. Consider (24) and (25):

(24) He left early; he wanted to be on time.

(25) He left early. The reason is he wanted to be on time.

In these pieces of discourse each sentence is a unit (discourse segment), as there is no grammatical connection between them. The conceptual relation connecting them is one of (a subtype of) causality; it may remain implicit, as in (24), or it can be marked in some way, as in (25). It is important to notice that such a conceptual relationship is always present, even if it is not explicitly marked; without a coherence relationship the two sentences in (24) would not constitute a meaningful piece of discourse, but just two isolated sentences. It is now clear that analyzing the conceptual structure of (24) and (25) at the discourse level but restricting the analysis of (22) to the level of grammar misses a generalization: *because* is 'just' one of several linguistic devices for constraining the interpretation of coherence relations in discourse.

Matthiessen and Thompson (1988) formulate and substantiate the general claim that all relations between so-called main clauses and adjunct clauses correspond to 'rhetorical relations' that hold between pieces of discourse that are larger than sentences (e.g. paragraphs and other discourse units). Following Halliday (1985), they also argued that there are significant grammatical differences between adjunct clauses and complement clauses, indicating that the former are much less tightly integrated into their matrix clauses than the latter. They adopted Halliday's category of hypotactic relationships, as intermediate between 'embedding' (real subordination, so to speak) and paratactic relations (i.e. coordination). This distinction allowed them to choose the clause, rather than the sentence, as their unit of discourse structure, with the exception of embedded clauses. With this definition, (24) and (25), *as well as* (22), can be analyzed as consisting of two discourse segments entering into a coherence relation, which may be marked in different ways. As Matthiessen and Thompson (1988) indicate, hypotactic grammatical relations are a special, 'grammaticalized' kind of coherence relations.

It appears that this approach has not gained wide acceptance outside functionalist traditions comprising the study of discourse, but I believe it is on the right track. However, recent work by Thompson (2002) on the role of complementation in conversation, as well as work by Diessel and Tomasello (2001) on the acquisition of complementation, points to a possible problem in the conceptualization of complements in these usage-based approaches. Both Thompson and Diessel and Tomasello challenge the traditional assumption that complementation constructions should, generally or prototypically, be viewed as instances of subordination of the complement clause to the matrix clause. Thompson does so for conversation, using both interactional and grammatical evidence to argue that the complement clauses are not in any insightful or useful sense 'subordinate' to the matrix clauses. She formulates her view in contrast to that of many grammarians, including cognitivists and functionalists; for example, Langacker's (1991: 436 ff.) view that the profile of a complement clause 'is overridden by that of the main clause', illustrated with '*I know she left* designates the process of knowing, not of leaving'. Thompson demonstrates that complement clauses in conversation function to 'profile' the situations they denote with at least the same degree of prominence as their matrix clauses. To give an example, consider the excerpt in (26) (= (11) in Thompson 2002: 132):

(26) (talking about a photo collage on the wall)
 TERRY: I think it's cool.
 ABBIE: it i = s cool.
 MAUREEN: it i = s great.

The observation that exchanges such as these are perfectly normal makes it impossible to maintain, Thompson suggests, that a complement clause (here: *it's cool*) has lower prominence than the matrix clause (here: *I think*). Instead, the complement provides an assessment of a common object of attention, while the matrix clause provides an epistemic stance on that assessment. Thompson proposes that this is typical for relations between complements and their matrix clauses. We will return to this alternative view later, but for the moment this suffices to illustrate what is meant by the claim that applying the notion of 'subordination' to the relationship between complement and matrix clauses is problematic.

Development
Diessel and Tomasello (2001) argue the same point for young children's earliest complementation constructions, which correlate with the most frequent patterns of such constructions in the language use they encounter. They make slightly different distinctions than Thompson does, but their general claim is similar:

in most of children's complex utterances that seem to include a finite complement clause, the main clause does not express a full proposition; rather, it functions as an epistemic marker, attention getter, or marker of illocutionary force. The whole construction thus contains only a single proposition expressed by the apparent complement clause. (ibid. 97.)

These studies contain important contributions to a better understanding of the structure and function of complementation. I will ultimately argue that the view of complementation that I will propose for (mostly) written discourse can be insightfully integrated with those of Thompson (2002) and Diessel and Tomasello (2001). Still, it should be recognized that this view leads to at least a conceptual problem. In the older work on the topic, which led to the view of adjunct clauses as 'hypotactic', the only remaining cases of 'real' embedding were complement clauses. The recent work just mentioned also sees complements as normally not instantiating 'subordination' either. So if the difference between adjunct and complement clauses does not involve a degree of subordination, we face the question: What *is* the difference between adjuncts and complements? It still seems to be true that complements and their matrix clauses are more 'tightly' integrated than adjuncts and their matrix clauses; but if a complement clause may profile a situation independently of its matrix clause, then at least another explication is needed of what is meant by 'tightly integrated'.

A related issue, especially evoked in the study by Diessel and Tomasello, is the following. Ultimately people do develop the ability to construe matrix and complement clauses in a way that may involve the expression of two propositions, but how is that kind of use related to the apparent single-proposition character of their initial (seeming) complementation constructions? The authors propose that the latter are concrete instances—learned early, stored separately, and with specific properties of their own—in a Langackerian network of constructions that, in adults, also contains more abstract, rule-like schemas (Diessel and Tomasello 2001: 133–5). But this implies that there are *conceptual* relationships between the different nodes in the network, presumably as a result of the developmental process. The different subconstructions in such a network are connected by relations of extension and schematization (Langacker 2000: 12–13). So it must be possible to specify these conceptual connections; an analyst has the task of hypothesizing and testing such relationships.

Analogously, a conceivable objection to Thompson's claim is that her findings may be a product of 'performance' factors in spoken language (e.g. limited working memory, which puts constraints on processing complex constructions). Perhaps the fully productive rules constituting linguistic competence are better observable in writing, and these might conform to the traditional view of complementation as subordination. Whatever force one may want to attribute to such objections and their theoretical presuppositions, form and function of complement clauses in written language as used by adult readers and writers are at least *related* to those in spoken language. Even if they are not exactly the same, it is a valid and interesting question what the connection is; a situation in which no plausible link between them can be formulated remains unsatisfactory.[7]

In brief, the status of complements is problematic in several respects. There are some long-standing problems of grammatical analysis, including unresolved inconsistencies, as well as some questions of consistency and completeness in modern functional and cognitive approaches. Thus there are good reasons to reopen the issue of how to analyze complementation constructions in a comprehensive way.

3.3 Use and structure of complementation constructions

3.3.1 *The special role of complementation in discourse structure*

At the end of the previous section we saw that recent discourse-oriented research into the function of distinct clause types that were traditionally all labeled 'subordinate' seems to leave the question of the difference between adjunct and complement clauses unanswered. It is this issue that I want to take as a starting point. Consider the text fragment in (27), in which hypotactic clause combinations dominate, and finite complements are absent:

(27) Studentenverenigingen beleven tegenwoordig weer een behoorlijke opbloei, nadat ze in de jaren '80 door een dal zijn gegaan. Tegenwoordig worden studenten weer vaker lid van een gezelligheidsvereniging, juist omdat de studieduur inmiddels zo sterk beperkt is: ze hebben minder tijd om hun sociale contacten helemaal zelf te organiseren, en dus is het zinnig om bij een club te gaan waar dat allemaal al tot op zekere hoogte geregeld is.

'Student fraternities are prospering again, after they went through a serious decline in the eighties. Nowadays, students generally join a social association, precisely because the duration of college programs has been so strongly reduced: they have less time to organize their social relationships all by themselves, and so it makes sense to join a club where such things have all been pre-arranged to some extent.'

---

[7] To some extent, the questions raised here are similar to those discussed in Boye and Harder (2007). While several aspects of their approach are in the same spirit as mine, I think the network conception of complementation constructions developed below, and especially the central role attributed to intersubjectivity, offer better perspectives for an integrated analysis than distinguishing different, although related, 'levels' of usage and of structure.

In (27′) the contents of the 'main' and 'subordinate' clauses have been distributed over distinct columns.

(27′)

'Main' clauses	'Subordinate' clauses
Student fraternities are prospering again	after they went through a serious decline in the eighties
Nowadays, students generally join a social association	precisely because the duration of college programs has been so strongly reduced
they have less time to organize their social relationships all by themselves[8]	
and so it makes sense to join a club	where such things have all been pre-arranged to some extent

Notice that the series of clauses in the left-hand column—that is, the concatenation of the main clauses by themselves—constitutes a kind of summary of the entire text in (27). Thus the main clauses can indeed be said to provide the 'skeleton' of the discourse, determining its overall structure, with the other clauses providing additional pieces of information. This is in accordance with the idea, put forward in Matthiessen and Thompson (1988), that a hypotactically connected clause relates to its main clause as a satellite discourse fragment to its nucleus (with the nuclei constituting the text's main line).

Now consider (28), in which complementation constructions dominate, and (28′), where the contents of the 'main' and 'subordinate' clauses are again represented separately:

(28) Eerder vertelde ik dat het al gelukt is om klonen van zoogdierembryo's te kweken. Uit het bovenstaande valt nu af te leiden dat het binnenkort mogelijk wordt om ook met het DNA van volwassen dieren nieuwe embryo's te maken. De directeur van GenTech verwacht zelfs dat dit reeds volgend jaar zal gebeuren. Anderen zijn van mening dat het misschien wat langer zal duren, maar niemand twijfelt eraan dat het klonen van een volwassen schaap of paard binnen 10 jaar een feit is. De vraag is of de samenleving hier mentaal en moreel aan toe is, of dat we voor de zoveelste keer hopeloos achter de technische ontwikkelingen aanlopen.

---

[8] For ease of exposition I include non-finite verb phrases (sometimes considered reduced clauses) in their finite main clauses. It will be clear that the question of to what extent they should be considered as adjunct and complement clauses (i.e. share properties with finite clauses) is one that should be reconsidered completely independently from existing analyses, given that we are developing a new understanding of what *finite* clauses are.

'I have reported before that there has already been success in breeding clones of mammalian embryos. From the above it may now be concluded that it will become possible in the near future to make new embryos with the DNA of full-grown animals as well. The director of GenTech even expects that this will happen as soon as next year. Others believe that it may take somewhat longer, but nobody doubts that the cloning of a full-grown sheep or horse will be a reality within ten years. The question is whether society is mentally and morally ready for this, or whether we will once again be hopelessly overtaken by the technical developments.'

(28') | 'Main' clauses | 'Subordinate' clauses |
|---|---|
| I have reported before that[9] | there has already been success in breeding clones of mammalian embryosit |
| From the above it may now be concluded that | will become possible in the near future to make new embryos with the DNA of full-grown animals as well |
| The director of GenTech even expects that | this will happen as soon as next year |
| Others believe that | it may take somewhat longer |
| but nobody doubts that | the cloning of a full-grown sheep or horse will be a reality within ten years |
| The question is whether | society is mentally and morally ready for this |
| or whether | we will once again be hopelessly overtaken by the technical developments |

There is a striking difference between (27') and (28'). While the string of main clauses in the former contained the main line of the discourse, this is not at all the case in the latter. Quite the contrary. Example (28') shows that, if anything, it is the series of 'subordinate' clauses that represents the basic content of the discourse; the series of 'main' clauses, on the other hand, does not even seem to constitute a coherent whole.

[9] I include the 'subordinating conjunctions' in the left-hand column, with the matrix clauses. For the present argument nothing hinges on this, but I believe there is actually good linguistic motivation for doing so. In the case of adjuncts, with conjunctions like *because*, the clause elaborates a salient subpart ('e-site', in terms of Langacker 1991) of the conceptual structure defined by the word itself, whereas here the subordinate clauses elaborate e-sites of the structure defined by the main *predicate* (see Schilperoord and Verhagen 1998).

It appears therefore that a discourse perspective shows a fundamental difference between adjunct and complement clauses that remains invisible as long as we stick to a constituent view of such clauses. Whereas adjunct clauses can be insightfully characterized as a form of grammaticalization of coherence relations, it seems that complement clauses have to be viewed as relating to a fundamentally different aspect of discourse structure. What I want to propose is that complementation be viewed as a form of grammaticalization of a dimension of discourse structure that is 'orthogonal' to its informational content; namely, the fact that, as language in use discourse involves the intersubjective coordination of cognitive systems.

In Chapter 2 I argued that the key to understanding several properties of expressions of negation in human language is that negation's primary function involves the coordination between conceptualizers by means of language, rather than the coordination between a conceptualizer and (a model of) the world. Intersubjectivity is the dimension in which negation and negation-related elements operate. Here I want to argue similarly. Complementation constructions are another family of constructions operating primarily in that dimension, although in their own specific way.

In the constituent view, as I suggested, an utterance of the type *X thinks/ promises/hopes that Y* is taken to represent an event of some sort (indicated by the verb) as an object of conceptualization. However, when one thinks of the utterance as a communicative event, it should be clear that it may just as well be taken as an instruction, from speaker/writer to addressee, that Y is to be conceptualized in a particular way; this is the intersubjectivity view. I will argue that this holds for complements traditionally considered as objects of their matrix clause, as well as for complements traditionally analyzed as subjects (as in *That Y is obvious/unfortunate/dangerous* or *It is...that Y*). However, I will first focus on so-called object complements, and integrate so-called subject complements in Section 3.3.6.

Recall the basic construal configuration introduced in Chapter 1, Fig. 1.2 repeated on p. 98 for convenience.

In terms of this configuration I propose that complementation constructions have the primary function of instructing the addressee of an utterance (performing role 2 in the Ground) to coordinate cognitively—in a way specified by the matrix clause—with another subject of conceptualization in construing the object of conceptualization (the latter being represented by the complement clause), and not that of representing an object of conceptualization. I will call the conceptualizer that is explicitly mentioned in the matrix clause (the referent of the subject of the matrix predicate) the 'onstage conceptualizer', in order to distinguish this role from those

O: *Object of conceptualization:*

S: *Subject of conceptualization (Ground):*

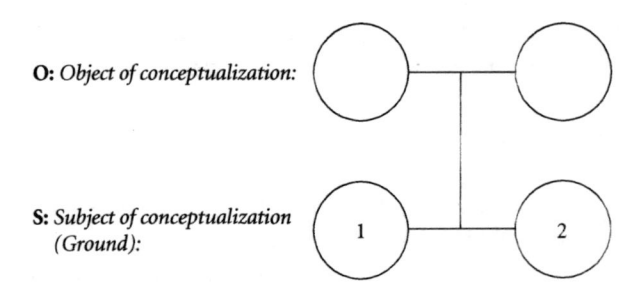

FIGURE 1.2 The construal configuration and its basic elements

of the conceptualizers that are inherent in the Ground of the construal configuration.

When the matrix clause contains present-tense first-person and second-person expressions (of the type *I think* and *You know*) the onstage conceptualization is minimally distinct from the Ground, and the expression relates to the coordination relation between conceptualizers 1 and 2 in a maximally direct way. With non-pronominal third-person matrix clauses (of the type *The director expects that...*) it may seem that the addressee just has to coordinate with this third person. However, there are good reasons (to be discussed in the next section) to assume that also in the latter case the ultimate point of a complementation construction concerns cognitive coordination between the addressee and the producer of the discourse, albeit more indirectly.

It is in this sense that matrix clauses of complementation constructions in general relate to another dimension of discourse structure than the matrix clauses of hypotactic constructions. Whereas 'clause combining' constructions with adverbial clauses may be viewed as grammaticalized expressions for rhetorical relations (Matthiessen and Thompson 1988; see Sect. 3.2.3 above), complementation constructions may be viewed as general grammaticalized expressions for intersubjective coordination.

Recursion

Notice that this view provides a basis for understanding why complementation constructions can be so easily embedded in each other; that is, recursively. They are the most straightforward expressions for making perspective-taking explicit; unlike negation, for example, they do not necessarily impose a particular structure (opposition) on the relationship between perspectives. Thus they constitute a direct linguistic reflection of the specific human ability to identify deeply with conspecifics, understood as intentional and mental agents (see Ch. 1, Sect. 1.2.1). This basic cognitive capacity is inherently recursive. My taking another person's perspective as if it were my own implies that I attribute to this other person the same cognitive capacities that I have, and these include the capacity to take another person's perspective. More specifically, it implies that I attribute to other persons the capacity to take *my* perspective. The capacity to engage in cognitive coordination involves the recognition that I have the ability to think about other people's thoughts, that they can also have thoughts about my thoughts, and thus that I can think about their thoughts about my thoughts (and so on). In other words, it follows that a construction dedicated to putting perspectives 'on stage' should exhibit recursion. This explains the fact, I think, that sentences of the following type (the examples are from the Eindhoven Corpus) are used so frequently in the linguistic literature to illustrate the occurrence of recursion in syntactic structure:

(29) Ik wil   wel dat de   mensen weten dat ik eerlijk ben.
     I want-to PRT that the people know that I honest am
     'I do wish people to know I am honest.'

(30) Waarom denkt die meneer   dat ik niet weet dat het een pop is?
     Why   thinks that gentleman that I not know that it a   doll is
     'Why does this gentleman think that I don't know this is a doll?'

What this suggests is that recursiveness of complementation reflects recursion in the relevant conceptual domain, and is independent of its linguistic expression. It need not be a feature of linguistic form per se. Now we may expect recursion to occur in linguistic structures that function in a conceptual domain exhibiting recursion, but the converse is not a necessary consequence; at the end of Section 3.3.7 we will in fact find a situation where complementation does appear to be used only non-recursively.[10]

In view of their separate status, I will from now on, following suggestions by Diessel and Tomasello (2001) and Thompson (2002), use the term 'complement-taking clause/predicate', or briefly 'CT-clause/predicate', instead of 'matrix clause/predicate (of a complementation construction)'.

---

[10] It will be clear that I am using the term 'recursion' here in its strict mathematical sense of 'a procedure calling itself'. One sometimes finds the term also used more loosely, for the more general notion of 'indefinite embedding' (rather than 'self-embedding'). This concerns the phenomenon of grammatical dependencies over indefinite distances (Hauser, Chomsky, and Fitch 2002; see Pinker and Jackendoff, 2005 for comments). An example is the fact that in an *if... then* construction there is no well-defined limit on the amount of material intervening between the two elements. Notice that such a 'long distance dependency' can be the result of recursion in the strict sense, but it need not: *if... then* itself, for example, cannot be self-embedded (*If, if gold is a metal, then it conducts electricity, then it conducts heat as well*). Recursion entails indefinite embedding, but the reverse does not hold. Long-distance dependencies are more common in language (and, presumably, general cognition; see Comrie (2003) on 'chunking') than recursion in the strict sense.

3.3.2 A template and its meaning

Let us now turn to the question about the nature of the grammatical pattern of which complementation sentences are instantiations. How should that be characterized? One consequence of the ideas developed so far is that the schema *X-verb-Y* is too high a level of abstraction for a proper characterization of complementation constructions. *X-verb-Y* is prototypically instantiated by transitive clauses, with nominal constituents *X* and *Y*, and, as we have seen, it is treating complement clauses on a par with constituents that leads to analytical problems (Sect. 3.2.2). The fact that prototypical transitive verbs (e.g. *make, build, give*) do not take complement clauses (see n. 1) also suggests that the transitive-clause schema does not provide the proper level for their characterization. This raises the question of the delineation of the class of complement-taking verbs: Is there any coherence to it, which makes it possible to set them off from prototypical transitive verbs? Consider the following overview of subtypes of verbs said to take 'direct object clauses', from the comprehensive reference grammar of Dutch, the *Algemene Nederlandse Spraakkunst* (*ANS*), and especially the kind of concepts these verbs express:

(31) Semantic types of verbs taking 'direct object clauses' according to the *ANS* (Haeseryn et al. 1997: 1156–8):
   (*a*) Verbs denoting a statement, question, command, promise, etc., i.e. with communication as part of their meaning;
   (*b*) Verbs denoting some form of knowing, believing, supposing, etc.;
   (*c*) Verbs (and verbal expressions) indicating evaluation (e.g. *appreciate, regret*, but also expressions of the type *find it a pity/strange*, etc.);
   (*d*) Verbs denoting a wish or desire;
   (*e*) Verbs denoting a way of perceiving;
   (*f*) Verbs denoting causation.

The generalization over subtypes *a–e* is clear: such predicates all evoke a mental state or process of a subject of consciousness (sometimes a process *comprising* a mental state, as in the case of communication), and the content of the complement is associated with this subject's consciousness in a particular manner. In other words, with the exception of subtype *f*, these predicates are all 'mental-space builders' in the sense of Fauconnier (1994 (1985)). We can express this generalization in the form of a 'constructional schema' (in the sense of Langacker 1991: 546; Goldberg 1995; Croft and Cruse 2004): a construction consisting of a CT-clause and a clausal complement involves entertaining the content of the complement in the way the subject of conceptualization referred to in the CT-clause entertains it:[11]

(32) *Complementation Construction 1* (Dutch)[12]
    construction form: [$_A$Y[X$_{Predicate}$]dat[$_B$ ...]]
    construction meaning: ENTERTAIN CONTENT OF B IN THE MANNER OF Y: AS X

I intentionally formulate the meaning of this pattern in this way in order to highlight its function at the level of cognitive coordination between subjects of conceptualization. An alternative would have been to formulate it as a *description* of Y entertaining the content of the clause. However, that form would suggest that the function of the construction is to present some object of conceptualization; this has been demonstrated to be the source of several problems. I will provide further justification for this formulation in the following sections (3.3.3 and 3.3.4).

Notice that subtype *f* cannot be directly analyzed as an instance of (32). In (33), for example, the CT-clause indicates a cause, and the complement the result. This cannot easily be seen as a case of the instruction specified as the meaning of the pattern in (32):

(33) Dat   maakte dat je   je   deel voelde van je   volk.
     This made   that you you part felt   of   your people
     'This made you feel part of your people.'

I will return to this special subtype in Section 3.3.7.

---

[11] It does not have to be specified at the form level that the predicate has to be of a certain type ('Mental-Space Builder'): this requirement is effectively incorporated in the formulation of the construction's meaning, which comprises a generalization over the meanings of the CT-predicates. In a different terminology, a similar insight has been formulated for *that*-clauses by Wierzbicka (1988: 132–40): 'reference to knowledge is present in all sentences with THAT' (p. 137; Wierzbicka in turn cites a few other linguists who have proposed partly similar analyses, notably Bolinger). Complement clauses with the (Dutch) complementizer *of* (English *whether/if*), rather than *dat*, do not refer to knowledge, of course, but precisely to lack of knowledge, or uncertainty, on the part of the speaker (e.g. *My father will hear whether I passed sooner than I will myself*). The general meaning of (32) is applicable in these subcases as well; namely, that the content of the complement is to be entertained in the way of the CT-predicate.

[12] Unlike English, Dutch does not have the possibility of complementation without a complementizer: *dat* is the 'unmarked' complementizer, in the sense that it does not contribute a specific meaning beyond the meaning of the construction, and also that it is an obligatory element. Thus any functional load carried by absence vs. presence of *that* in English cannot be conveyed in the same way in Dutch. It seems reasonable to suppose that *in general* the pattern in (32) may be more parallel, functionally, to English constructions without *that* than to those that do contain this 'linker'. In any case, this demonstrates that the concrete, actual patterns of use of words and constructions cannot be wholly predicted on the basis of the general conceptual space they operate in. Ultimately all such patterns are usage-based, and they represent stages in historical processes of grammar formation (see Bybee 2003), so that any accurate description must ultimately be data-based.

Productivity

A question that may be raised with respect to (32) is whether it really represents a construction. That is, is it an independent symbolic unit, or a general formulation of a property of a number of lexical items (verbs)—a so-called lexical rule?[13] It is arguable that this is a type of question that in principle cannot and need not always be answered (Croft 2003). But it is interesting to point out, for this specific case, that the assumption that (32) represents an independent piece of linguistic knowledge is supported by the fact that it appears to exhibit some productivity. It may be used to 'license' expressions without the verb itself being subcategorized as a complement-taking one. For example, the verb *somberen* is a relatively recent addition to the Dutch language, and if dictionaries mention it at all it is only as intransitive (meaning 'be in a dark mood', 'behave gloomily'). But an issue of the newspaper *de Volkskrant* of 1995 contained the following sentence:

(34) Twee ruiters... die nog vóór de beslissende rondgang somberden
Two riders who still before the decisive tour gloomed
dat de titel hun ook dit keer niet vergund zou zijn.
that the title them also this time not granted would be
'Two riders... who were glooming, even before the decisive round, that they wouldn't be granted the title this time either.'

The fact that this is unproblematically understood in the sense that the content of the complement clause is attributed to the riders cannot be based on any general, conventional use of the verb, so it presumably derives from the recognition of the general *pattern* as a conventional way of doing so. This supports the claim that it is entrenched as an independent processing unit.

Type and token frequency

Such a status is also to be expected in view of the high number of distinct CT-predicates that occur in the pattern. Bybee (1995) has argued that high type frequency (repeated occurrence of the same pattern with different lexical elements, each of which has a relatively low token frequency) leads to entrenchment of the general pattern rather than entrenchment of specific instances. Such a schema with an open 'slot' is applicable to a *category* of items, including elements that are recognized as members of the category even if they have not been used with the pattern before; in other words, such a schema is productive.[14] Table 3.1 lists the frequencies of CT-predicates with

---

[13] This is actually just another instance of a much more general question on the relationships between verbs and the structural patterns they occur in; see Goldberg (1995: 9–23) for some types of argument in favor of a constructional analysis, and Croft (2003) and Langacker (2005) for discussion.

[14] See Croft and Cruse (2004, ch. 11) for an overview of the literature, and a generalization of this idea about productivity from the domain of morphology to that of syntax.

'object'-complement *dat*-clauses in the first 2,000 sentences in a corpus of Dutch newspaper fragments.[15]

First of all, it is clear that the frequency of 'object' complements in this material is high: 151 instances of the same pattern in 2,000 sentences is of the same order of magnitude as that of personal pronouns; more precisely, it is in between that of the pronouns *ik* ('I'; 129) and *hij* ('he'; 197) in the same set of 2000 sentences—in itself already an indication that finite complementation is a well entrenched pattern. Even more telling is that the type frequency for the predicate slot is high: more than half (47 out of 89) of the predicates occurring in this set[16] have a frequency of 1, and the most frequent single verb accounts

TABLE 3.1. CT-predicates used with 'object' complements in the first 2,000 sentences in the Eindhoven Corpus (Dutch newspaper fragments)

Tokens per predicate	Predicates (types)	Total no. of tokens
15	*zeggen* ('say')	15
11	*geloven* ('think', 'believe')	11
6	*vaststellen* ('decide', 'conclude'), *stellen* ('state', 'argue')	12
5	*vertellen* ('tell'), *het eens zijn* ('agree'), *weten* ('know'), *betekenen* ('mean', 'imply')	20
3	*aannemen* ('assume', 'suppose'), *horen* ('hear'), *vinden* ('think', 'be of the opinion'), *verklaren* ('declare', 'state'), *zorgen* ('see to it', 'manage'), *hopen* ('hope')	18
2	*antwoorden* ('answer', 'reply'), *bewezen achten* ('hold proven'), *concluderen* ('conclude'), *het gevoel hebben/krijgen* ('have/get the feeling'), *meedelen* ('inform', 'let know'), *menen* ('think', 'suppose'), *ontdekken* ('discover'), *tot gevolg hebben* ('result in'), *uitwijzen* ('reveal'), *voorkómen* ('prevent'), *vrezen* ('fear'), *willen* ('want to', 'wish'), *zich ervan bewust zijn* ('be aware', 'appreciate'), *zien* ('see')	28
1	(47 different predicates)	47
Total no. of types	89	151

[15] Data from the Eindhoven Corpus, in the version available from the Free University in Amsterdam (including a subcorpus of 'officialese'); it is described in Uit den Boogaart (1975) and Renkema (1981).

[16] This set of predicate types includes a small number of causal expressions: *zorgen* ('see to it', 'manage'), with a frequency of 3, *tot gevolg hebben* ('result in'), *voorkómen* ('prevent'), with a frequency of 2, and *ertoe bijdragen* ('contribute to', 'stimulate'), *gedaan krijgen* ('get done'), and *maken* ('make', 'cause'), with a frequency of 1—, a total of 10 cases. See Sect. 3.3.7 for further discussion.

for only 10 per cent of the cases. As a result, the pattern *should* be well-entrenched as a schema, and productive, which it is, as we have just seen.

'Exceptions' are regular

The insight that the pattern of the form given in (32) must be entrenched as a productive schema also provides a solution to the problem noted in Section 3.2.2; namely, that clausal complements can be freely combined with predicates that do not take nominal arguments. Consider examples (5a) and (6a) (for ease of exposition I only give the English translations):

(5) (a) He was afraid that he was not going to make it.

(6) (a) Experts warned that the profit would turn out to be lower.

Since *be afraid* denotes a mental state, and *warn* an act of communication, the clauses involved satisfy both the formal and the semantic requirements of (32). In other words, the hypothesis that (32) is an entrenched pattern predicts that sentences such as (5a) and (6a) are normal instances of language use, without the need of any 'detour' such as deletion of dummy prepositional objects (see Sect. 3.2.2). The fact that this prediction is borne out thus supports the hypothesis that (32) is an independently accessible unit of linguistic knowledge.

3.3.3 *Third-person conceptualizers and degrees of directness in intersubjective coordination*

Let us now return to the proper characterization of the function of the complementation construction. At the end of Section 3.3.1 I claimed that even when the CT-clause does not refer to a speech-act participant it still involves cognitive coordination of the addressee with the producer of the discourse, though less directly than with a first- or second-person CT-clause. I will now provide support for this claim.

A first indication is the well-known fact that the reference point for the interpretation of first-person deictic elements in complement clauses is provided by the speaker/writer, not by the referent of the subject of the CT-clause, that is the onstage conceptualizer. This is a major feature that differentiates 'direct' from 'indirect' speech or thought (Banfield 1982; Sanders 1994):

(35) She said: 'I should have stopped here.'

(36) She said that I should have stopped here.

The referent of *I* is 'She' in (35), while it is the speaker/writer in (36). Similarly, the position indicated by *here* is determined via the point of view of 'She' in

(35), while it is determined via the point of view of the speaker/writer in (36). In Sanders's terms (ibid.): although the validity of the information in the complement clause is attributed to the onstage conceptualizer, the speaker/writer is responsible for the wording.[17]

Complementation and argumentativity
Secondly, the speaker/writer normally adopts a certain degree of responsibility for the validity of the information as well. We can show this using the notions of argumentative orientation and argumentative strength introduced in Chapter 2. The fact that we can do so demonstrates that the conceptual configuration with respect to which complementation constructions operate is the same as that for negation-related expressions, namely, the construal configuration depicted in Figure 1.2.

Consider the exchanges in (37), supposing it is 2 p.m. at the time of the exchange and the distance to the launch site is 1 mile:

(37) A: Will we be in time for the launch?
B_1: It was scheduled for 4 p.m.
B_2: I think it was scheduled for 4 p.m.
B_3: Someone said that it was scheduled for 4 p.m.

Each of the three responses by B in (37) is a coherent follow-up to the initial utterance by A; that is, each constitutes a possible answer to A's question. In the given context each of them can be interpreted as inviting the inference that the answer is 'Yes, we will probably be in time'. Crucially, in B_2 and B_3 it is the complement that contains the basis for the answer, not the CT-clause. Thus, in line with Thompson's observation (2002: 131–2), we can say that complements contain the issues or claims being discussed, while their CT-clauses in one way or another mark the speaker's stance towards the issue or claim. The fact that B_1, B_2 and B_3 basically function in the same way in terms of discourse coherence can be represented in terms of the construal configuration as shown in the Figures 3.1, 3.2, and 3.3.

The similarity between Figures 3.1 and 3.2 represents the fact that the addressee and the speaker/writer are engaging in cognitive coordination with respect to the same object of conceptualization. The difference indicates that the CT-clause of B_2's utterance marks this object as a thought of conceptualizer 1. The CT-clause does not operate at level O of the construal configuration, but at level S and its relation to O.

---

[17] See Pit (2003), sect. 3.3, for an overview of somewhat different characterizations of these phenomena in the literature, and of related phenomena (esp. free indirect discourse), as well as conceptual similarities between the different approaches.

106   *Finite complements*

O: *Object of conceptualization:*

S: *Subject of conceptualization*
  (Ground):

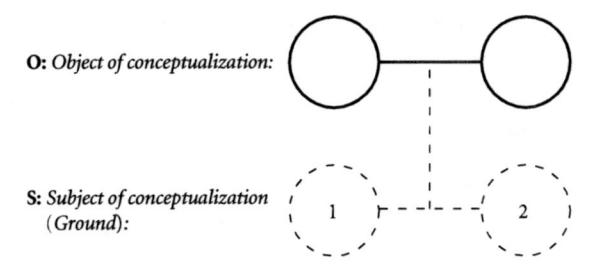

FIGURE 3.1. Construal configuration for non-perspectivized utterance (B₁ in (37)).

O: *Object of conceptualization:*

S: *Subject of conceptualization*
  (Ground):

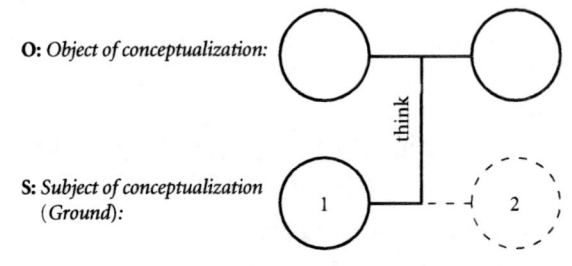

FIGURE 3.2. Construal configuration for first-person perspective (B₂ in (37)).

But not only B₂ (mentioning the speaker's own state of mind) suggests 'Yes' as the answer. Example B₃, mentioning an unidentified third person having said something, does so as well. This can be represented as in Figure 3.3.

In a complementation sentence the addressee is invited to adopt the perspective of the onstage conceptualizer. When this is a third-person the utterance exhibits the same argumentative orientation as when it is a first-person, and when there is no onstage conceptualizer (a 'non-perspectivized' report from the speaker/writer). By presenting a particular perspective to an addressee, the speaker/writer is adopting this perspective, at least temporarily. It is in this sense that A in (37), as the addressee of B's utterance, is engaging in cognitive coordination with B concerning the claim 'It was scheduled for

O: *Object of conceptualization:*

S: *Subject of conceptualization*
  (Ground):

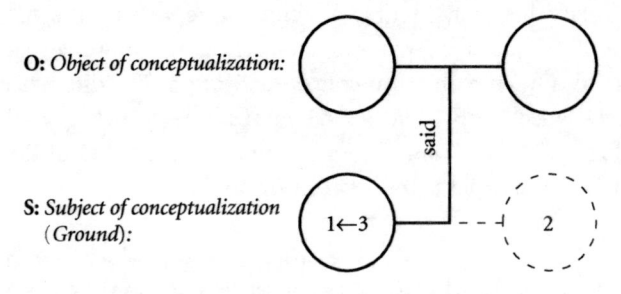

FIGURE 3.3. Construal configuration for third-person perspective (B₃ in (37)).

4 p.m.' in all three cases. However, with a third-person onstage conceptualizer the cognitive coordination of conceptualizer 2 with conceptualizer 1 is indirect (which I indicate by means of the arrow in Figure 3.3). Still, the content of the CT-clause concerns level S and not level O.

While B's utterances in (37) share their argumentative orientation, they certainly differ in argumentative *strength*. The force with which the addressee is invited to take 'Yes' for an answer is less in B_2 than in B_1. In the latter—the non-perspectivized report—the relevant information is straightforwardly introduced into the shared mental spaces of A and B. But the former (*I think*...) relates it explicitly to B's point of view, activating the possibility of a difference between one's perspective and reality; such an indirect introduction into the shared mental space has less force. The relation of the complement to the Ground is still less direct and less forceful in B_3, in which there is the possibility of a difference between the perspective of the onstage conceptualizer and that of the speaker.

The report of someone saying or thinking something, when actually *used*, thus always also has a function in the dimension of cognitive coordination between the addressee and the (assumed) producer of the utterance. The existence of these orientations can be illustrated in the same way as the argumentative orientations of scalar operators such as *almost* and *barely* discussed in Chapter 2. Consider the extended responses in (38), assuming the same context (time of exchange 2 p.m., distance 1 mile):

(38) (*a*) I think it was scheduled for 4 p.m., so we still have lots of time.
(*b*) John said it was scheduled for 4 p.m., so we still have lots of time.
(*c*) I think it was scheduled for 4 p.m., but there might be a traffic jam.
(*d*) John said it was scheduled for 4 p.m., but there might be a traffic jam.

The parallel use of the concluding connective *so* in (38*a*) and (38*b*) shows that both do indeed have the same argumentative potential. In (38*c*) and (38*d*), the final clause contains an argument for the negative conclusion that we might *not* be in time for the launch; the fact that it is only coherent to connect it to the preceding piece of discourse with the contrastive connective *but* indicates that the first part has a positive orientation itself (otherwise it could not be contrasted to the second part). Notice that it is very strange to use *and* instead of *but* here (certainly in the context of the question 'Will we be in time?').

Performativity
This insight allows for a reduction of the difference between so-called performative and non-performative uses of speech-act verbs (Austin 1962; Searle

1969) as compared to the standard view. In this view the use of the following two sentences exhibits an important qualitative difference:

(39) Ik beloof dat ik om 2 uur met de auto voor de deur sta.
 I promise that I at 2 hour with the car in-front-of the door stand
 'I promise that I'll have the car at the door at 2 o'clock.'

(40) Jan heeft beloofd dat hij om 2 uur met de auto voor de
 John has promised that he at 2 hour with the car in-front-of the
 deur staat.
 door stands
 'John promised that he'll have the car at the door at 2 o'clock.'

The point is, according to Austin, Searle, and others, that it makes no sense to characterize (39) in terms of truth conditions; that is, to treat it as a *description* of an act of promising. In uttering (39) one *performs* an act of promising, and the performance of an act can be felicitous or infelicitous, but not true or false. An utterance such as (40), on the other hand, constitutes a description of an act of promising, and thus its semantics can be characterized in terms of truth conditions. Accordingly, the two sentences seem to belong to two wholly distinct categories of speech acts, (39) being a commissive one, and (40) an assertive one.[18] What I want to propose, however, is that the difference is a matter of degree rather than of kind. In accordance with the analysis above, (40) invites an addressee to adopt John's perspective on the content of the complement clause; that is, as a promise. So the speaker/writer and the addressee are *indirectly* engaging in the same type of cognitive coordination, at this point in the discourse, as when the utterance is a first-person, present-tense one;[19] from the perspective of an addressee, the difference is a matter of degree. Consider the way (39) and (40) function in the context of (41):

---

[18] See Nuyts (2001a, 2001b) for a generalization of this distinction to modal expressions, in which he includes impersonal and first-person matrix clauses of the type *It is probable that...* and *I think*. According to Nuyts such expressions are used 'performatively' (in the sense that the speaker 'peforms' an epistemic evaluation by uttering these expressions), while third-person ones (*Mary thinks that...*) are used 'descriptively': 'the speaker reports on someone else's epistemic evaluation of a state of affairs without there being any explicit indication as to whether the speaker personally subscribes (i.e. is committed) to the veracity of the evaluation or not' (Nuyts 2001a: 385). Although I agree with the suggestion of treating speech-act predicates and mental state predicates on a par, it will be clear that my analysis differs from Nuyts's in that mine also brings out the parallel between first- and third-person uses: although the speaker is not committing *herself* as strongly in the latter case, she is orienting the addressee in the same direction as with first-person use. See the discussion in the text below.

[19] This phenomenon may also be described as a case of presupposition float from lower to higher mental spaces (Fauconnier 1997: 60–4). John's commitment to having the car at the door can be considered a presupposition in his mental space, which then floats up to the 'base space' (the Ground). However, I consider the present proposal more adequate, because it also accounts for the observed

(41) A: Can I be in Amsterdam before the match starts?
    B$_1$: I promise that I'll have the car at the door at 2 o'clock. [= (39)]
    B$_2$: John promised that he'll have the car at the door at 2 o'clock.
    [=(40)]

Both can count as an affirmative answer. Both can felicitously be followed by the explicit reassurance *So don't worry* (notice the use of *So*). That is, both saying *I promise that X* as well as saying *John promised that X* count as arguments for an addressee to strengthen the assumption that X will happen; they have the same argumentative orientation.[20] The difference is one of force: whereas the argumentative strength of the first-person, present-tense utterance is maximal, the strength of the third-person, past-tense utterance is less, as the cognitive coordination between author and addressee is indirect. Consequently, it is possible to cancel the invited inference (with a subsequent, contrastively marked utterance) in the latter case, but not in the former:

(42) John promised that he'll have the car at the door at 2 o'clock. But he might have forgotten the route to your new home.

(43) #I promise that I'll have the car at the door at 2 o'clock. But I might forget the route to your new home.

The fact that the contrastive conjunction *but* has to be used in (42) once again illustrates that the first sentence by itself has the argumentative orientation that I ascribed to it. The difference between performative and non-performative use of speech act verbs is parallel to that between maximally and less strong argumentative operators, observed in Chapter 2, Section 2.3.2. Consider the parallel of the difference between (42) and (43) with the difference between (44) and (45):

(44) He barely made it in time for the launch. But he did.

(45) # He did not make it in time for the launch. But he did.

This parallel confirms the idea that third-person matrix clauses of complementation constructions differ only in strength from first-person ones, not in

---

differences in argumentative strength, and because it is more general: it does not invoke different mechanisms (performativity and presupposition float, respectively) for the similar rhetorical effects of B$_1$ and B$_2$ in (41), and it also covers cases like (37), which does not contain a speech-act verb but a verb of cognition.

[20] In Verhagen (1995; see also Ch. 1, Sect. 1.3.2 above) it is argued that it is precisely this constant argumentative orientation of the report of someone promising something that provides the basis for the development of the epistemic/evidential use of *promise* as in *The debate promises to be interesting*; in such cases the verb *only* functions as a speaker-oriented marker of argumentative orientation, and does not designate (performatively or descriptively) an act of promising.

kind. In this analysis the difference between 'performative' and 'descriptive' uses of speech act verbs appears to be not categorical (they have the same argumentative orientation) but a matter of degree (they differ in argumentative strength). It thus avoids the discrepancy, in the standard analysis, between the fact that they are formally (lexically and grammatically) very similar but supposedly very different functionally. I consider this a welcome consequence.

Likewise, the present approach also accommodates similarities in use between performative utterances and first-person indications of mental states. Austin (1962) restricted his discussion to speech-act verbs, but others, noticing the parallels in use and structure of expressions like *I think*, have extended it (e.g. Nuyts 2001a, 2001b; Diessel and Tomasello 2001: 103–4). Benveniste (1958) had already classified both speech-act formulas and first-person present-tense uses of verbs of cognition as 'subjective' utterances.[21] I have shown above that these expressions share their argumentative orientations, which are manifest in phenomena of discourse coherence. Thus, (42) and (43) have parallels with verbs of cognition:

(46) John believes that the mission has been successful. But in fact it has failed.

(47) #I believe that the operation has been successful. But in fact it has failed.

Developing a network of complementation constructions

More generally, this approach makes it possible to connect the findings of Thompson (2002) for conversation and those of Diessel and Tomasello (2001) for young children's language to the structure and use of complementation constructions in 'advanced' types of discourse such as literary narrative and newspaper reports (see the discussion in Sect. 3.2.3). The latter can be seen as an extension of the former, with some of the effects, in particular the strength of their discourse function, toned down or qualified, but basically with the same general rhetorical character. The extension may be considered to be directly related to the high type-frequency for the predicate slot that we observed in Section 3.3.2 (Table 3.1). Learning to process such language inevitably involves the experience of an increasingly large number of predicates used with complements. With growing linguistic experience, also as a function of the expansion of this experience into the realm of reading and writing, the increasing type-frequency of CT-predicates (as well as the type frequency of subjects, beyond first- and second-person pronouns) leads to the

---

[21] It will be clear that I do not agree with Benveniste's classification of third person expressions as objective, or Nuyts's characterization of them as descriptive. Anachronistically from the present perspective, argumentative force is mistaken for orientation in such classifications.

entrenchment of increasingly schematic patterns in the language user's memory, and thus to the 'upward' and 'outward' growth of a network of complementation constructions of the sort suggested by Diessel and Tomasello (ibid. 134–5). Consider Figure 3.4, representing a small part of such a network for Dutch complementation constructions.

The boxes with round corners represent instances of use. The high token-frequency of a communicatively relevant specific pattern (a large number of highly similar utterances) leads to entrenchment of the representation of that pattern in memory (indicated by boxes with sharp corners; the most prototypical schemas are in boxes with heavy lines). An increasing number of similar but slightly different usage events leads to the entrenchment of a somewhat more general pattern for *denken* taking different subjects (i.e. also second-person and especially different kinds of third-person). The experience with even more different usage events, each of which has a rather low frequency itself (such as *concluderen*, 'conclude', and *beloofde*, 'promised'), raises the type-frequency, leading to stronger entrenchment, for the general complementation pattern (32) (besides certain 'intermediate' patterns).

A condition for this process to work is that the semantic and/or pragmatic functions of the different patterns are related. Otherwise they would not contribute to this particular network, but perhaps to another one. The claim here is that it is precisely the specification of some aspect of intersubjective coordination that provides semantic coherence to this network. The concrete, 'formulaic' complementation patterns which are acquired early do have connections to the rest of the growing network, but they remain stored separately and are retrieved (i.e. used) frequently, and may have specific properties not shared with other nodes in the network. The schematic

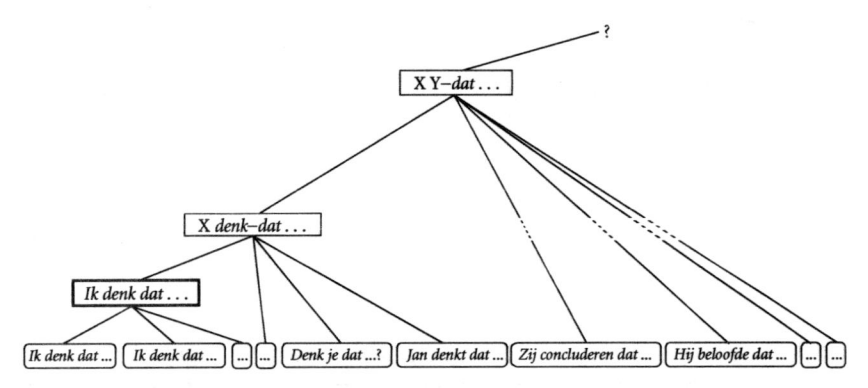

FIGURE 3.4. Partial network for 'object' complementation constructions in Dutch

construction (32) is certainly near the 'top' of this network (but see Sect. 3.3.6). Both its form and its meaning are more abstract than those of specific expressions. But there is still an important conceptual connection between the abstract pattern and the specific ones, so that even instances of the abstract pattern resemble the specific cases more than they resemble instances of other abstract patterns—for example, the transitive-event pattern. It is only when we no longer look at the way complementation constructions function in the cognitive coordination between addressee and speaker/writer (and just focus on the relation between a subject and an object of conceptualization) that we perceive qualitative, substantive differences between different types of CT-clauses—on the one hand those that simply cannot be analyzed as specifying an object of conceptualization (the ones that always function as markers of stance or illocutionary force), on the other hand those that can in principle be conceived as specifying an object of conceptualization. But it is this perspective, or rather the absence of the discourse dimension in this perspective, that makes the difference seem larger than it is.

Thus the extension of CT-clauses to other than first- and second-person, present-tense ones does allow for the possibility of construing the content of such a CT-clause as an event that can itself be an object of conceptualization. But instead of regarding children and conversationalists as using descriptions of (mental and communicative) events in a particular way (as markers of stance and illocutionary acts), we can say that advanced language users (especially in writing) have developed the ability to construe extended versions of certain stance and speech-act markers as descriptions of a particular kind of event. However, as the discussion of text fragment (28) has demonstrated, it is not necessary or even normal for a CT-clause to function in such a way in discourse. The events and situations constituting the object of discussion in this text are not the ones denoted by the CT-clauses, but the ones in the complement clauses. Put differently, the CT-clauses do not by themselves enter into coherence relations with other discourse segments: raising questions, addressing issues, or answering questions raised (implicitly or explicitly) in other segments of the discourse. Such usage does occur sometimes, but it is quite rare. The first 2,000 sentences of the Eindhoven Corpus (see n. 15) contain 215 instances of complementation constructions (including 'subject' complements). In at most 7 of those the CT-clause may be considered to enter into a coherence relation with other discourse segments. One example is (48):

(48) Deelt   de   minister de mening dat deze commissie heel goed
     Shares the   minister the opinion that this committee very good

werk   doet?
work   does

'Does the minister share the view that this committee is doing very good work?'[22]

The MP asking this question is not asking about the good work of the committee (although he does present it as probably his own opinion). What he is focusing on is the minister's opinion about it; that is, the point addressed in the CT-clause. The question really is: 'Does the minister agree?' This is evident from the question that follows (48), which is whether the minister would be willing to try to prevent the abolition of the committee. This depends on the answer to the question as to the minister's opinion. Thus the CT-clause of (48) enters into a causal/conditional relation with the sentence following it: 'If the minister shares my view, then he may be willing to do something I want.'

Notice that this paraphrase does not contain a complement clause but a nominal object ('shares my view'). In (48) the complement clause functions to identify the object of agreement between the MP and the minister (see n. 22). But, as stated, this is a rare type of use. The standard function of the CT-clause is to specify the manner in which the addressee is to coordinate cognitively with another subject of conceptualization, without this process of coordination being made into an object of conceptualization itself.

3.3.4 *Manipulating the relation between Ground and onstage conceptualizers*

It has already become apparent that speakers/writers can manage their co-ordination relationship with the addressee by modifying the content of the matrix clause. While in early stages of development children have only a limited range of options in this respect, adult language users can in principle manipulate this relationship in many subtle ways, by modifying the connection between the Ground and the onstage conceptualization. In this section I will explore these degrees of possible distinctness and identification further.

As noted at the beginning of Section 3.3.3, complementation constructions differ from direct speech (quotation) in that the speaker/writer is held

---

[22] One can imagine that this might be a case of a nominal direct object containing a modifying clause instead of a complementation construction. However, in making this selection a 'liberal' attitude was adopted in order not to prejudge the case. Since verbal expressions of the type 'have/hold the view that', 'be of the opinion that' were counted as complementation constructions, this one was included as well. There is clearly not an obvious cut-off point. In fact, I suspect that the feeling that there is something like a 'real' direct object here is a consequence of the relatively independent status of the CT-clause. Below I will argue that syntactic roles have no independent part to play in the interpretation of complementation constructions, which automatically eliminates the need to determine which grammatical roles are present in this case.

responsible for several features of form and content of a complement clause; that is, the piece of information the validity of which is attributed to the (third-person) onstage conceptualizer. The speaker/writer is taken as providing the point of view from which to construe the interpretation of first-person deictic elements, and in general the responsibility for the wording may be attributed to her. I then provided arguments for the conclusion that the argumentative orientation of the author, and not just the view of the onstage conceptualizer, is also an important factor in the way complement clauses contribute to the coherence of discourse.

These two aspects are related. The responsibility of the speaker/writer for the wording allows her to identify the source of the content of certain ideas as another mental space than her own, and at the same time present them in a way that suits her communicative purposes optimally. Notice, for example, that 'indirect speech' often involves leaving things out from someone else's discourse and summarizing it, such that its size and content best fit the present discourse.

Thus complementation constructions provide another illustration of the generality of what Ducrot (1996) calls 'polyphony': the presence of multiple 'voices' in a single linguistic utterance. In mental-space terminology, a complementation construction with a third-person onstage conceptualizer is an instrument for incorporating elements and structure from the mental space of this onstage conceptualizer into the mental space of the speaker/writer and the addressee (first- and second-person).[23] Which elements of the utterance are to be attributed to one mental space and which to the other is not completely fixed. In indirect speech, as we noticed, the author is responsible for the choice of words, also in the complement clause, but without indications to the contrary it is normal to assume that the words chosen are at least a good approximation of the onstage conceptualizer's own words. In fact, it is also possible to attribute the content of the *CT-clause* to some extent primarily to the onstage conceptualizer rather than to the present author of the discourse. Consider (40), repeated here for convenience (English only):

---

[23] This characterization may evoke the notion of 'blending' from recent work in mental-space theory (see Fauconnier 1997; Coulson and Oakley 2000; and others). Thus complementation constructions exhibit not only the phenomenon of conceptual integration that is typical for blending, but also that of 'compression' (Fauconnier and Turner 2000), in view of the summary effect mentioned in the text. However, the examples of blending and compression given in the literature involve more radical forms of these phenomena than can be observed in complementation constructions. Therefore I prefer to remain agnostic on the issue of whether complementation should be considered as involving blending, and to treat them as 'just' a particular way of manipulating mental spaces. Notice that Fauconnier (1997: 40) also presents the CT-clauses *Max hopes...* and *Susan believes...* only as examples of elementary instructions for space building.

(40) John promised that he'll have the car at the door at 2 o'clock.

Following Cornelis (1997: 189–93), we may observe that this is not only a proper report if what John has said is: 'I promise I'll have the car at the door at 2 o'clock', but also if he has said: 'I'll have the car at the door at 2 o'clock.'[24] In the latter case the qualification that the content of the complement clause must be entertained as a promise stems entirely from the present speaker/writer; in the former, it stems from the onstage conceptualizer, John. This indeterminacy is a general feature of many complementation constructions.[25] Specifically, it is also observable in cases of CT-predicates indicating mental states rather than speech acts, such as (49):

(49) GenTech's director believes that cloning of full-grown animals will be possible soon.

Although saying *I believe X* strictly speaking does not amount to performing a speech act of believing (simply because believing is not an act), (49) exhibits the same indeterminacy as (40) with respect to the question of who is primarily responsible for the choice of the predicate *believe*: it may well be that the author of (49) is 'shadowing' the director's own words ('I believe that...'), but it could also be that it is only the author who is characterizing the director's propositional attitude with respect to the complement clause's content as a belief—for example, on the basis of something else the director said or did (e.g. make an investment in a particular project or company).

The possibility of attributing the choice of a CT-verb to the onstage conceptualizer clearly represents the default situation. However, there are a number of CT-predicates which allow the speaker/writer to indicate that the way a complement clause relates to the Ground (the way it should be entertained by the addressee) differs from the way it relates to the mental space of the onstage conceptualizer. For example, consider (50):

(50) De   boeren   dreigden   dat   de   acties   nog   veel   grimmiger
The farmers threatened that the actions still much vicious-COMPAR
zouden worden.
would become
'The farmers threatened that the actions would become much more vicious.'

---

[24] Notice that in both cases the exact wording of what was promised may also differ without (40) becoming an incorrect report.
[25] Namely those in which the difference between first/second-person use and third-person use is only a matter of strength, with the argumentative orientation being the same; as we will see below, there are also CT-verbs that have the specific function of 'dissociating' the perspective of the onstage conceptualizer from the Ground.

Unlike the choice of *promise* in (40), the choice of the main verb in (50) cannot be attributed to the onstage conceptualizer; that is, (50) cannot be interpreted as a report by the speaker/writer of the farmers having said 'We threaten that the actions will become much more vicious'. One cannot use *threaten* performatively (as has already been observed by Searle (1976: 6)). The verb is related to *promise* as a kind of negative counterpart. It is parallel to *promise* in that its use counts as an argument inviting the addressee to conclude that the situation mentioned in the complement will be realized as a result of the intention of the 'threatener', but it differs from *promise* in that this situation is evaluated negatively. In first-person usage this combination would be self-defeating (see Verhagen 1995: 121). To evaluate the effect negatively (implying 'I think this is a bad thing, so it should preferably not happen') and simultaneously say that one is going to do it in the future (implying: 'I am not going to refrain from doing it') results, if not in theory then in any case for all practical purposes, in irrelevance and/or complete confusion. This is what distinguishes *threaten* from *warn*. Like *threaten*, the use of *warn* evaluates a possible future event negatively, but its meaning involves a condition ('Something bad will happen *unless* you take measures to prevent it'), so that it may be used performatively, because it is not commissive, as *promise* is. Notice that (50) can be read as a report both of the farmers saying 'The actions will become much more vicious', and of them saying 'We warn you that the actions will become much more vicious'. In either case the categorization of the event as a threat is the responsibility of the speaker/writer as *distinct* from the onstage conceptualizer.[26]

The use of *threaten* as a CT-predicate thus invites the addressee of the utterance to entertain the content of the complement as a threat, but this is not in the same way as it will have been entertained by the onstage conceptualizer. So this verb indicates a difference between the way a clause is to be entertained in the Ground, and the way it may be attributed to a third person. Some other verbs and expressions of this kind are *vergeten* ('forget'), *verzwijgen* ('conceal, keep silent about'), and *over het hoofd zien* ('overlook, fail to notice'). In cases such as (51) the mental space of the onstage conceptualizer is evoked, but as differing from the Ground with respect to the status of the complement clause:

---

[26] In Verhagen (2000a) I suggest that this difference between *threaten* and *promise* may have contributed to the fact that Dutch *dreigen* developed into an epistemic/evidential marker much earlier than *promise* (see n. 20): even when denoting a speech act, *threaten* always evokes the speaker/writer's point of view as distinct from that of the onstage conceptualizer.

(51) He has $\begin{Bmatrix} \text{forgotten} \\ \text{left out} \\ \text{failed to notice} \end{Bmatrix}$ that the building has no elevator.

There are also differences among these verbs, of course. For example, with the mental-state expressions *forget* and *fail to notice* the onstage conceptualizer does not entertain the content of the complement at all, while the communication verbs *threaten* and *leave out* imply that the subject does entertain it, but in a way that is different from the role it plays in the Ground. What they have in common is that they mark a difference between the status of the complement as entertained by the onstage conceptualizer and its status in the Ground; the choice of verbs in (50) as well as in (51) cannot be attributed to the onstage conceptualizer, and is always the responsibility of the speaker/writer.

It is also possible for the speaker/writer to indicate that the onstage conceptualizer has a negative epistemic stance towards the content of the complement clause, thus contrasting it with the Ground (examples are verbs like *doubt* and *deny*), or, conversely, to indicate explicitly that the content of the complement clause is being entertained by the onstage conceptualizer and is a part of the (common) Ground (examples are *know, regret, discover, realize*). The latter are typical examples of so-called factive predicates, presupposing the truth of their complement.[27] Factivity is an operation on the relation between a third person's mental space and the Ground with respect to the status of a proposition, but it is not the only one. As we have already seen, there are others with which it cross-classifies (for example, *forget* is factive, but its complement is not attributed to the onstage conceptualizer).

The choice of these verbs may be attributed to the onstage conceptualizer (unlike *forget* and *threaten*), although they still differ from each other as to what they specify about the relationship between the mental space of the onstage conceptualizer and the Ground, and the status of the complement clause in each of these.

Notice that a verb (factive or not factive) that implies that the content of the complement is not being entertained by the onstage conceptualizer cannot be used to introduce 'direct' speech or thought, of course:

(52) (*a*) She might be angry, but he doubted that she would launch an investigation.
 (*b*) ??She might be angry, but he doubted: 'She will launch an investigation.'

---

[27] i.e. if that is not a *whether/if*-clause, which is inherently marked as uncertain in the Ground, witness the difference between *to know that X* and *to know whether/if X*.

(53) (a) He forgot that is was Sunday.
    (b) ??He forgot: 'It is Sunday.'

This supports the view that complementation constructions should not be seen as just an instrument for presenting someone's thoughts or words in a 'compressed' way. At least in the language of adults, the same grammatical construction (of complementation) can be used to specify various sorts of relationships between the onstage conceptualizer's mental space and the Ground, independently of the way in which the onstage conceptualizer herself entertains the relevant idea.

Besides lexical means, there is also at least one grammatical instrument operating on the relation between the onstage conceptualizer's mental space and the Ground; namely, the passive, as proposed by Cornelis (1997: 193–8). Notice that one does not *perform* an act of promising with the passive clause in (54). It is also hard to interpret it as a kind of detached report of a presently occurring promise, so such an utterance just sounds rather strange:

(54) ??It is promised by me that the taxi will be on time.

Consequently, when a promise by a *third* person is presented in the passive voice, that form of presentation is certainly not the one used by the promisor. So the formulation will be taken to be the speaker/writer's responsibility, not that of the onstage conceptualizer. This holds in general for verbs whose lexical meaning does not imply a distinction between the view of the speaker/writer and the view of the onstage conceptualizer; that is, the large majority of CT-verbs.

CT-clauses can thus be seen as specifying, in some respect, the relationship between the onstage conceptualizer's mental space and the Ground, thereby managing the coordination relationship between speaker/writer and addressee. In several cases, as we have just seen, the content of the complement is not (just) being attributed to the onstage conceptualizer, since it may be presented as being denied, doubted, or refuted; as a kind of process that the onstage conceptualizer cannot have predicated of herself (threaten, forget); or as being present in both the onstage conceptualizer's mental space and in the Ground (know, regret). These cases thus all presuppose distinctness of these two mental spaces, with some of them emphasizing it. Therefore the generalization over the function of different subtypes of complementation constructions cannot be that the content of the complement clause is always directly *attributed* to the onstage conceptualizer. This is part of the reason why (32) was formulated the way it was; that is, as an instruction to the addressee to entertain the content of the complement in the way indicated by the CT-clause. This is also valid for the special cases considered above.

3.3.5 Wh-*extraction 'in the wild'*
Clausal constituents again

I now want to turn to a specific issue in the syntax of complementation, the phenomenon known as *Wh*-extraction (or 'long-distance *Wh*-movement'). This has been a continuous topic of central concern in syntax since the early days of generative grammar, especially since Chomsky's seminal paper (1977). Some examples given by Chomsky are (55) and (56):[28]

(55) Who did Mary say that John kissed *t*.

(56) Who did Mary hope [$_{\bar{S}}$ that Tom would tell Bill [$_{\bar{S}}$ that he should visit *t*]]

The theoretical interest of such examples lies in the fact that the question phrases ('*Wh*-elements') appear to occupy a position in a clause that does not determine their syntactic role. In (55), *Who* is the first element of the matrix clause ('Mary said that...'), while the verb to which it bears the relation of direct object is not *said* but *kissed*, in the subordinate clause; thus it seems to be extracted out of 'its own clause'; its assumed original position is indicated by *t* (for 'trace'). In (56), the preposed *Wh*-element even seems to have originated more than one clause 'down'. Normally, a constituent can only receive a role from an element (typically the verb) in the same clause, so these phenomena are intriguing. Because they appear to violate the normal structural integrity and autonomy of clauses, they offer an opportunity for identifying the factors that cause clauses to behave syntactically in the way they do.

Notice that this way of describing the phenomenon presupposes the constituent view of complements that I have been criticizing in this chapter. The only difference between the clauses that is considered relevant concerns their hierarchical relationship: the clause in which the *Wh*-element plays a syntactic role is properly contained ('embedded') in the one where the element is actually positioned. Otherwise, they are both just clauses, each viewed as an abstract structural unit characterized by the presence of a verb and its participant noun phrases. I have been arguing, however, that matrix clauses differ systematically from complements in that the former operate in the intersubjective dimension of the construal configuration. In this analysis complement clauses and matrix clauses are not viewed as instances of a single abstract grammatical category ('S', 'InflP',...); rather, they perform very

---

[28] These are examples (32) and (10) in Chomsky (1977), respectively.

distinct roles, determined by a relatively specific grammatical template (from a connected network of such templates). It is therefore relevant to consider the question of whether and how the present framework can deal with these phenomena, and whether it does not cast a different light on them. This is what I will be exploring in this section. As we will see, the results will turn out to be rather remarkable.

The specific nature of complementation questions in the construal configuration
We have seen that in prototypical complementation constructions, including the formulaic types that are first acquired and most frequently used in conversation, the onstage conceptualizer is minimally distinct from the Ground. What I will argue is that this notion of minimal vs. non-minimal distinctness of the onstage mental space from the Ground is crucial for understanding what is going on in 'Wh-extraction' as it occurs in actual language use. More specifically, any additional special machinery, whether formal or functional, to constrain the extraction of question phrases will not be needed.

To begin with, notice that the distance between an onstage conceptualizer and the actual Ground is minimal when the onstage conceptualizer is first-person and the utterance is a statement. In the case of questions, the distinction is of course minimal with *second*-person usage; a question 'probes' the addressee's (second person's) mind. So the addition of the second-person question *Do you think?* makes explicit which of the two epistemic stances in the Ground is relevant, just as the addition of the first-person expression *I think* does for statements. As we saw in (37), in response to the question *Will we be in time for the launch?*, the answers *It was scheduled for 4 p.m.*, *I think it was scheduled for 4 p.m.*, and *Someone said it was scheduled for 4 p.m.* have the same argumentative orientation, with the distance between the onstage conceptualizer and the Ground being minimal in the second case. Notice that the initial question in (37) does not put a conceptualizer on stage. What is the formulation with an onstage conceptualizer that is minimally distinct from the Ground for a question? Clearly, that must be (57):

(57) Do you think we will be in time for the launch?

This is the utterance with an explicit conceptualizer that is minimally different from the question *Will we be in time for the launch?*, not the utterance *I ask you if we will be in time for the launch*, let alone *Do I think...* or *I don't know if we will be in time for the launch*. The construal configuration evoked by (57) is indicated in Figure 3.5, with both the speech-act features and the CT-clause relating to level S.

Finite complements 121

O: *Object of conceptualization:*

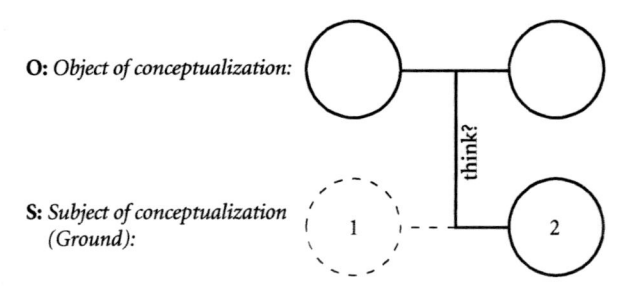

S: *Subject of conceptualization (Ground):*

think?

1 — 2

FIGURE 3.5. Construal configuration for second-person perspective in questions

What is marked in the intersubjective dimension in (57) is, as indicated in Figure 3.5, the mirror image of what is marked in *I think we will be in time for the launch*; that is, B₂'s declarative utterance in (37) (see Fig. 3.2).

In view of this, it is revealing to look at the following corpus examples of '*Wh*-extraction' in Dutch and English; that is, sentences with a question-word ('*Wh*-word') in first position that appears to be associated with a grammatical role in a subordinate clause:

(58) *Wh*-extraction in Eindhoven Corpus (Dutch)²⁹
    (*a*) Hoe denkt u dat de AKV-gedachten in de gemeenten
        How think you that the AKV-thoughts in the communities
        zullen landen?
        will land
        'How do you think the local councils will react to the ideas of the AKV?'
    (*b*) En wat denk je dat ie zei, die prins?
        And what think you that he said that prince
        'And what do you think this prince said?'
    (*c*) Wat denk je dat ie zei?
        What think you that he said
        'What do you think he said?'
    (*d*) Wie denk je dat je voorhebt, om me zo te tekenen?
        Who think you that you have-in-front-of for me thus to draw
        'Who do you think I am, drawing a picture of me like that?'

---

²⁹ The lack of clause boundary markings in the corpus makes it impossible to search directly for *Wh*-sentences with more than one clause, let alone for clauses with 'extracted' *Wh*-phrases. The way this set was obtained then, was as follows: searches were done for *Wh*-words followed by some form (present or past tense) of the verbs *denken* ('think'), *zeggen* ('say'), *vinden* ('find', 'think'), and *willen* ('want to'), which all take finite complements, and are generally used in the literature to illustrate *Wh*-extraction; two more verbs included in the search were *geloven* ('think, believe') and *beloven* ('promise'). From the results, the instances of *Wh*-extraction were selected manually.

(e) Waarom dacht   je   dat dit geslacht tot nu   toe alleen
    Why   thought you that this lineage till now to only
    maar vrouwen voortbracht? Voor de *lol*?[30]
    PRT women   produced   For the fun
    'Why do you think this family has produced so many women up to now? For the fun of it?'

(f) Wat denk je   dat moeder en vader voor cadeau voor je
    What think you that mother and father for   present for you
    hebben?
    have
    'What do you think that mother and father have got you as a present?'

(59) *Wh-extraction in Brown Corpus (English)*[31]

(a) 'Fools', he bayed, 'what do you think you are doing?'

(b) What does he think a remark like this 'lousy' one does to our prestige and morale?

(c) What conclusions do you think he might come to?

(d) What you think I care about that?

(e) 'I don't know what you think you've been doing about my clothes', he said.

(f) What did she think he could do?

(g) What do you think I did with them?

(h) What the hell do you think baseball is? [*twice*]

(i) What the hell do you think it'll be like up there?

(j) Who do you think pays the rent?

(k) And what would you say he wants to do?

Notice that all of the six Dutch cases involve the verb *denken* ('think'), and have a second-person singular subject (one case of the polite form *u*, five of the unstressed default form *je*). Ten of the eleven English examples also

---

[30] In principle, this sentence could also be interpreted as the question: 'What is the reason that you have this idea?', in which case the *Wh*-word would not be related to the complement clause. As the rhetorical question 'For the fun of it?' indicates, however, that is not how it should be read here; the question concerns the reasons for producing only women. Below, another interesting case of such a 'Why do you think' question is discussed in greater detail.

[31] In this case a search was done for one of the elements *what, who, whom, how, when, where, why,* with one of the verbs *think, believe, say,* and *tell* following it (in the same sentence, i.e. before a full stop). The final selection was again done manually.

contain *think*, one case ((59k)) has *say*; the second-person subject is also dominant in these examples: nine cases of *you*, two cases of third-person pronouns ((59b) and (59f)). The set of verbs included in the corpus searches (see nn. 29 and 31) comprised other verbs as well, and there were no conditions on the nature of the subject of the CT-clause searched. But in the Dutch corpus no instances of *Wh*-extraction with verbs other than *denken* were found, and in the English corpus only one; furthermore, in Dutch no other subjects were found than second-person pronouns, and in English only two, both of which were pronominal, not lexical. This might raise the question, especially for the Dutch corpus, of whether this lack of variation is perhaps due to the limited size of the corpus. It might be too small to uncover the relevant patterns; a sentence such as (60) sounds completely standard, but even this is not found in the Eindhoven Corpus:

(60) Wat wil je dat ik voor je doe?
What want you that I for you do
'What do you want me to do for you?'

A search through the material of *de Volkskrant* from 1995 reveals some instances of verbs other than *denken* as well as subjects other than second-person pronouns. Examples are given in (61)–(66):

(61) En wat zei je nou dat die Cornell had bereikt?
And what said you now that that Cornell had achieved
'And what did you say now that this Cornell had achieved?'

(62) Hoe vind je dat Kok het in de laatste verkiezingen heeft gedaan?
How find you that Kok it in the latest elections has done
'How do you think Kok performed in the last election?'

(63) Waar wil je dan dat ik het over heb?
Where want you then that I it about have
'What do you want me to talk about then?'

(64) Wat denken B en W dat onze burgers zullen denken
What think Mayor and Aldermen that our citizens will think
van zo'n dure buitenlandse reis?
of such-a expensive foreign trip
'What do Mayor and Aldermen think that our citizens will feel about such an expensive trip abroad?'

(65) Hoe denkt Oudkerk dat dit in zijn werk is gegaan?
How thinks Oudkerk that this in its work is gone
'How does Oudkerk think this was done?'

(66) Hoe denken zij   dat het voelt om als juist teruggekeerde militair
     How think they that it feels for as just returned   military
     te moeten lezen dat het zojuist meegemaakte niets   voorstelde?
     to must   read that the just   experienced   nothing represented
     'What do they think it feels like for a soldier who has just returned to
     have to read that what he just went through meant nothing?'

However, it is clear that the verb *denken* is much more frequent than any other verb and that second-person subjects are much more frequent than others. Consider the numbers in Tables 3.2 and 3.3.

First of all, we may conclude that the results from the Eindhoven Corpus (only second-person-subject cases of one verb, *denken*; see (58)) were not really a coincidence. The corpus may indeed have been too small to show that more than one verb occurs with '*Wh*-extraction', but the exclusiveness of *denken*, as well as that of second-person subjects, does in fact reflect a significant regularity of language use, as shown by a comparison with the much larger *Volkskrant* corpus. The extremely high frequency of the specific pattern '*Wh-denk*-2ndPerson-*dat*-X' that is evident in the larger corpus is manifested as an exclusive occurrence in the smaller one.

Type and token frequencies

Furthermore, there is a remarkable difference between complementation constructions in general and '*Wh*-extraction'. The general abstract complementation pattern 'X-verb-*dat*...' (see (32)) is supported by a high

TABLE 3.2. CT-predicates used with '*Wh*-extraction' in *de Volkskrant* (1995)

Tokens per predicate	Predicates (types)	Total no. of tokens
34	*denken* ('think')	34
5	*willen* ('want to')	5
2	*zeggen* ('say'), *vinden* ('find', 'think')	4
Total number of types	4	43

TABLE 3.3. 'Matrix' subjects used with '*Wh*-extraction' in *de Volkskrant* (1995)

Tokens per subject	Subject types	Total no. of tokens
36	Second-person pronoun (*je*: 25, *u*: 10, *jij*: 1)	36
3	Third-person pronoun (*ze*: 2, *zij*: 1)	3
3	Definite noun phrase with lexical head	3
1	First-person pronoun (see text below)	1
Total number of types		43

type-frequency of items occurring in the verb slot (see Table 3.1), as well as a considerable variation in kinds of subjects. It may thus be assumed to have a strong memory representation. But there is no such support from high type frequency for a general, abstract pattern '*Wh*-verb-X-*dat*...'. In fact, the connection of the pattern of '*Wh*-extraction' with the lexical item *denken* and second-person pronouns is very tight, as can be shown by comparing their frequency in this pattern with their general frequencies. Consider Table 3.4.[32]

It is immediately obvious that the high frequency of *denken* in '*Wh*-extraction' cannot be explained by its general frequency; that is, the hypothesis that this verb is more frequent than the other ones *in general* is not true. In fact, *denken* is much less frequent than *zeggen* (the numbers from the relatively small Eindhoven Corpus already suffice to show this), while it occurs seventeen times more often than *zeggen* with '*Wh*-extraction'.

Something similar holds in the case of the subjects, as is evident from Table 3.5. (Here the general frequencies are given for the Eindhoven Corpus, as they are too frequent in *de Volkskrant* to be included in its index; the numbers are high enough to be considered representative.)[33]

TABLE 3.4. Comparative frequencies of CT-verbs in '*Wh*-extraction'

Verbs	Total in Eindhoven Corpus	in *de Volkskrant*	in '*Wh*-extraction' (*de Volkskrant*)
zeggen ('say')	2,998	70,980	2
willen ('want to', 'wish')	1,561	40,094	5
denken ('think')	920	14,302	34
vinden ('find', 'think')	<181	<17,914	2

[32] The form *wil* is not only the singular present-tense form of a verb, but also the noun *wil* ('will', 'desire'), and the *Volkskrant* material is not tagged. In the Eindhoven Corpus, 6 per cent of the instances of *wil* are nominal. On this basis, only 94 per cent of the cases of *wil* in *de Volkskrant* were included. Similarly, 12 per cent of the forms of *wilde* in the Eindhoven Corpus are adjectives ('wild'), so the number of those forms in *de Volkskrant* was also reduced with that percentage. For the verb *vinden* only the 'opinion' sense is relevant, not the sense 'come across (as a result of searching or not)', but this distinction cannot be made in either corpus; hence the indication in Table 3.4 that the numbers mentioned with this verb constitute a maximum.

[33] The number of definite noun phrases was estimated by counting the number of finite verbs and subtracting the number of 'base-form' (mostly subject) pronouns and the average percentage of proper nouns in the set of nouns (43%), and then dividing the result by two (i.e. as if half of these either involved an impersonal construction or had an indefinite subject). Especially because of the latter assumption, the estimate is highly conservative (the actual number must be considerably higher), but that does not affect the point here. For the subject forms of the personal pronouns exact numbers can be given, as these have been specifically tagged in the corpus.

In terms of a network as in Figure 3.4, the high-frequency specific pattern mentioned above has a position near the 'bottom', as represented in Figure 3.6.

It is remarkable that instances of '*Wh*-extraction' in the corpus material never deviate in more than one respect from this pattern: when the subject is not a second person, the verb is *denken* (see examples (64)–(66)), and when the verb is not *denken*, the subject is second person (see examples (61)–(63)). Thus even the pattern '*Wh*-V-X-*dat*...' appears not to be strongly entrenched. Rather, the specific pattern '*Wh-denk*-2ndPerson-*dat*...' should be considered the template on the basis of which analogical extensions are built.[34]

This result has dramatic consequences for the role of the phenomenon in syntactic theory. The properties of '*Wh*-extraction' do not follow from *general* properties of complementation, and thus also should not be accounted for in such general terms. The template licensing such constructs constitutes a relatively concrete, low-level pattern, which has some properties that do not percolate upwards in the network to the level of productive rules. In other words, the fact that certain complementation sentences seem to contain displaced constituents is no evidence that such displacement follows from any general property of complementation; in this case, they instantiate a low-level template. Instances that do not fully conform to it can be seen as analogical extensions from this prototype. Only if the degree of deviation from the prototypical pattern would frequently be large, might a situation arise in which the displacement could generalize to a more abstract level. However, the actually occurring extensions in the present corpus never deviate from the prototype in more than one respect, as we have seen. Cases

TABLE 3.5. Comparative frequencies of 'matrix' subjects in '*Wh*-extraction'

	Total	
Subjects	in Eindhoven Corpus	in *Wh*-'extraction' (*de Volkskrant*)
Definite noun phrase with lexical head	>14,100	3
Third-person pronoun	6,704	3 (*ze, zij*)
Second-person pronoun	1,655	36 (*je, jij, u*)

[34] It is worth noting in this respect that the frequency of the exact combination '*Wh- denk*-2ndPerson - *dat*...' in *de Volkskrant* (namely 28) is of the same order of magnitude as that of other combinations that are well entrenched, such as the default case of the Dutch *way* construction, with the unique verb *banen* (Verhagen 2002: 412).

Finite complements 127

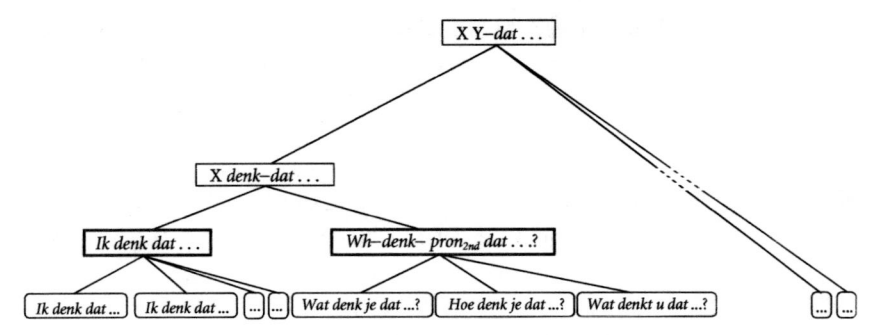

FIGURE 3.6. '*Wh*-extraction' in the complementation-construction network

like (55) and (56) are not instantiated in this material. Example (55) deviates the least from the prototype, as it can be constructed out of features of actually occurring instances ('blending' a third person subject with a verb other than *think*), so that it constitutes a rather easy analogical extension. The construction of an example like (56) requires blending it with another template (for embedding complements), a feature not instantiated in actual usage for this phenomenon at all, and it thus appears artificial.

Pursuing this line of thought, further support for the present analysis comes from the phenomenon that invented examples of '*Wh*-extraction' are judged worse to the degree that they deviate more from the specific pattern. Consider the series of cases in (67):

(67) (*a*) What did you say that the workers had done?

 (*b*) What did he say that the workers had done?

 (*c*) What did the trade union leader say that the workers had done?

 (*d*) What had the trade union leader said that the workers had done?

 (*e*) What did the trade union leader concede that the workers had done?

 (*f*) What did the trade union leader concede to a journalist after the press conference that the workers had done?

 (*g*) What had the trade union leader conceded to a journalist after the press conference that the workers had done?

The further one goes into this series, the worse the examples become. In groups of freshmen in Dutch linguistics over a number of years, subjects who were asked to rank these examples in terms of acceptability always agreed completely that (*a*) and (*b*) were fine, and that (*f*) and (*g*) were unacceptable. Judgments varied for (*c*), (*d*), and (*e*), both across and within individuals (people who find (*d*) unacceptable sometimes nevertheless consider it 'not as bad' as (*g*), but never the other way around). Discussion about the judgments led to increased agreement about the *relative* acceptability, but not about the absolute acceptability, of (*c*), (*d*), and (*e*).

The point is that from (67a) to (67g) there is an increasing number of respects in which the onstage conceptualizer's mental space is linguistically distinguished from that of the Ground. The more this is the case, the harder it is to conceive of the CT-clause as an indication of the way the addressee should engage in cognitive coordination with another subject of conceptualization with respect to the content of the complement clause, and not as at least partly presenting an object of conceptualization itself. When the subject is referred to with a lexical description (*the trade-union leader*) rather than a pronoun, his point of view is apparently not yet related to the Ground (see Van Hoek 2003: 175); when the CT-clause is formulated in the present or past *perfect*, we have to conceive of a relation between two situations (one situation happening before the other; see Boogaart (1999) 133–4), one of which is thus necessarily distinct from the Ground; when a particular subtype of an argumentative discourse is involved (with *concede*), this additional feature beyond pure 'entertaining' (thinking or communication) is apparently relevant; when other third-person participants (not participating in the Ground) in the onstage conceptualizer's space are mentioned, this creates a further distinction between that space and the Ground. So judgments about such invented examples correlate with the 'distance' between the examples and the standard pattern observed in usage, despite the fact that these sentences all have the same general structure. This fact is another indication that only this particular pattern is actually entrenched in speakers' mental grammars, and that special properties of '*Wh*-extraction' do not say much about the abstract structure of complementation.

This view is corroborated, in a surprising way, by evidence from language acquisition presented by Dąbrowska (2004: ch. 9). Although the phenomenon is not very frequent in children's speech, young children do understand and produce instances of '*Wh*-extraction'. Understandably, their appearance follows that of simpler 'matrix clauses' of the type *I think*, as well as that of simpler *Wh*-questions. But the interesting point is that such utterances occur at around age four, while children have not even mastered the full generality of the network of complementation constructions at age five. Diessel and Tomasello (2001: 134) claim that by that age children have only learned the templates at the bottom of the network. This implies that they cannot have constructed their (understanding of) apparent extraction *utterances* on the basis of general rules. As Dąbrowska observes, these utterances are highly formulaic. The fact that they are also highly formulaic in adult language use, as shown in the present study,[35] suggests that while adults do develop knowledge of general templates for complementation constructions, the '*Wh*-extraction' template remains a kind of 'island' in the ultimate network of constructions (see Verhagen 2002: 414–15), with specific properties that do not percolate upwards.

Frequency and subjectivity
On the other hand, the fact that '*Wh*-extraction' does not involve complementation constructions in general does not imply that the phenomenon is 'just lexical', in the sense of being governed by some *arbitrary* (set of) lexical item(s). It is no coincidence that actual instances of '*Wh*-extraction' look so similar in different languages, as shown by the corpus data from Dutch and English. Nor is it a coincidence that the matrix clauses have the kind of content that they have. Recall that I started this discussion by pointing out that, for questions, a matrix clause like *Do you think*... creates the kind of utterance in which the distinction between the onstage conceptualizer and the Ground is minimal, as it is the addressee's mind that is being probed by a question. This kind of clause is the interrogative variant of *I think* in the case of declaratives, and thus it is intimately connected to the specific, well entrenched 'complementation' patterns that are acquired early, and used frequently in conversation to mark the speaker's epistemic stance (Thompson 2002). Instances of '*Wh*-extraction' belong to a subset of prototypical patterns for explicitly signaling aspects of the intersubjective dimension of the construal configuration (see Fig. 3.6). So even though they are located at a low level in the network of complementation constructions, the region that they occupy is a central one.

This particular phenomenon provides a good example of what Bybee and Hopper (2001) notice about the relationship between function and frequency in general. While frequency has a profound effect on the way language units are stored and processed, this frequency in turn is 'governed by the content of people's interactions, which consist of a preponderance of subjective, evaluative statements' (ibid. 3).

The importance of the conceptual factor 'minimal distinctness between mental spaces of onstage conceptualizer and addressee' can be demonstrated further by taking a somewhat closer look at the instances that have an onstage conceptualizer other than a second-person. Recall example (64) (for convenience, only the translation is repeated below):

(64) How do Mayor and Aldermen think that our citizens will feel about of such an expensive trip abroad?

---

[35] They are also highly formulaic in the adult input speech in Dąbrowska's material.

This is a question, quoted in the newspaper, asked by a member of the city council and addressed to the Mayor and Aldermen. Conceptually, the onstage conceptualizer therefore *is* the addressee of the question. So even though the latter is not linguistically referred to with a second-person form, the mental spaces of the addressee and the onstage conceptualizer are minimally distinct. Something similar holds for the other instances. Questions (65) and (66) are not addressed to the readers, but to their onstage conceptualizers: these sentences are from letters to the editor responding to statements from Mr Oudkerk and the writers of another letter, respectively. Of course, the reader is not really supposed to be able to answer the question, for example, of how something was done, as represented in the mind of Oudkerk. This is what gives these instances the flavor of rhetorical questions, unlike a second person question such as (62) ('How do you think Kok performed in the latest election?').

Particularly revealing is the case of the first-person onstage conceptualizer in (68):

(68) Waarom denk ik dat die twee elke avond rondhangen in
 Why think I that those two each evening hang-around in
 het hotel?
 the hotel
 'Why do I think these two hang around in the hotel every night?'

Notice that this sentence on its own cannot be interpreted as a case of '*Wh*-extraction' (a question about the reason for 'these two' to hang around), but only as a question about the reason for my thinking that they are hanging around in the hotel. However, the context in which it occurs, given in (69), is of a special kind. It is a story from a reporter about a meeting in Tripoli with a Libyan man:

(69) Ik mag hem Eunice noemen [...] Doet iets in hotels, iets bij een bank— en die twee vrouwen daar moest ik maar eens in de gaten houden. Marokkaansen. Waarom denk ik dat die twee elke avond rondhangen in het hotel? Juist. Libische vrouwen doen dat niet.

'I may call him Eunice [...] Does something in hotels, something with a bank—and I'd better keep an eye on those two women over there. Moroccan. Why do I think these two hang around in the hotel every night? Right. Libyan women don't do that.'

This text has the character of free indirect speech (Banfield 1982; Sanders 1994): the writer functions as the deictic center ('I'), but the sentences represent not the writer's words but a character's, in this case the man named Eunice. So here the question is actually asked by Eunice and addressed to the writer, referred to with a first-person pronoun. Again, then, the addressee of the question and the onstage conceptualizer are the same person, with minimal distance between the onstage conceptualizer's mental space and the Ground as a result. So the matrix clause does nothing more than putting the addressee's perspective on stage. It is only in this interpretation that the sentence is a case of '*Wh*-extraction', asking about the reasons for these women to hang around in the hotel.

Finally, recall that the templates in the central region in the network of complementation constructions, with the CT-clauses marking epistemic stance, do not involve subordination (see Sections 3.2.3 and 3.3.3; Thompson 2002; Diessel and Tomasello 2001). There are only mono-clausal structures involved. There is not really any extraction going on, as there is no embedded (clausal) constituent to extract from. Contrary to what the term 'extraction' suggests, '*Wh*-extraction' is neither a phenomenon occurring at a very abstract level of grammatical structure, nor a particularly strange, structure-destroying kind of operation. But the way it works, especially the crucial role of the relation between the onstage conceptualizer's mental space and the Ground, once again demonstrates how central the dimension of cognitive coordination is to the function and structure of complementation constructions.[36]

I started this section with the observation that '*Wh*-extraction' phenomena appear to instantiate the constituent view of complements in a particular way, so that the question must be asked if and how the intersubjectivity approach can deal with them. As we have seen, the answer sheds new light on the phenomenon itself.

3.3.6 *Impersonal intersubjectivity and the irrelevance of syntactic relations*

So far I have only considered complementation sentences with what are traditionally called 'object complements'; that is, sentences in which the complement clause seems to occupy a direct object slot. However, I have suggested that it is not at all clear that syntactic relations like 'subject' and 'object' are of any use in the characterization of such sentences, and that they

---

[36] In this respect the present analysis is also different from, and superior to, previous semantic/pragmatic explanations of constraints on '*Wh*-extraction' employing notions of information structure, which can be traced back to Erteschik-Shir (1973). In terms of Erteschik-Shir (1997): 'islands [configurations from which elements cannot be 'extracted'] are environments which cannot provide the main focus of the sentence' (ibid. 225, see esp. pp. 230–2 on *that*-clauses). The strong correlation between '*Wh*-extraction' and the verb *denken* ('to think') and especially second person subjects that can be observed in actual usage, is an empirical phenomenon not accounted for in 'focus-structure' terms, while it finds a natural explanation in the present approach.

may even be the source of inconsistencies (see Sect. 3.2.3). And so far the notion 'direct object' has not played a role in the characterization of the complementation construction either. The questions I want to address now are: can this characterization be extended to complementation constructions in which the complement is traditionally considered to be the 'subject' of the matrix clause, and does the notion 'grammatical subject' play any role in their characterization? Recall from Section 3.2.1 that the term 'subject complement' is used for the complements in sentences such as (3) and (4), on the basis of the fact that (3) is similar to clauses with a prototypical (i.e.(pro)nominal) subject (*Something was obvious to George*), and that (4) in turn is similar to (3):

(3) That his opponent was closing in, was obvious to George.

(4) It was obvious to George that his opponent was closing in.

Impersonal complementation constructions—extensions from the prototype
In terms of the present framework, the main difference between these cases and the ones considered so far seems to be that (3) and (4) do not have to contain an explicit, onstage conceptualizer. The conceptualizer mentioned in these sentences is an adjunct, and its presence is not obligatory. But the characterization that the addressee is invited to entertain the object of conceptualization in the same way as *some* other subject of conceptualization is doing also fully applies to *It was obvious that his opponent was closing in*. This suggests the hypothesis that this type of complementation construction also operates in the intersubjective dimension of the construal configuration, the difference being that it is 'impersonal'. Hence, I will from now on talk about 'personal' and 'impersonal' complementation constructions, rather than about 'object' and 'subject' complement clauses.

In view of the analysis given so far, the difference is not totally unimportant. Impersonal complementation constructions never attribute a thought *directly* to one of the conceptualizers in the Ground, as there is no onstage conceptualizer, or only in an adjunct. Thus the distance between the onstage conceptualization and the Ground is never minimal, and these sentences do not form part of the prototype region in the network of complementation constructions. Still, they share, by hypothesis, the important function of managing the intersubjective coordination between participants in the Ground.

The first issue to look into, then, is whether the paradigm of predicates used in impersonal complementation constructions comprises the same semantic classes as are found in personal ones. To begin with, notice that an important category of CT-clauses of impersonal constructions consists of passives of the predicates listed in (31): *It was argued...*, *It has been claimed...*, *It can be seen...* These are as much mental space builders as the corresponding active clauses, even if they do not mention the 'owners' of the mental spaces involved explicitly.

Another set consists of CT-clauses with copular verbs and a nominal predicate indicating evaluation or epistemic stance. Examples of the evaluating expressions are *It is important that...*, *It is a bad thing that...*, *The problem is that...*, *It is puzzling that...* Even though such CT-clauses do not explicitly mention a conceptualizer either, as evaluating expressions they denote a cognitive stance and thus evoke the idea of a conceptualizer entertaining it. Some examples of copular epistemic CT-clauses are *It is likely that...*, *It is only a hypothesis that...*, *The accepted opinion is that...*, *It is clear that...* Such epistemic stances can also be marked with a few non-copular predicates; for example (Dutch) *Het blijkt dat...*, (English) *It appears that...*, (Dutch) *Het lijkt/schijnt dat...*, (English) *It seems that...* (see Sanders and Spooren 1996 for an analysis of their specific semantics in Dutch). Though their subjectivity may not be as immediately obvious as in the case of evaluative expressions, it is undeniable that they evoke the idea of a conceptualizer. Only a subject of conceptualization can entertain something as clear, just as only a subject of conceptualization can consider something a problem. Being clear, problematic, etc. is never a property of an object of conceptualization as such, but always an aspect of the way it is being entertained; that is, of the construal relation *between* levels O and S in the construal configuration. It is this relation that is also specified in the case of the impersonal constructions, but without being explicitly anchored to a particular subject of conceptualization. This general character of impersonal complementation constructions is represented in Figure 3.7.

Whereas personal complementation constructions explicitly invite the addressee to entertain the object of conceptualization in the way someone else does (see Figs. 3.2 and 3.3), impersonal ones 'just' invite the addressee to entertain it in a particular way, while non-perspectivized clauses straightforwardly introduce the object of conceptualization in the shared mental space (see Fig. 3.1). The default is that the addressee engages in cognitive coordination with the speaker/writer, the assumption being that since this is the person who presents the object of conceptualization as clear, problematic, etc. to the addressee, she may be taken as holding those views in the absence of evidence to the contrary. Consider (70), for example:

Finite complements

O: *Object of conceptualization:*

S: *Subject of conceptualization (Ground):*

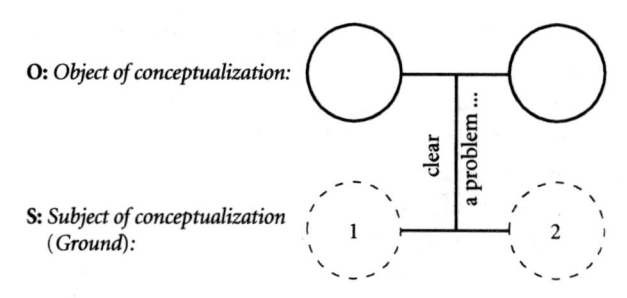

FIGURE 3.7. Construal configuration for 'subject' (impersonal) complementation constructions

(70) Er is echter dringend behoefte aan nieuwe modellen. De twee-relatie is weliswaar een ideaal voor zeer veel homofielen, maar het is duidelijk dat dat dan heel iets anders is dan het traditionele huwelijk.

'However, there is an urgent need for new models. It is true that the duo-relationship is an ideal for many homosexuals, but it is clear that this will be quite different from the traditional marriage.'

In interpreting this fragment a reader will normally ascribe responsibility for the claim that something is clear directly to the writer of the text, conceptualizer 1 in the construal configuration. But, as indicated in Figure 3.7, this is not an obligatory semantic feature of the construction as such, as the clause itself contains no reference to a participant who is the source of the judgment. Rather, it is a default option given the fact that the conceptualizers 1 and 2 are always available for use in interpretation. If the context contains an explicit reference to another subject of conceptualization, then the attribution of responsibility for the claim is easily changed. Suppose that this fragment was a report about someone delivering a speech on types of homosexual relationship, then it could be formulated as in (70'):

(70') Er is volgens de spreker echter dringend behoefte aan nieuwe modellen. De twee-relatie is weliswaar een ideaal voor zeer veel homofielen, maar het is duidelijk dat dat dan heel iets anders is dan het traditionele huwelijk.

'However, according to the speaker there is an urgent need for new models. It is true that the duo-relationship is an ideal for many homosexuals, but it is clear that this will be quite different from the traditional marriage.'

Note that the reference to a third person is not included in the CT-clause (e.g. as an adjunct). The second sentence in this fragment is completely identical to the one in (70). Nevertheless, the opinion expressed in it is now ascribed to the referent of 'the speaker' in the previous sentence.

Still, the difference between the CT-clause of an impersonal complementation construction and that of a personal one is that identification of the latter's subject of conceptualization is constrained linguistically, while this may be left completely open in the former. In both cases the addressee is invited to engage in cognitive coordination with another subject of conceptualization in a particular way, but this subject is only specified, to some extent, in the personal constructions.

Recall the formulation of the complementation construction that I proposed in section 3.3.2, repeated below:

(32) *Complementation Construction 1* (Dutch)
construction form: $[_A Y[X_{Predicate}] dat[_B \ldots]]$
construction meaning: ENTERTAIN CONTENT OF B IN THE MANNER OF Y: AS X

In view of the characterization given above and represented in Figure 3.7 it will be clear how this may be generalized to include 'subject' complementation constructions; namely, as in (71):

(71) *Complementation Construction 2, generalized* (Dutch)
construction form: $[_A [X_{Predicate}] dat[_A \ldots]]$
construction meaning: ENTERTAIN CONTENT OF B AS X

The formulation in (71) and Figure 3.7 also apply straightforwardly to a set of CT-clauses that can perhaps best be seen as an extension of the epistemic-stance indications mentioned above; namely, expressions of the type *Another argument/reason is that...*, *The alternative is that...* Unlike expressions such as *likely, clear, a problem*, these do not indicate a particular *kind* of epistemic evaluation themselves, but they do mark explicitly that *some* epistemic stance is being entertained. Their use means that the addressee is invited to entertain the content of the complement clause as an argument, an alternative, etc., and to connect this content in that way to the present discourse.

Some Dutch expressions of this type do not have direct equivalents in English. Examples are *Daarbij komt dat...* (literally 'There-to comes that...', meaning 'It should be added that...,' or 'Additionally,...'), and *Hier staat tegenover dat...* (lit. 'To this stands opposite that...,' meaning 'On the other hand,...' or 'Conversely,...'). As the translations indicate, sometimes the translation equivalent of a seemingly 'complex' sentence in one language is a simplex sentence with a speaker-oriented adverb tagged on to it in another language. It is consistently the complement clause which is rendered as the simplex, independent clause in the translation. This is another piece of evidence that the complement in complementation constructions is actually doing the same kind of work as grammatically simplex (main) clauses.

Another point demonstrated by these observations is that the actual use of words and constructions in a particular language cannot be fully predicted on the basis of the general conceptual space they operate in. Complementation constructions in Dutch as well as in English can be characterized well in terms of the basic construal configuration, but this does not mean that the exact patterns of use can be predicted, or that they should be the same in the two languages. As indicated before (see n. 12), all such patterns are ultimately usage-based conventions, resulting from historical processes. Both a complementation construction and a speaker-oriented adverb may provide a good solution to the problem of marking the construal relation. There are no non-historical, non-language-specific 'principles' that determine which one should be used in a specific case (just as there are no universal, non-species-specific principles that determine that birds should use feathers and bats skin for flying). Another example of such a difference is the fact that in Dutch, CT-clauses occur without the subject pro-form *it*, with verbal as well as adjectival and nominal CT-predicates. In English, this is only possible with nominal CT-predicates. Besides clauses of the type *It is a problem that...* there are also clauses of the type *The problem is that...*, and the same is true for Dutch. But in Dutch it is also possible to have sentences such as *Duidelijk is dat...* (lit. 'Clear is that...') and *Daaruit blijkt dat...* (lit. 'From-this turns-out that...'), and this is not true for English. The pronoun *it* is always obligatory (*It is clear/turns out that...*, etc.).

Type and token frequencies, and an extended network
Table 3.6 lists the frequencies of the CT-predicates in impersonal complementation sentences in the first 2,000 sentences in a corpus of Dutch newspaper fragments.[37]

It is clear that the type–token ratio is even higher here (49 : 60 = 0.82) than in the case of CT-predicates of 'object' complements (89 : 151 = 0.59; see Table 3.1). In Table 3.1, 47 of 151 tokens occurred only once, but here 44 of 60 tokens

---

[37] Like the set of CT-predicates of 'object' complementation constructions (see n. 16), this set also includes a few causal expressions: *te danken zijn aan* ('be due to') with a frequency of 2, and *zo komen* ('come about', with manner adverb ('thus', 'how') obligatory in this meaning), *vandaar* ('hence', 'that's why'), and *voorkomen worden* ('be prevented') with a frequency of 1—a total of 5 cases. See Sect. 3.3.7 for further discussion.

have a frequency of 1. So the prominence of the *general* pattern relative to that of specific ones is more conspicuous here than in the case of 'object' complementation constructions. This is in line with the theoretical claim that impersonal cases are extensions from the prototype.[38] On this basis, we can add the general complementation schema (71) at the top of the network of complementation constructions from Figure 3.4; that is, as depicted (with only a few instances of use and low level schemas) in Figure 3.8.

Against syntactic relations in complementation
The general schema at the top of this network is also supported by a number of patterns that actually lack a finite verb in the CT-'clause' (two of which, namely (72) and (73), are among the 44 single-token CT-predicates of Table 3.6):

(72) Jammer dat alles   in een emotionele sfeer   is getrokken.
     Pity   that everything in a   emotional atmosphere is pulled
     'Pity that everything was made into an emotional issue.'

(73) Vandaar dat we besloten hulp in te roepen.
     Hence   that we decided help in to call
     'That's why we decided to call in help.'

(74) Niet dat het makkelijk was.
     Not that it easy   was
     'Not that it was easy.'

(75) Dat je zoiets   durft!
     That you such-a-thing dare
     'Amazing that you dare to do something like that!'

TABLE 3.6. CT-predicates used with impersonal complementation sentences in the first 2,000 sentences in the Eindhoven Corpus (Dutch newspaper fragments)

Tokens per predicate	Predicates (types)	Total no. of tokens
7	*blijken* ('appear', 'turn out')	7
3	*duidelijk zijn/lijken* ('be/seem clear, obvious')	3
2	*gezegd worden/dienen* ('(must) be said'), *waar zijn* ('be true'), *te danken zijn aan X* ('be due to X')	6
1	(44 different predicates)	44
Total no. of types:	49	60

[38] Presumably, they are also acquired later, and more representative of written than spoken discourse. This seems entirely plausible, but I have not investigated it.

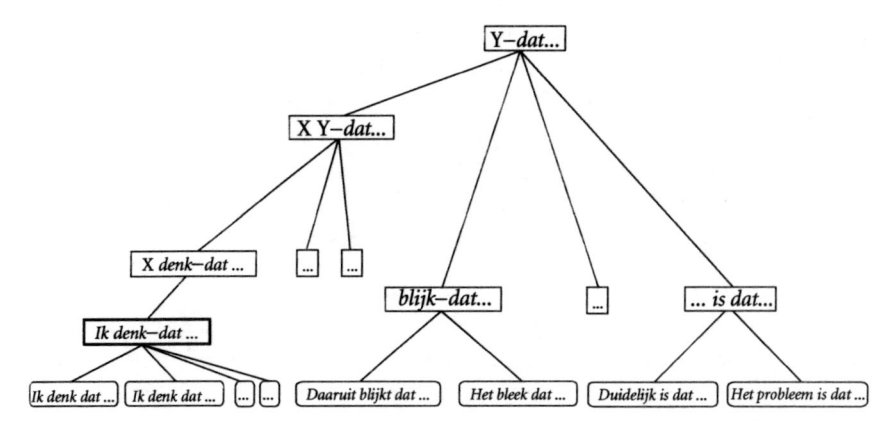

FIGURE 3.8. Partial general network for complementation constructions in Dutch

It is difficult to analyze the complement clauses in these expressions as fulfilling a 'subject' role in a CT-clause. With some effort (72) could be regarded as containing an 'elliptical' CT-clause, with the finite verb deleted, but that is impossible for the other cases.[39] But all of them straightforwardly satisfy the conditions of (71). Clearly, the fact that it is not possible to assign these complement clauses a syntactic role poses no obstacle to their interpretation, indicating that such a role is actually irrelevant.

This observation makes it possible to generalize a point made for 'object' complementation constructions, namely, why it is that complement clauses can occur with a number of CT-predicates that do not take nominal arguments. The hypothesis that the construction in (32) represents an independently accessible unit of linguistic knowledge explains, as noted at the end of Section 3.3.2, why a sentence such as *He was afraid that he was not going to make it* is acceptable despite the fact that a copular predicate such as *be afraid* does not take a direct object. Similarly, the hypothesis that the general construction (71) is an independent unit of linguistic knowledge solves the remaining issues from Section 3.2.2. The point was that there is a long-standing controversy concerning the proper analysis of sentences such as (13) (English *The danger is that things will escalate*). One possibility was to call the complement clause the subject (in view of the parallelism with sentences of the type *What is dangerous is that things will escalate*, cf. Dutch (18)), but there seem to be equally good reasons to call the nominal phrase the subject (in view of the parallelism

---

[39] For example, the only acceptable form for a full CT-clause corresponding to (74) is *Het is niet zo dat...* (lit. 'It is not thus that...', i.e. 'It is not the case that...'), with an obligatory element *zo* that would also have to be deleted, just for this specific case.

with (20), *The danger exists that things will escalate*). The presupposition of all these dilemmas and problems is that it is necessary for all sentences, including complex ones, to be analyzable exhaustively in terms of such syntactic relations as 'subject' and 'object'. For impersonal complementation constructions too we have now established that there are good reasons to assume instead that a schema such as (71) is used *directly* to categorize complex sentences that satisfy its formulation. A clause such as 'The danger is...', no matter which syntactic role (if any) is assigned to it, expresses an evaluation, and thus can be seen as instantiating schema (71), and be interpreted in terms of it.[40]

Combining this argument with that of Section 3.3.2, we are in a position to conclude not only that the assumption of general syntactic relations as essential for grammatical analysis poses a problem for the analysis of complementation constructions, but that such relations are irrelevant for producing and understanding such constructions. (See Croft 2001, esp. chs. 4 and 6, for general arguments against construction-independent syntactic roles and relations.)

To conclude, the irrelevance of syntactic 'parsing' for these constructions is confirmed by the existence (and rise during the twentieth century) of a particular subpattern, reported in Van der Horst and Van der Horst (1999: 213–22). Recall that in Dutch the pronoun *it* is not obligatory when the lexical content of a CT-predicate consists of an adjective ((76)) or noun phrase ((77)) in first position:

(76) Belangrijk is dat de provincie een commissie in het leven riep.
     Important is that the province a committee in the life called
     'What is important is that the province set up a committee.'

(77) Een feit is wel dat weinig vrouwen een maatschappelijke loopbaan
     A fact is PRT that few women a social career
     zoeken.
     seek
     'It is certainly a fact that few women seek a social career.'

---

[40] In the framework of generative grammar, Koster (1978) has suggested abandoning the idea that 'subject' clauses occupy the same structural position as a nominal argument. Instead, he proposes analyzing them as a kind of adjunct to their matrix clause, 'binding' the position of an argument in the structure (whether filled with a pronoun, or phonologically empty). While this is preferable to earlier (and some recent) accounts according to which all complement clauses occupy 'argument positions', and solves certain problems concerning the distribution of 'subject' clauses with respect to constituents of their 'matrix' clauses, it is also clear that it maintains the problematic one-to-one-relationship between an alleged subject role and the complement clause. Furthermore, it does not generalize to 'object' complements, and it does not take semantic constraints on complementation constructions into account.

Van der Horst and Van der Horst (ibid.) show that in present-day Dutch, nouns can also be used in this subpattern without a determiner. Two examples are (78) and (79):

(78) Feit is dat de kijkcijfers tegenvielen.
    Fact is that the ratings   fell-short
    'Fact is that the ratings were disappointing.'

(79) Gunstig neveneffect is dat corrupte ambtenaren hun handel wordt
    Favorable side effect is that corrupt officials their business is
    ontnomen.
    taken-away
    'A favorable side effect is that corrupt officials are deprived of their business.'

Leaving out a determiner is impossible in a different order, when the pronoun *it* is in the initial position, as illustrated by the difference between (78′) and (78″).

(78) *Het is feit dat de kijkcijfers tegenvielen.
    It is fact that the ratings fell-short

(78″) Het is een feit dat de kijkcijfers tegenvielen.
    It is a   fact that the ratings   fell-short
    'It is a fact that the ratings were disappointing.'

This suggests that the pattern 'nominal predicate-*is-dat*...' is relatively well entrenched, is directly associated with a particular meaning, and can be activated independent of other patterns, especially patterns that would require processing of grammatical relations such as subject. Even the category 'noun phrase' does not have to play a role here, in view of the occurrence of determiner-less nominals in the front position in this construction.[41] This phenomenon makes the conclusion inevitable that the sentence pattern as a whole is not necessarily 'composed' of syntactic phrases that can be built up on the basis of category information about the phrase's lexical head alone and then enter into relations with each other to form the entire sentence. If processing the noun as (the head of) the clause's subject or predicate were a necessary component of processing this type of sentence, then this pattern could not have emerged; the fact that it is now quite general shows that it

---

[41] The phenomenon is actually not limited in Dutch to complementation constructions. It also occurs with other kinds of complements than finite clauses. The consequences of this fact for the conception of relations between constructions and their parts in grammar are quite far reaching, but I will not pursue that issue here.

must have been possible, at earlier stages of the language, to activate the template without invoking syntactic relations. As I have shown above, there are independent reasons for making this assumption anyway.[42]

3.3.7 *Perspectival and causal connections*

I will now turn to a final category of extensions from the prototype in the network of complementation constructions. In Section 3.3.2 I noticed that there seems to be one type of CT-predicate, namely causal ones, that apparently cannot be characterized as a mental space builder. What I want to suggest here is that these should be considered a kind of 'extreme case' of extension from the central cases.

In the corpus material summarized in Tables 3.1 and 3.6 the CT-predicates listed in Table 3.7 were marked as causal (see nn. 16 and 37). These predicates do not belong to the most frequent ones, and it is only 7 per cent of all complementation constructions that have a causal CT-predicate. More importantly, however, a relatively large number of even these few cases still involve some aspect of subjectivity. When something is 'prevented' (3 cases), for example, this implies that the possibility of something bad happening

TABLE 3.7. Causal CT-predicates in the first 2,000 sentences in the Eindhoven Corpus (Dutch newspaper fragments)

Predicates with 'object' complements	Predicates, with 'subject' complements	Total items
zorgen ('see to it', 'manage')		3
tot gevolg hebben ('result in')		3
voorkómen ('prevent')		2
	te danken zijn aan X ('be due to X')	2
ertoe bijdragen ('contribute to', 'stimulate')		1
gedaan krijgen ('get done')		1
maken ('make', 'cause')		1
	voorkomen worden ('be prevented')	1
	zo komen ('come about')	1
	vandaar ('hence', 'that's why')	1
Total		16

---

[42] While it may be less widespread, the same phenomenon does in fact occur in English, so that the same argument may be made for that language. Two examples found on the Internet are: *Fact is that more and more photo's* [sic] *of pro-taliban demonstrations show up around the world* and *Biggest problem is that there is no obvious organization that represents the domain name side of things.*

has been projected, which presupposes a subject of conceptualization entertaining this idea. Conversely, to 'see to it that something happens' and to 'get something done' (4 cases) implies goal-directedness and planning, so again a subject of conceptualization is involved. The Dutch phrase *te danken zijn aan* (literally 'be thanks to', 2 cases), expresses a positive evaluation of a causal relationship. The negative counterpart is *te wijten zijn aan* (literally 'is to be blamed to'). The expressions *vandaar* [*dat*] ... ('hence', 1 case) and *zo komt* [*het dat*] ... ('that is how it comes about that...', 1 case) both mark conclusions and explanations, which presupposes a subject of conceptualization capable of reasoning and entertaining problems.

It should also be noted that many other CT-predicates in one way or another presuppose some form of causal reasoning as part of their meaning. Interestingly, this is not true for the predicates with the highest frequencies in Tables 3.1 and 3.6, with the meanings 'say', 'think', 'appear', 'be clear'. These simply assign the content of a complement clause to a subject of conceptualization or mark it as cognitively accessible, without further specification. But as one moves on to less frequent and more specific predicates, a semantic dimension in which their meaning is specified is often that of causality. Examples are *vaststellen* ('decide', 'conclude'), *concluderen* ('conclude'), *aannemen* ('assume', 'suppose'), *menen* ('suppose'), *ontdekken* ('discover'), *uitwijzen* ('reveal'), *voorzien* ('anticipate'), *aantonen*, ('prove'), *bevestigen* ('confirm'), *toegeven* ('admit'). If someone concludes, proves, or anticipates something, the conceptual content of the complement clause is not only associated with some subject of conceptualization, but also presented as participating in a chain of causes and consequences; that is, as being licensed by knowledge of the causal structure of the world. If one assumes or supposes something, the notion of background knowledge about a chain of causes and consequences is also activated. The complement clause may express a possible (but as yet hypothetical) consequence of certain facts, and also (even at the same time) the starting point for reasoning about further consequences. In other words, the use of these CT-predicates evokes the idea that some topos (see Ch. 1, Sect. 1.2.3 and Ch. 2, Sect. 2.3.2) is relevant at this point in the discourse for connecting a new discourse segment to the rest. They not only invite the addressee to engage in cognitive coordination, but they do so on the basis of shared, common knowledge about the causal structure of the world.

It seems then that other causal CT-predicates can be regarded as a further extension from the class in which some aspect of causation is a semantic specification of a subjective construal. In the in-between cases just mentioned ('anticipate that...', etc.), causality is presupposed, not something that the words designate.[43] In predicates such as 'prevent that...' or 'see to it that...' subjective projection of a possible event and actual causation of an event are more or less on a par. (In the first case what is considered and what is done are contrary to each other, in the other case they coincide.) For cases such as, finally, 'That's how it happened that...' and 'The consequence is that...' the marking of causation can be said to constitute all that the expressions designate. Thus we can assume a semantic extension along the line indicated in Table 3.8, starting with the predicates that are closest to the central category of complementation constructions and ending with the most peripheral ones.

This is not the only dimension of extension from the 'core' of saying and thinking (consider, for example, verbs of communication). Here the transition between the first and second columns, especially with the transitive predicates, is closely tied to the difference between narrative discourse on the one hand, and written, informative or argumentative discourse on the other. General background knowledge about the causal structure of the domain under discussion is essential to the coherence of informative and argumentative discourse—much more so than for narrative discourse. Seen this way, the use of even the most peripheral, apparently purely causal CT-predicates still shares certain features with perspectival ones that makes them different from verbs of causation in simplex clauses. Consider (80), which indicates that the preceding sentence in the discourse expresses the cause of the situation described in the complement clause of this one:

(80) Zo   komt het dan, dat goed   opgezette politieke gedragslijnen
     Thus comes it then that well   arranged political courses-of-action
     ontaarden in irrationele onrustverwekkende reacties, die de verwarring
     degenerate in irrational trouble-producing reactions that the confusion
     alleen maar vergroten.
     only   PRT increase

TABLE 3.8. From perspectival to causal CT-predicates

Purely subjective >	Causal reasoning ('topos') >	Reasoning + causation >	Causal relation between two situations
say, think (appear, be clear)	decide, conclude, assume, suppose, discover, anticipate, prove, admit,...	prevent, see to it, hence...	cause that..., consequence is that...

---

[43] But notice that in certain institutional contexts (e.g. judicial) to conclude or decide that something is the case can have very real consequences.

'So this is how it happens that well-conceived lines of political conduct degenerate into irrational responses which create turmoil and only increase the confusion.'

In principle, it is possible to give a paraphrase of this sentence that expresses the same causal relationship in a single clause, using a grammatical causative construction (See Stukker et al. 1999, Stukker 2005, ch. 8); an example is (81):

(81) Dit doet goed opgezette politieke gedragslijnen ontaarden in
This makes well arranged political courses-of-action degenerate in
irrationele onrustverwekkende reacties, die de verwarring alleen
irrational trouble-producing reactions that the confusion only
maar vergroten.
PRT increase
'This makes well-conceived lines of political conduct degenerate into irrational responses which create turmoil and only increase the confusion.'

However, a clear difference appears when we insert such a paraphrase into the original text; (82a) contains (the English translation of) the original version of the text;[44] in (82b) the complementation construction has been replaced by (81):

(82) (a) The Superpowers are just as much dragged along in a chaotic state of confusion that is practically beyond their control, as the states in these regions themselves. This is how it happens that well-conceived lines of political conduct degenerate into irrational responses which create turmoil and only increase the confusion.

 (b) The Superpowers are just as much dragged along in a chaotic state of confusion that is practically beyond their control, as the states in these regions themselves. This makes well-conceived lines of political conduct degenerate into irrational responses which create turmoil and only increase the confusion.

With the formulation in (82a) it is clear that the text is an argumentative one. There are two situations: the Superpowers not being in control of a chaotic

---

[44] For completeness, the Dutch original is: 'De grote mogendheden worden kennelijk al evenzeer als de staten van deze gebieden zelf meegesleept in een chaotische verwarring waarover zij maar weinig controle hebben. En zo komt het dan, dat goed opgezette politieke gedragslijnen ontaarden in irrationele onrustverwekkende reacties, die de verwarring alleen nog maar vergroten.' Strictly speaking, the translation of the first sentence should have contained the adverb 'apparently' (translating *kennelijk*), but as that is itself typical for argumentative discourse, I left it out in order to bring the effect of the formulation of the second sentence into greater relief.

situation, and the degeneration of political conduct. The two are presented as causally linked, and this link has the character of an explanation. The first situation does not just make the second happen; the text also claims that it is *understandable* for it to happen. The formulation is that of an answer to a question, namely what the source of the degeneration is, and suggests that there is some general principle behind the answer, which is itself provided in the complement clause. Notice that the causal clause does not indicate a causal *event* happening, but just the fact of a causal relationship ('This is how it happens') holding between being dragged down into chaos and the degeneration of political conduct.

In the case of (82*b*), on the other hand, the causality is part of the event being presented. The second sentence is not formulated as an answer to a question, but straightforwardly presents the situation mentioned in the first as affecting political conduct, and the reader may take it as simply the next link in a chain of events. The text has more of a narrative character. Thus even though a causal CT-clause does not have to specify an aspect of the Ground, it normally does not directly specify an aspect of the object of conceptualization either. It does not describe a causal event happening, but instructs the addressee to construe a causal relation between the situation described by the complement clause and the preceding discourse.[45] What a causal CT-clause shares with CT-clauses in general is how to construe the content of the complement clause.

The similarity between perspectival CT-clauses and causal ones in the domain of construing a coherence relation between the complement clause and the rest of the discourse reflects a similarity between the *conceptual* roles of perspective and causality in discourse coherence. This link was noticed in Boogaart (1991; see also Boogaart 1999: 15–17, 81–5) in connection with the problem of how to relate discourse level temporal relations between situations to the lexical and grammatical (esp. aspectual) properties of the clauses presenting these situations.[46] Consider (83) and (84):

(83) Hij deed de deur open. De sneeuw waaide naar binnen.
     He did the door open The snow   blew   to   inside
     'He opened the door. The snow was blown in.'

---

[45] For more discussion of similarities and differences between expressing causality in a mono-clausal causative construction and in a multi-clausal piece of discourse see Stukker (2005, ch. 8).

[46] More specifically, of how to explain restrictions on the interpretation of temporal ordering that have to do with differences between states and events. As this issue is not directly relevant to my point here, I will pay no further attention to it.

(84) Hij deed de deur open. Het sneeuwde.
    He did the door open It snowed
    'He opened the door. It was snowing.'

In (83) the conceptual relation tying the two discourse segments together is a causal one.[47] His opening the door made it possible for the snow to be blown in. In (84) such a causal relation is, given our knowledge of the world, not conceivable, but there is still a connection between the discourse segments. His opening the door made it possible to *see* that it was snowing. This relation is thus one of perspectivization. In order to construct a coherent discourse representation the addressee takes the character's perspective, and interprets the second clause as representing this character's experience, or perhaps even his thoughts. When neither a causal nor a perspectival relationship seems available, the discourse is not coherent, as can be illustrated with (85):

(85) ??Hij deed de deur open. Hij had zwart haar.
      He did the door open He had black hair
      'He opened the door. His hair was black.'

It is not clear how opening the door could lead to the person involved having black hair (a causal connection), nor how this could enable his perception of his black hair (a perspectival connection), and thus this discourse is not coherent. However, as Boogaart points out,

it is a sufficient condition for a coherent interpretation if the second sentence can be interpreted as the thought or observation of *another* character in the story. Suppose, for instance, that Mary had been waiting for her blind date to enter the room while secretly hoping that his hair was not black because of her bad experiences with black-haired men in the past. (ibid. 84–5).

In retrospect, it is also clear for (84) that it does not have to be the character's perspective in which the second sentence is interpreted.

As *discourse* relations, causality and perspectivization thus have an important function in common. In the former case, the situation of the first clause is understood as enabling the occurrence of the one mentioned in the second. In the latter case, the situation of the first clause is understood as enabling the *conceptualization* of the one mentioned in the second. From the perspective of an addressee (the reader of the text), the latter in fact encompasses the first. In other words, understanding two situations as causally linked is a way of *conceptualizing* them as connected, and thus of satisfying the goal of constructing a coherent discourse representation.

[47] With causality understood in the sense of force dynamics (Talmy 1988), so including relations of enablement and blocking.

Recall that for many (low-frequency) mental-space-building CT-predicates causality is a part of their meaning. I suggest that the conceptual link between causality and perspectivization in the construction of coherent discourse representations provides additional support for the extension of CT-clauses—prototypically operating on intersubjective coordination—to the expression of 'purely' causal relationships. Notice that complementation constructions can be used to make the relationship between the sentences explicit, both for (83) and (84), for example as in (83') and (84').

(83') Hij deed de deur open. Het gevolg was dat de sneeuw naar binnen
He did the door open The result was that the snow to inside
waaide.
blew
'He opened the door. The result was that snow was blown in.'

(84') Hij deed de deur open. We stelden vast dat het sneeuwde.
He did the door open We concluded that it snowed
'He opened the door. We concluded that it was snowing.'

Still, purely causal cases remain a special, peripheral subcategory in the whole network of complementation constructions. Normally, the use of a complementation construction is an attempt to manage the relationships between the conceptualizers, and between the Ground and the object of conceptualization. It operates on a complement's argumentative orientation or force (see Sect. 3.3.3). Causal complementation constructions, on the other hand, exhibit such effects only weakly (with CT-predicates such as 'prevent' and 'be due to'), or do not do so at all. While they do instruct the addressee to entertain the content of the complement clause as a causal factor or a consequence, their relevance for the dimension of intersubjective cognitive coordination is quite limited, and sometimes reduced to explicit marking of a simple coherence relation. This is also reflected in the fact that causal CT-predicates not evoking any notion of mental projection (so, others than 'prevent', 'see to it', and 'get done') are never used with animate subjects, but only with inanimate nouns referring to other facts, especially neuter pronouns.

One more indication for their relatively peripheral status is the fact that they are apparently not used recursively. The Dutch Eindhoven Corpus does not contain instances of recursive use for any combination of the causal CT-predicates mentioned in Table 3.7, and a constructed example such as (86) is also highly forced:

(86) ?Het kapitalisme leidt ertoe dat de toegenomen welvaart tot
The capitalism leads there-to that the increased prosperity to

>   gevolg heeft dat het milieu   vervuild raakt.
>   result has that the environment polluted gets
>   'Capitalism has the effect that the growing prosperity leads to the environment getting polluted.'

Note that the conceptualization of a recurrence of cause–effect relations is not in itself problematic; capitalism producing prosperity producing pollution (etc.). But that is not what (86) seems to (attempt to) express. Rather, the second causal *relation* (prosperity producing pollution) itself seems to be the effect of capitalism. Recall that I attributed the fact that complementation may be used recursively to the fact that recursion is a property of the conceptual structure involved. (The cognitive capacities attributed to another person comprise the capacity to attribute cognitive capacities to others; see the discussion of recursion in sect. 3.3.1.) An example was (30), repeated here for convenience:[48]

> (30) Waarom denkt die meneer   dat ik niet weet dat het een pop is?
>   Why   thinks that gentleman that I not know that it a doll is
>   'Why does this gentleman think that I don't know this is a doll?'

In this recursive embedding of mental spaces it is the *relation* of my not knowing that something is a doll that constitutes what the gentleman is thinking. Notice that the embedding of perspectives is not necessarily a transitive relationship. If A thinks that B thinks that X, it does not follow that A thinks that X; such an inference is defeasible. But embedding of causality seems to be conceptualized as strictly transitive. If A causes that B causes that X, then it is legitimate to conclude that A causes that X; there is no way to annul the inference that A is a cause of X. The *specific* features of recursive causation appear to be different from those of mental-space-embedding, and the present observations thus again show that marking intersubjective coordination is a central function for complementation constructions, while marking causality is not.[49] Recursive causation occurs in other kinds of expressions. For instance, the Eindhoven Corpus contains five cases where a clause with the conjunction *omdat* ('because') is embedded in another one; one example is (87):

---

[48] Notice that this has the same structural complexity as (86), but is much easier to process.

[49] One might want to add here that '*Wh*-extraction' is not possible in causal complementation constructions (*What did she prevent/take care that her child ate?*), but given the analysis in Section 3.3.5, this can hardly be considered telling, as it is just a part of the large area of the network outside that covered by the '*Wh*-extraction' pattern (cf. Fig. 3.6).

(87) Bovendien werd   ik doodeenzaam, omdat ik geen kennissen   en
    Moreover became I dead-lonely   because I no   acquaintances and
    vrienden kreeg en ginds iedereen kwijtraakte, omdat ik weg was
    friends   got   and yonder everyone lost   because I away was
    of thuis zat.
    or home   sat
    'What's more, I became very lonely, because I didn't make any acquaintances and friends and lost everyone over there, because I was away or stayed at home.'

In conclusion, the expression of causality can, it seems, be connected to the network of complementation constructions. One basis for this extension is the fact that background knowledge of the causal structure of the world is often part of the meaning of CT-predicates of cognition and communication, especially in non-narrative discourse. An additional source is the functional overlap between the conceptualization of perspective and that of causality in the construction of discourse coherence. It is also clear that the expression of causality is not a function of central members in the network of complementation constructions, both in terms of its frequency and in view of some special grammatical limitations which do not hold for cases closer to the prototypical ones. Nevertheless, the two mechanisms discussed in this section suffice to show that there is a natural path of extension from the marking of intersubjective coordination to that of causality.[50]

3.3.8 *Clauses as discourse segments revisited*

I started my analysis of complementation in the framework of the intersubjectivity approach with a discourse perspective. It is appropriate to end this chapter by returning to that perspective. The point of Sections 3.2.3 and 3.3.1 was that the role of complement (so-called subordinate) clauses in the structure of discourse is very different from that of (so-called subordinate) adjunct clauses, and especially that the role of matrix clauses of complementation constructions is different from that of simplex (main) clauses. Distributing the CT-clauses and the complement clauses of text (28) over two columns resulted in the two-dimensional segmentation of the text in (28′), which demonstrates that it is a systematic feature of the CT-clauses that they do *not* provide the main line of the discourse.

---

[50] As in the case of special manipulations of the coordination relationship (see n. 39), we should also expect this kind of case to be acquired relatively late, and to be closely connected to the development of literacy.

150 *Finite complements*

(28′) CT-clauses (level S)	Complement clauses (level O)
I have reported before that	there has already been success in breeding clones of mammalian embryos
From the above it may now be concluded that	it will become possible in the near future to make new embryos with the DNA of full-grown animals as well
The director of GenTech even expects that	this will happen as soon as next year
Others believe that	it may take somewhat longer
but nobody doubts that	the cloning of a full-grown sheep or horse will be a reality within ten years
The question is whether	society is mentally and morally ready for this
or whether	we will once again be hopelessly overtaken by the technical developments

In the rest of this chapter I argued that the content of a CT-clause does not designate an object of conceptualization, but rather instructs the addressee to construe it in a particular way and thus to engage in cognitive coordination with another subject of conceptualization, ultimately the speaker/writer. What a CT-clause designates is some aspect of the Ground and the construal relation in the basic construal configuration, rather than something in the object-dimension. These distinctions were motivated in the first place by the consideration that any actual linguistic-usage event comprises an addressee engaging in cognitive coordination with a speaker/writer. Applying this idea to the interpretation of discourse, that is of *connected* utterances, we can conclude that this proceeds at the two levels of the construal configuration in parallel.[51] We can now identify the right-hand column of (28′) as representing the way the discourse develops in the object-dimension, and the left hand column as representing its development in the intersubjective dimension. The basic function of complementation constructions is that of connecting these two intrinsic dimensions of language use.

This explains why CT- and complement clauses are tightly integrated—more so than combinations of matrix clauses with adjunct clauses (see the issues raised in Sect. 3.2.3). A CT-clause specifies how to engage in cognitive

---

[51] We have already seen another demonstration of this phenomenon in Chapter 2 (Sect. 2.3.2), where it was observed that even the interpretation of coreference could be dependent on argumentative orientation.

coordination with another subject of conceptualization. But without some specification of an object of conceptualization with respect to which this should be done, it does not constitute a complete, relevant contribution to a discourse. It is the content of a complement clause that provides the material without which a CT-clause cannot perform its role in the discourse.[52] In contrast, an adjunct clause is more loosely connected to its matrix clause; each of these constitutes a separate discourse segment, instead of specifying another dimension of a single segment. In this way we have removed the risk of not being able to account for the fact that the degree of integration into a matrix clause is higher for a complement clause than for an adjunct clause.

Complementation and topic continuity
The reality of CT-clauses and complement clauses operating in different dimensions of discourse structure can be demonstrated in an interesting way by means of some phenomena of thematic continuity in discourse; that is, the way the topic or 'theme' of a particular discourse segment is linearly connected to previous segments. In Onrust et al. (1993, ch. 2) two ways are distinguished in which the initial and final positions of sentences (in Dutch) contribute to the thematic cohesion of texts. Given two adjacent sentences S1 and S2, then:

(1) when the initial constituents of S1 and S2 refer to the same piece of information, we have a so-called 'constant pattern' (two statements are being made about the same topic);

(2) when the initial constituent of S2 refers to the same piece of information as a constituent that is (more or less) final in S1, we have a so-called 'chaining pattern'.

This is indicated schematically in Figure 3.9.

These patterns are not obligatory, but when used they do contribute positively to the cohesion of texts (Onrust et al. 1993: 39–45). As they have

Constant pattern:
[$_{S1}$ A...B] [$_{S2}$ A...C]

Chaining pattern:
[$_{S1}$ A...B] [$_{S2}$ B...C]

FIGURE 3.9. Two patterns of thematic cohesion

[52] The combination of a CT-clause with *one* complement actually suffices to produce a complete discourse segment. Further complements may be added separately which do not have to be integrated into the CT-clause (see Schilperoord and Verhagen 1998; Verhagen 2001b). Schilperoord (1996, ch. 6; 1997) provides evidence that this analysis also predicts the boundaries of planning units in actual language production.

been defined, these notions only apply to the initial and final positions of (complete) sentences. This sometimes restricts their usefulness, giving rise to conflicts with language users' intuitions about discourse cohesion. Subjects quite generally view a case like the following (a fragment from (28)) as an instance of the chaining pattern:

(88) Uit het bovenstaande valt nu af te leiden dat het binnenkort mogelijk wordt *om ook met het DNA van volwassen dieren nieuwe embryo's te maken.* De directeur van GenTech verwacht zelfs dat *dit* reeds volgend jaar zal gebeuren.
'From the above it may now be concluded that it will become possible in the near future *to make new embryos with the DNA of full-grown animals as well.* The director of GenTech even expects that *this* will happen as soon as, next year.'

According to the definitions in Onrust et al. (ibid.), however, this cannot be an instance of any pattern, because the demonstrative anaphor *dit* is not in the initial position of a sentence.

Notice that what is in between the final position of the first sentence in (88) (the italicized part 'to make new embryos...') and the demonstrative in the second sentence is the CT-clause 'The director of GenTech expects that'. If we assume, as I have proposed, that a CT-clause relates to the intersubjective dimension of discourse interpretation and only the complement clause designates a relevant object of conceptualization, then it is immediately apparent from (28′) above that *as far as the object-dimension is concerned*, the demonstrative *is* adjacent to its antecedent. In this dimension we do have a chaining pattern, followed by a constant pattern (with *it* in initial position in the next segment in the right-hand column).

Once the distinction between the intersubjective and object dimensions has been adopted for discourse analysis, we can restrict the conditions for patterns of thematic continuity, which are essentially anaphoric relations, to the object dimension. Given the distinction between the two dimensions, material that is *linearly* intervening but that relates to the intersubjective dimension is effectively 'invisible' to the formation of patterns of thematic cohesion.

In order to see if this would account for the actual use of discourse anaphors in spontaneously produced texts, a search was undertaken in the entire Eindhoven Corpus (see n. 15), collecting all instances of the complementizers *dat* and *of* that were immediately followed by a demonstrative with an antecedent elsewhere in the discourse (not in the same sentence). In this corpus there were 62 instances satisfying this criterion—thus all of them 'violating' the thematic continuity patterns as formulated by Onrust et al.

(ibid.). However, under the present proposal 39 of them turn into straightforward examples of the chaining pattern. There are 3 more cases that also conform to the pattern in the sense that the antecedent is in a final position and the anaphor in an initial one in the object dimension, but there is another independent clause intervening. Moreover, 9 cases constitute examples of the constant pattern in this analysis, with 1 more possible case with a clause intervening. So there are at least 48, and arguably 52, out of 62 'exceptional' cases that turn out to be regular ones as an immediate consequence of distinguishing the intersubjective and object dimensions of discourse structure.

An example of the most frequent pattern, that of chaining, is given in (89). At the end of one sentence the idea is expressed of the government taking over the entire production machinery. What follows next is a CT-clause mentioning economists who used to believe something on theoretical grounds. (In order to indicate that this piece of the discourse belongs to the intersubjective dimension it is underlined.) Subsequently there is an anaphor as the first element of a new segment in the object dimension. This refers to the idea at the end of the previous segment in the object dimension. It is noteworthy that such pieces of discourse are completely natural and unproblematic, which suggests that restricting the cohesion patterns to the object dimension is a desirable move:

(89) [...] Wanneer wij, in de rug gesteund door de moderne economie, het laissez faire afwijzen, dan staan wij voor de keus tussen twee alternatieven. In de eerste plaats kan *de overheid het gehele produktieapparaat overnemen.* Sommige economen meenden vroeger op theoretische gronden, dat *dit* niet tot gevolg kon hebben dat de welvaart op gunstige wijze zou worden verdeeld, maar dit standpunt is thans door de meeste economen verlaten.

'[...] When we, with the support of modern economics, decline the principle of 'laissez-faire', we face a choice between two alternatives. On the one hand, the *government could take over the entire production machinery.* Some economists used to believe on theoretical grounds that *this* could not lead to an advantageous distribution of wealth but this opinion has now been abandoned by most economists.'

Fragment (90) contains an example of a constant pattern that can be analyzed in a similar way:

(90) De EEG-raad van ministers van landbouw heeft maandag in Luxemburg in beginsel overeenstemming bereikt over de methodiek van een regel-

ing voor vlas: er zal een forfaitaire toeslag per hectare worden gegeven [...]. *Over het bedrag van die toeslag* zal de Europese Commissie nog een voorstel doen. <u>Minister Lardinois verwachtte wel dat</u> *deze* iets hoger zal worden dan de huidige Nederlandse toeslag.

'On Monday, the European council of ministers of agriculture reached agreement in Luxembourg about the method of regulation for flax: a standard surcharge per acre will be given [...]. *As to the amount of the surcharge*, the European Committee will produce a proposal. <u>Minister Lardinois did expect that</u> *this* will turn out somewhat higher than the present surcharge in the Netherlands'

Thus there is evidence not only from readers' intuitions, but also from the distribution of discourse anaphors in spontaneously produced texts, that language users treat these devices for cohesion across sentence boundaries in a way that takes the distinction between the intersubjective and object dimensions into account and that respects the boundaries of CT-clauses and complements. This finding thus provides another piece of independent support for the present analysis, which links the parts of complementation constructions to different parts of the construal configuration, and thus to different dimensions of discourse structure.

3.4 Conclusion

Complementation constructions belong to the 'core' of syntax, the study of the ways linguistic symbols are combined into phrases and sentences. One of the reasons why complementation is generally considered one of the central problems in the study of syntax is that the phenomenon is both general and at the same time known to pose a number of challenges. At the end of this chapter it is possible to claim that an important aspect of the analytical problems has its source in the tendency to use simplex clauses as the structural model for the analysis of complementation constructions. Moreover, this is in turn based on the neglect of the dual structure of normal language use, which involves not only the construction of an object of conceptualization, but always also an addressee coordinating cognitively with another subject of conceptualization. The syntax of simplex clauses typically concerns the structure of an object of conceptualization: an event or state, the participants involved in it in their distinctive roles, the predication of properties, etc. Using simplex clauses as a model for complementation constructions thus implies imposing the structure of an object of conceptualization on these constructions. This has the effect of obscuring the fact that their conventional function is to link the intersubjective and objective dimensions of linguistic communication.

The traditional view is maintained, or even reinforced, when the empirical material used in the study of the syntax of complementation essentially consists of sentences considered in isolation, and sentences that are typical for 'advanced' forms of written discourse, such as *In a televised speech, the Prime Minister yesterday promised that*... Such sentences *allow* for an interpretation as designating an object of conceptualization. But as soon as we stop looking at complementation sentences in isolation it becomes clear that they normally do not do the same kind of work in discourse as simplex sentences and that this 'objective' use is the exception rather than the rule.

Instead, I have proposed in this chapter analyzing the function of matrix clauses in complementation constructions as related to the intersubjective dimension of the construal configuration. Cases that do not immediately appear to designate elements of the Ground in this sense (and thus may look like just descriptions of an event of thinking, etc.) are still better understood as extensions from patterns that do than as representations of objects of conceptualization. They relate to a specific, separate dimension of the structure of discourse, in which different perspectives on situations are organized, while the situations involved are themselves systematically encoded in the complement clauses.

The idea of 'extension' is crucial here. It allows us to see the network of complementation constructions as solidly based on patterns of language use with a function that is completely orthogonal to that of presenting an object of conceptualization, but which nevertheless can develop, in certain non-central areas, groups of subcases which allow a descriptive kind of use in special circumstances. It also allows us to explain how certain properties of patterns in central parts of the network, where the function of organizing intersubjectivity is realized in the most basic way, are *not* extended to the most general level of the network (as in the case of '*Wh*-extraction'). The fact that the network of complementation constructions has this kind of structure, including extensions and non-central areas, does not take anything away from its autonomous position in the whole of the grammar as a particularly prominent set of linguistic instruments that we use to establish, maintain, modify—in sum, to manage—mutual understanding at the level of basic units of discourse.

4

Discourse connections—managing inferences across perspectives

4.1 Introduction

The main focus of Chapters 2 and 3 was on linguistic expressions operating in a single discourse segment. In Chapter 2 I argued that negation and related expressions should be analyzed as instruments for managing the relationship of cognitive coordination between subjects of conceptualization, rather than as instruments for describing an object of conceptualization. In the course of that chapter some instances of usage consisting of more than one segment were also discussed, especially in the argumentation for the analysis. In Chapter 3 I analyzed complementation as a special grammatical construction for managing the intersubjective coordination relation by putting subjects of conceptualization on stage. In an abstract, purely structural sense, complementation sentences contain another clause as a constituent; but in fact we were concerned with single discourse segments here as well. And here too discourse fragments consisting of multiple segments played a role in the argumentation. The present chapter will be entirely concerned with linguistic expressions marking *relations* between discourse segments. In terms of the construal configuration: while the previous chapters focused on the analysis of linguistic expressions that in principle relate *one* situation from dimension O to dimension S, we will now focus on linguistic expressions connecting at least *two* situations in dimension O. Some examples are given in (1):

(1) (*a*) This feature is uninformative and irritating. It has been removed from the output report.

   (*b*) This feature is uninformative and irritating. It has therefore been removed from the output report.

   (*c*) This feature is uninformative and irritating, and it has been removed from the output report.

(d) This feature is uninformative and irritating, but it has been removed from the output report.

(e) This feature is uninformative and irritating. So it has been removed from the output report.

(f) This feature is uninformative and irritating, so that it has been removed from the output report.

(g) Since this feature is uninformative and irritating, it has been removed from the output report.

(h) Although this feature is uninformative and irritating, it has not been removed from the output report.

The structural relations involved comprise paratactic, coordinating, ones (see (1c–e)), as well as hypotactic ones (see (1f–h)), in the sense of Halliday (1985), Matthiessen and Thompson (1988), and other text-oriented studies of clause combining. These two types are essentially characterized by the presence of a linguistic expression—often a word—that is not a constituent of a clause, that linearly introduces one of the connected clauses, and that provides an indication about the conceptual nature of the connection; these are traditionally labeled 'conjunctions', either coordinating or subordinating.[1] However, the same kinds of relations also occur between clauses that are not linked in a paratactic or hypotactic construction but juxtaposed, with (see (1b)) or without (see (1a)) an element that serves to mark the conceptual nature of the relationship. In fact, such relations also hold between pieces of text that consist of multiple segments. That is, paratactic and hypotactic constructions may well be considered a kind of 'grammaticalization' of relations between discourse segments, at least in the sense of 'specifically grammatical ways of marking' such relations (see Matthiessen and Thompson 1988). But the conceptual relation marked by a grammatical conjunction is not necessarily different from a relation that is marked by a lexical element, or not marked at all. Thus it will not be necessary, in the discussion to follow, to make a systematic distinction between relations marked by lexical items on the one

---

[1] I use this formulation in order to make explicit that such words are precisely called conjunctions because they occur in this type of construction, rather than the other way around. Sometimes the same word, e.g. Dutch *dus* ('so'), can appear in the connecting 'slot' of a coordinating or subordinating construction as described here and as a constituent of a clause; in the former case it is traditionally classified as a conjunction, in the latter case as an adverb. Notice that the distribution of such an element cannot be described without circularity by saying that it occurs in one position *because* it is a conjunction, and in the other because it is (also) an adverb; that is, the part of speech to which the element is supposed to belong is actually not identifiable independently of its distribution over constructions. See Croft (2001) for general arguments for the primacy of constructions with respect to (e.g.) parts of speech.

hand, and those marked by grammatical items (conjunctions) on the other; this is just one other area exemplifying the absence of a really sharp boundary between grammar and lexicon. Both traditional 'conjunctions' (*but, because, although*, etc.) and traditional 'adverbs' (*therefore, consequently*, etc.) provide constructional templates requiring text segments to be connected, with the former imposing more strict restrictions on the position of the lexical element involved and on the form of the connected segments. A full description of any language must somehow mention all the specifics of the different constructions, but that does not concern me here. Following standard practice in discourse studies, I will therefore use the term 'connective' to generalize over paratactic and hypotactic conjunctions as well as other linguistic expressions that conventionally establish a conceptual relationship to another discourse segment.[2]

The construal configuration defines a limited number of possible ways in which two conceived situations can be connected in discourse. Figure 4.1 represents the basic configuration for such an instance of language use: conceptualizer 2 is engaging in cognitive coordination with conceptualizer 1 with respect to two situations, A and B, which are both objects of conceptualization. It is essentially the same as the basic construal configuration from Chapter 1, with the addition that we are dealing with two distinct situations represented linguistically in (at least) two distinct clauses (indicated by the heavy lines of the circles around A and B). This configuration would correspond to example (1*a*): two situations A and B are profiled, but not the relation

O: *Object of conceptualization:*   A - - - - - B

S: *Subject of conceptualization*   1 - - - - - 2
   (Ground):

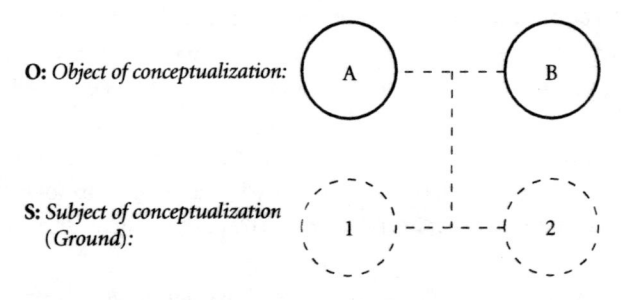

FIGURE 4.1. Construal configuration for connecting O-situations in discourse

[2] This does not mean that there are no differences between, in particular, paratactic and hypotactic relations between clauses. It only means that any systematic difference between these ways of connecting clauses is independent of the conceptual character of the relation. In Dutch and German the difference between parataxis and hypotaxis is reflected in a clear formal difference (the position of the finite verb), so that the question of a possible functional difference is especially relevant in these languages. For a proposal relating this difference to the hierarchical aspect of discourse structure see Verhagen (2001*a*; in prep.).

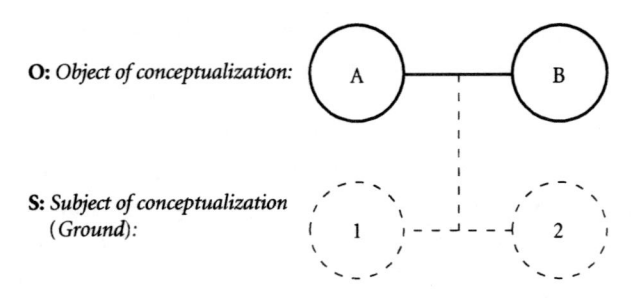

FIGURE 4.2. Theoretical configuration for 'objective' connection between segments

between them, nor any relations to and between the conceptualizers in the Ground.

What are possible roles of connectives in this configuration? Theoretically, there are clearly two extremes: a connective may mark a relation that is itself part of the object of conceptualization, resulting in a configuration as depicted in Figure 4.2.

But it may also mark a relation that is entirely restricted to the intersubjective dimension, resulting in the configuration represented by Figure 4.3.[3]

While the configuration of Figure 4.2 seems straightforward, it may not be immediately obvious what kinds of situation are characterized by the one in Figure 4.3. Consider the relation marked by *because* in (2), from an on-line review of a computer game:

(2) Well, the title says it all, really. And too bad if it doesn't, because it's late and we don't feel like explaining it.

Clearly, 'too bad' does not constitute an object of conceptualization. It is an instruction to readers for whom 'the title says it all' does not hold as to how to

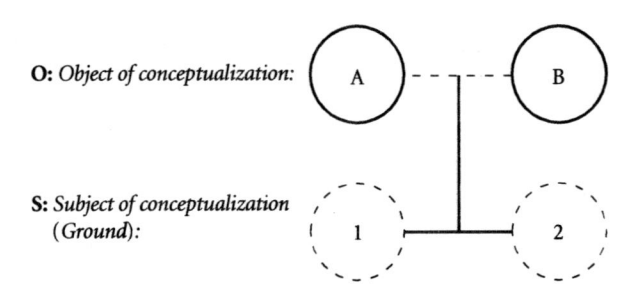

FIGURE 4.3. Theoretical configuration for 'subjective' connection between segments

[3] The difference corresponds to the factor 'source of coherence' in the classification of discourse coherence relations proposed by Sanders et al. (1993).

relate to this fact; they will have to resign themselves to their lack of understanding. This is the result component in the causal relation. The other component is, apparently, that the writer 'does not feel like' explaining, which has something to do with the fact that it is late. So the relationship marked with *because* here entirely involves the management of the mutual expectations and obligations of the subjects of conceptualization. The causality strictly concerns the coordination between the latter: if an unresolved misunderstanding arises and communication breaks down, this is 'because it's late and we don't feel like explaining'. What the whole utterance indicates is an instruction to the reader not only to consider the conceived situation a pity, but especially not to expect anything more from the speaker/writer.

On the other hand, the intersubjective connection in such a configuration is not entirely disconnected from the contents of the clauses. It must of course be possible to construe the contents of the conceived situations A ('it's late') and B ('the title is unclear') in such a way that their combination supports the causal relationship in the intersubjective dimension. In this case this support can be constructed by invoking some background reasoning about the communicative situation, for example along the following lines:

I just asserted that the title says it all; if a reader does not understand my assertion, he is normally justified in requiring a clarification; normally, I am obliged to provide such an explication to support my assertion (a topos about communication); in this particular situation there is a counteracting force (hence *because*) as to why my obligation and the reader's rights are overridden; namely, it is late.[4]

Thus it seems to me that there must always be some particular way of construing an object of conceptualization with respect to the Ground when the linguistically marked discourse relationship is located in dimension S. This is why the construal relationship (the vertical line) in Figure 4.3 is also represented as being profiled. One might wonder whether something similar should not hold in Figure 4.2. In fact, this may make sense for many relations, for example causal ones, which might be argued to induce reasoning processes in the conceptualizers. But providing an instruction for a particular construal

---

[4] To avoid misunderstanding: I do not wish to suggest that such a stepwise computation is actually carried out in producing or understanding utterances of this sort. On the contrary, I think their input and output conditions are mostly available as holistic schemas or frames for linguistic behavior, and a linguistic template such as *too bad if X because Y* may even function as a trigger for the entire frame. But that does not undo the fact that such behavior is ultimately governed by, and can be justified by, such norms. One does not, in the United States or on the European continent, constantly compute where to drive on a road, or how to take a left-hand turn, as a chain of inferences starting with the knowledge of the rule that one is supposed to drive on the right-hand side; but that does not change the fact that such driving behavior is ultimately governed by, and can be justified by, such a computation.

with an 'objective' discourse relation is not a matter of conceptual necessity, and there are exceptions. For example, the Dutch connective *ook* ('also', 'as well'), unlike *en* ('and'), marks the relation between two conceived situations as one of parallelism strictly in terms of the objects of conceptualization themselves (see Pander Maat 1999*a*: 171–4). Furthermore, we will encounter evidence in Section 4.3.2 indicating that some causal connectives precisely have to be distinguished from other ones along these lines.

Still, more often than not ordinary cases of discourse connectives involve a particular construal of the relation at level S of the basic construal configuration. This is especially true for markers of contrast and concession. Since they are also conceptually connected to the negation phenomena discussed in Chapter 2, the relevance of the different features of the construal configuration is most obvious. Because of certain complications in their interaction, starting with concession and negation will also be helpful for laying out some problems that should preferably be solved in an alternative analysis. The discussion of concessive relations will be seen to automatically lead to certain hypotheses about causal ones.

In the previous chapters an important role was played, at more than one point in the discussion, by the notion of argumentative orientation (direction and force). For example, I used the coherence or incoherence of sequences of discourse segments in my argumentation for making certain generalizations in terms of argumentative orientation, such as the one over *not* and *barely*, or over performative and non-performative uses of speech act verbs. In this chapter too argumentative orientation will play a role. But as the phenomena under consideration already consist of combinations of segments, I will mostly be concerned with the orientation of one of them with respect to the other (as in the discussion of (2) above), in order to clarify the nature of the relation, and less with the argumentative orientation of the entire constellation of segments in relation to the larger discourse context. In principle, this is also an important aspect, and it may well be crucial for some parts of the discussion to follow. Nevertheless, I believe that the main points will be sufficiently clear and well supported despite this limitation.

Let me, at this point, once more emphasize that my purpose in this book is to develop a particular theoretical view of language structure and language use, and to provide support for it. The goal is not to produce all-encompassing analyses of all the linguistic phenomena discussed. This is true for Chapter 2, where I paid little attention to all kinds of important semantic factors involving scales, minimizers, polarity, and so forth; it is true for Chapter 3, which (even though quite extensive) focuses on *that*-clauses and does not pay attention to *Wh*-complements or non-finite complements, to mention only two special cases. It is also true for the present chapter; I will be making claims about the meaning of connectives in terms of elements of the construal configuration, in particular the intersubjectivity dimension, but I will not claim that this is all one could say about the semantics of any of these elements.

4.2 Concession

4.2.1 *Two paradoxes*

It is well known that the meanings of causal and concessive connectives are related in interesting ways. Notice, for example, the parallelism in the possible interpretations of sentences such as the following (König 1991):

(3) The house is no less comfortable because it dispenses with air-conditioning.
(4) The house is no less comfortable, although it dispenses with air-conditioning.

In one of its possible readings (3) can be read as a paraphrase of (4). Saying that the lack of air-conditioning does not cause the house to be uncomfortable can be seen as equivalent to saying that despite the lack of air-conditioning it is not uncomfortable. A requirement for this equivalence is to read the negation as taking wide scope in (3), so that it includes the *because*-clause; in (4), on the other hand, the negation takes narrow scope.

Duality

König (ibid.) explores the idea that this connection might be captured in a very direct way; namely, by considering it an instance of so-called duality. An expression A is said to be the dual of another one B if A is equivalent to the 'external' negation of the 'internal' negation of B. For example, consider the verbs *force* and *allow*: if you force me to sit down, then it is not the case that you allow me not to sit down, and vice versa, so *force* is the dual of *allow*. Similarly, if everyone sits down, then it is not the case that someone does not sit down, and vice versa, so *everyone* is the dual of *someone*. König sees something similar in the relation between *although* and *because*. When X is the case 'although' Y is the case, then it is not the case that Y caused not-X, and vice versa; in other words: then it is not the case that not-X *because* Y. The above examples seem to illustrate this: if the house is comfortable although it lacks air-conditioning, then it is not the case that it is not comfortable because of the lack of air-conditioning. And an interesting feature of the analysis is that the paradox posed by the formulation of (3) and (4) can be explained. Notice that the main clause looks exactly the same in both cases, and that the relation between main and subordinate clause can be the same in both cases despite the difference in meaning between *because* and *although*. This paradox only arises if the first conjunct contains an instance of sentential negation— witness the fact that there is no reading of (5) which can be (more or less) equivalent to (6):

(5) The house is attractive because it dispenses with air-conditioning.
(6) The house is attractive although it dispenses with air-conditioning.

The solution lies in the observation that external negation is needed to create the required reading, and this can only be provided by the sentential negation operator, which then also has to include the internally negative *because*-clause in its scope.

However, the very same point also creates a problem. As König has already pointed out, at the end of his paper, some serious problems for this approach appear as soon as one goes beyond the very first examples that inspired it.[5] One of these is that, in view of the logical equivalence underlying duality relationships, the expressions should behave symmetrically under negation, but this is not the case for *because* and *although*: negation of causality may lead to an interpretation as concessive, but (wide-scope) negation of concessivity does not produce a causal reading. Consider an attempt like (7):

(7) It is not the case that John failed his exams although he worked hard.

This certainly cannot be interpreted as equivalent to 'John passed his exams because he worked hard'—if it is interpretable at all. It seems unavoidable to conclude that concession cannot be taken as negated causality in any simple sense.

Still, this should not lead to the conclusion that the original observation was misguided; there is an important conceptual connection, a 'complementarity' of some sort, between causality and concessivity, and this does require explanation. Some other examples, from English as well as Dutch, are the following:

(8) They're not the best team, just because they won 3–0.

(9) They're not the best team, although they won 3–0.

(10) Jan   is niet meteen   de beste kandidaat omdat hij
     John is not straight-away the best candidate because he

---

[5] Cf. sect. 3 of König and Siemund (2000). Criticisms of the duality view can be found in Pasch (1992a) and Iten (1998).

gepromoveerd is.
promoted   is
'John is not [automatically] the best candidate just because he has a Ph.D.'

(11) Hoewel Jan gepromoveerd is, is hij niet meteen de beste
     Although John promoted is is he not straight-away the best
     kandidaat.
     candidate
     'Although John has a Ph.D., he is not automatically the best candidate.'

Notice that in both languages some special marking is definitely preferred in such cases. The minimal combination of just *not* and bare *because* does not really suffice to readily evoke the concessive interpretation: in English, *just* is added to *because*, and in Dutch, *meteen* is added to the negation operator *niet*. Still, such additions do not cancel the semantic nature of the causal connectives and thus the challenge of explaining the specific relation between a causal connective in the scope of negation, and concessivity.[6] In fact, the asymmetry in this relation can best be seen as the main component of the phenomenon to be explained: Why is it, on the one hand, that the inclusion of a cause in the scope of negation can give rise to a kind of concessive reading, and, on the other hand, that a concessive relation cannot even be included in the scope of negation?

Domain theory

There is yet another interesting connection between causality and concessivity: they exhibit parallel ambiguities, in terms of different conceptual domains distinguished in Sweetser (1990). It is this connection that I will use as a starting point for an alternative analysis of the relationship between causality and concessivity.

One of the main motives for Sweetser's domain distinctions is that they provide a way to account for the fact that similar types of polysemy show up in different expressions. Consider the ambiguity of modal verbs in terms of deontic vs. epistemic interpretations. *He must come home* is an example of so-called deontic usage; it describes some obligation in the world (namely, in the person referred to); this is what Sweetser calls an application of the modal verb in the 'content domain'. *He must be home (by now)*, on the other hand,

---

[6] Notice also that in neither language do the formulations used in (8) and (10) *enforce* a concessive reading. They may also mark straightforward causal relations, as in *They are not the best team, just because they don't practice enough*, or *Omdat Jan nog studeert, is hij nog niet de beste kandidaat* ('Because John is still a student, he is not yet the best candidate'). So in principle, sentence (10) may also be read as 'Because John has a Ph.D., he is not yet the best candidate', but that does not make a lot of sense.

locates an obligation (namely, to conclude 'He is home' on the basis of the available evidence) in the conceptualizer rather than in the world being conceptualized; this is what Sweetser calls usage in the 'epistemic domain'. Notice that these distinctions resemble those between the levels O and S of the construal configuration. This is no coincidence. However, there are some respects in which the intersubjectivity approach differs from (and is, I think, superior to) the domains approach.

It is no coincidence that this type of polysemy resembles the difference between distinct types of usage of the English conjunction *because*, as exemplified in the contrast between (12) and (13):

(12) John passed his exams because he worked hard.
(13) John worked hard, because he passed his exams.

In (12) the causal relation holds between the facts that John passed his exams and that he worked hard (i.e. in the content domain). In (13) it holds in the conceptualizer's mind; that is, the proposition that John worked hard is epistemically caused by the knowledge that he passed his exams. Postulating a systematic conceptual distinction between content and epistemic domains for the application of the meaning of distinct expressions (modal verbs as well as connectives) provides a unified account for such phenomena, and thus has great explanatory power.

At first sight Sweetser's approach is further corroborated by the fact that it also applies to concessive connectives, which have an element of opposition or negation as part of their meaning. However, precisely this application also produces a conceptual dilemma. On the one hand, cases like (14) and (15) seem to be clear parallels to (12) and (13):

(14) John failed his exams although he worked hard.
(15) John lounged around, although he passed his exams.

Intuitively, one can say that in (14) the real-world causal connection between working hard and passing exams is in some sense denied, so this would be a case of concession in the content domain. Analogously, what is denied in (15) seems to be the validity of the *inference* from the knowledge of John's passing to the conclusion that he has been working hard; so this would be a case of concession in the epistemic domain (cf. the examples and paraphrases of 'adversative' conjunctions in Sweetser 1990: 79). Thus what we have here is another interesting connection between causality and concessivity: if the latter is the negative counterpart of the former, then, given the theory of domains, we should expect it to be applicable in a parallel fashion in the distinct domains, and this is precisely what appears to be the case.

On the other hand, Sweetser herself explicitly draws attention to the fact that for the adversative conjunction *but* (arguably even more general and semantically simpler than concessive *although*) it is hard to find clear examples of content usage. The point is that a contrastive relation always allows for a construal as a relation of reasoning, involving relations between arguments and conclusions, and is never clearly restricted to real-world relations. Consider the following parallel to the concessive examples above:

(16) John worked hard, but he failed his exams.

The contrast signalled by *but* cannot be sufficiently explained in terms of the real-world facts of working hard and failing; after all, these situations are not at all incompatible in the real world, as is clear from the fact that they co-occur quite regularly. In Sweetser's words:

> what does it mean to say that A and B 'clash' or 'contrast' in the real world? How can discordance or contrast exist outside of the speaker's mental concept of harmony or non-contrast? In a sense, if two states coexist in the real world (and conjunction with *but* does present both conjuncts as true), then they cannot be said to clash at the real-world level. (ibid. 103–4.)

Recall that I have described *but* in Chapter 2 (esp. Sect. 2.3.2) as a connective cancelling inferences licensed by the discourse up to the point where *but* is used. The first clause in (16) can trigger a reasoning process, based on general and specific knowledge, producing the inference that John may have passed his exams. Only then may a contrast be constructed: it holds between this inference and the actual fact of John's failing (see also Spooren 1989).

However, although this move seems absolutely right, it does create a dilemma. If we call the use of *but* inherently epistemic, based on the very general consideration that the concept 'contrast' requires reference to reasoning, then we are obliged to call *although* inherently epistemic as well, because this also involves contrast:[7] (14) is as contrastive as (16), and it does in fact seem to require reference to the same kind of inferences. But calling *all* uses of *although* epistemic would deprive us of a way of accounting for the difference between (14) and (15), as well as for the parallel between this pair on the one hand and (12) and (13) on the other. In other words: that parallel precisely seems to require that not all uses of *although* are called epistemic. Somehow, this dilemma should be resolved, or avoided, in a better analysis.

---

[7] Without cancelling the inferences associated with the contrasted conjunct; see below.

4.2.2 Background assumptions and mental spaces

It is a commonplace in the literature on concessives that in such a relation two propositions are asserted 'against the background of an assumption', to use König's relatively neutral wording (1991).[8] Consider example (14), repeated below:

(14) John failed his exams although he worked hard.

Both the propositions *John failed his exams* and *he worked hard* are presented as true, but the difference between (16) and a simple coordination of the two propositions seems to be that there is an additional proposition involved, the background assumption, say, that John was supposed to pass his exams because he worked hard; that is, a proposition that connects concessivity to causality.

Analyses explicating this idea in terms of logical operators have been undertaken by Pasch (1992a, 1992b, 1994: 16–27) and König (1991, 1994), among others. There are differences among these analyses, but the general idea is as follows:

(17) 'p although q' means:
 (a) Truth conditions: $p \& q$
 (b) Presupposition: $q \rightarrow \neg p$

That is, the background assumption is thought of as an entailment relation that functions as a presupposition, that is, it must be true for the conjunction of p and q to have a truth value.

Taken at face value this leads to an internal contradiction (implying both p and ¬p, or both q and ¬q), and it is thus minimally in need of additional mechanisms or assumptions. Pasch, acknowledging this, seems to assume that a speaker of anything of the form 'p although q' actually utters something that is necessarily false. Others are more hesitant to draw such a conclusion. In any case, what is needed is greater clarity about the exact content of the notion 'background assumption'.

König and Siemund (2000) undertake an attempt to improve their own as well as Pasch's analysis, and in the process drop the duality hypothesis (p. 355). One thing they notice is that the relevant background assumptions always 'involve some kind of quantification and generalisation', yet they do not seem to deny such a rule the status of 'material implication of propositional logic'

---

[8] There is quite a variety of labels for this concept, such as *(discourse) presupposition, conventional implicature, defeasible implication*. For some analysts these are probably not the same, as they belong to specific, distinct theoretical frameworks, but the differences do not have to concern us here.

(ibid. 353). But the idea of the background assumption being some kind of generalization is the same as Ducrot's concept of 'topos', introduced in Chapter 1, and subsequently used in Chapters 2 and 3. As noticed particularly in Chapter 2, Section 2.3.3, it is a matter of conceptual necessity that topoi are conceived as default rules, laying down what is *normally* the case; that is, rules such as 'Normally, working hard increases your chances of passing your exams'. Such rules do not have the same properties as singular statements p and q connected by some connective, such as *although*. As already noted by Popper (1972: 27, 33), for example, particulars allow for verification, but generalizations do not. So one makes a category mistake if one describes the background assumption as a 'presupposition' and formulates it as if it has the same logical properties as the *although*-conjunction itself (see (17)). A background assumption must furthermore be 'only' general and not universal. If it were universally quantified, with q in the 'presupposition' taken as '$\forall x(f(x))$', the use of a concessive, asserting p and q, would still entail a contradiction (p, because of (17a), and ¬p, because of (17b)). As noted in Chapter 2, the rule laid down by a topos cannot be conceived as material implication.[9] But it is still a rule licensing an inference, and recognized as such. So what is especially important to avoid the derivation of contradictions, even if the defeasibility of generalizations is recognized, is that a background *mental space, distinct* from that of the speaker/writer, is evoked in which the shared topos is construed as the basis for a causal inference.

Using the notion 'topos', we can say that a concessive construction allows a speaker to acknowledge the possible validity of some inference and the topos it is based on, and still propose a contrary conclusion. For sentence (14) (*John failed his exams although he worked hard*), for example, we can say that the speaker/writer:

(i) envisages the possibility, given that John worked hard, that someone might make the inference 'therefore, John must have passed his exams', on the basis of a mutually shared topos;
(ii) by uttering *He failed although he worked hard*, acknowledges the basic validity of the inference but overrides the conclusion ('failing' implying 'not passing').

In (18) this is formulated in a general way:

---

[9] This was the reason why in Figure 2.6 the topos was represented by means of capital letters, and the associated particular propositions that are 'on stage' in the *although*-sentence by means of lower-case letters. König and Siemund (2000) adopt this notation too, but, as I said, they do not explicitly draw any conclusion about the 'logical' status of the rules.

(18) The speaker/writer who produces a concessive sentence *r although p*:
   (i) envisages the possibility, given a proposition p, that someone might validly make the inference 'p, therefore q' on the basis of a mutually shared topos;
   (ii) while acknowledging the basic validity of the inference, overrides q by asserting r, which licenses ¬q.

As this formulation makes clear, what is going on in a concessive utterance does not only have to take the difference into account between general, default rules and singular propositions. It is also a matter of managing the relation between the perspectives, or mental spaces, of two distinct conceptualizers: one in which a potentially valid inference is made, and the speaker/writer's. In terms of the representation of mental spaces used in Chapter 2, the cognitive configuration associated with (14) can be given as in Figure 4.4.

The conventional function of *r although p* is that its use by conceptualizer 1 projects a second mental space in which the proposition p ('He worked hard'), which is valid in Space$_1$, is valid as well. Space$_2$ furthermore contains a topos relevant to both r and p, in this case that if you work hard you are more likely to pass your exams. In Space$_2$ the topos licenses a positive epistemic stance towards the conclusion q; that is, that John has passed his exams. Thus the speaker/writer acknowledges that this reasoning may be valid. But by the use of the statement r ('He failed') she displays a negative epistemic stance towards this proposition herself; that is, she invites the addressee to modify his stance. In brief: while the speaker/writer acknowledges that given p there may be good reasons to adopt q, she nevertheless invites the addressee to adopt r, which is incompatible with q.

Space$_1$ Space$_2$

r although p p

{P→Q} {P→Q}
{R↔¬Q} {R↔¬Q}

{¬q} {therefore q}

topos: 'Working hard (P) makes passing more likely (Q)'

p = 'He worked hard'
q = 'He passed his exams'
r = 'He failed his exams'

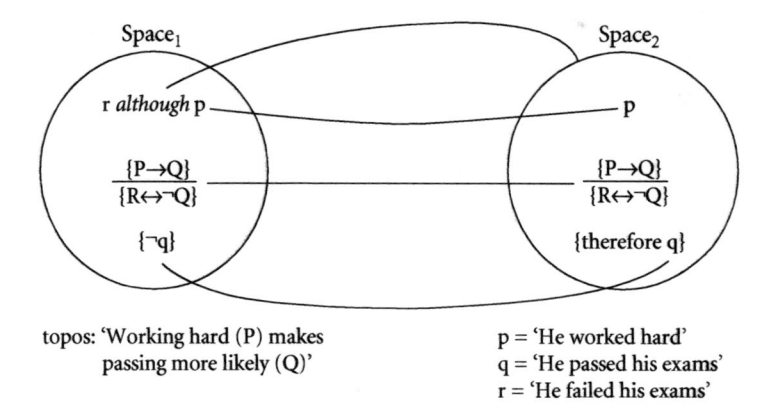

FIGURE 4.4. Mental-space configuration for *He failed his exams although he worked hard*

In this respect *p although q* differs from *p but q*. They are both contrastive, but whereas *p but q* cancels conclusions associated with p (q 'wins'), *p although q* cancels conclusions associated with q; in any case, q does not 'win', at least not at this point in the discourse—its validity is acknowledged, but the consequences are not accepted. Consider the difference in the degree of coherence in the following two pieces of discourse:

(19) John failed his exams, but he worked hard. So let's give him his birthday present anyway.
(20) ??John failed his exams, although he worked hard. So let's give him his birthday present anyway.

In (19) *but* simply undoes the argumentative force of the statement that John failed his exams, so that it can no longer counteract the proposal to reward him. Clearly, *although* in (20) does not have that effect. The elements differ in what the speaker/writer can use them for in managing the reasoning processes of the addressee; a difference, again, in the dimension of intersubjective coordination.

In view of this difference, it is not surprising that a large number of concessive clauses in actual language use *precede* the main clause (in the Dutch Eindhoven Corpus 55 per cent of the cases). In that position it can in the most straightforward way function to acknowledge a mutually shared, relevant piece of knowledge and reasoning, after which the speaker/writer can get to the point that she really wants the addressee to accept.[10] Apart from that, there is a perceptible functional difference between the order *p although q* and *although q, p*, though not as radical as the difference between *p but q* and *q but p*. Presenting a claim first and then acknowledging the validity of another inference, without accepting its consequences, can easily produce an effect of retreat, weakening the original claim—certainly not completely, but still somewhat. Putting the concessive clause in front does not have that kind of effect; at least, never to the same extent (see Van der Mast et al. 1994 for relevant observations).

---

[10] Provided, of course, that the content of the *although*-clause allows for a good connection to the topic of the preceding discourse. In written discourse that factor seems to be involved in many cases where the clause is not initial, but in spoken Dutch something special is going on. There are numerous instances of post-posed *hoewel*-zinnen, but many of these have verb-second word order; that is, the order of main clauses (the phenomenon also appears in print, but not so frequently, it seems, and then there is always a punctuation mark—comma, colon, or dash—following *hoewel*). There also seems to be a functional difference. Although with main-clause word order the effect of *hoewel* is still not as strong and immediate as that of *maar* ('but'), it does allow for (more) subsequent 'changes of mind', or 'corrections' initiated by the speaker. See Barth (2000) and Günthner (2000) for discussion of apparently similar phenomena in English and German, respectively.

As is clear from this description and from Figure 4.4 itself, the cognitive configuration associated with *although* is quite complex. The content of Space₂ can be kept relatively simple: in principle it only has to contain a proposition and a straightforward topos licensing an inference. But because the assertion in Space₁ is 'He failed' while the inference licensed in Space₂ is 'He passed', Space₁ must also employ the knowledge that failing and passing are complementary concepts, and the speaker/writer must assume that the addressee can activate and use the same knowledge—hence the rule below the line in the topos.

Notice that an attempt to remove this additional rule would make it necessary to introduce a complication elsewhere. If we change the topos to 'Working hard makes failing less likely', it is true that we no longer need the 'extra' rule about the complementarity of failing and passing, so it seems as if this can make things simpler. However, the topos itself then has to be negative ('P→¬R', e.g. working hard normally leads to *not* failing), and we also have to introduce negation into Space₂: conceptualizer 2 must be assumed to entertain the idea 'He has *not* failed', which is then supposedly contradicted by conceptualizer 1. But, as we have seen in the discussion of the differences between *on the contrary*, and sentential and morphological negation in Chapter 1, a positive statement (here: 'He failed') does not by itself project a mental space with a negative one; the *although*-clause, which does project a background mental space, is about working hard, not about causes and consequences of failing. So the alternative analysis suggested above must assume some other mechanism to introduce the negative epistemic stance into Space₂; for example, from the context.

Interestingly, there *is* a way to reduce the complexity of the configuration in Figure 4.4 while retaining its overall content, but this involves introducing an *explicit* negative element into the utterance. Suppose we consider (21) rather than (14):

(21) He did not pass his exams although he worked hard.

The mental space configuration for this is given in Figure 4.5.

Since the speaker/writer herself utters *not q*, there is no need for an extra rule to license the inference of ¬q as in Figure 4.4. The single, positive topos suffices, both in Space₁ and in Space₂. Moreover, the negation in Space₁ does not open an extra mental space, but relates to the same one as *although*; after all, the latter already contains q (complementary of *not* q), licensed by the topos and p.

172   *Discourse connections*

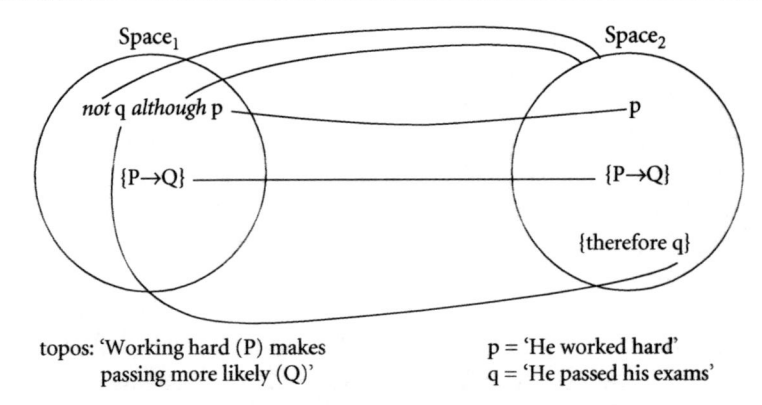

[Figure 4.5 diagram: Space₁ contains "not q although p", {P→Q}; Space₂ contains p, {P→Q}, {therefore q}]

topos: 'Working hard (P) makes   p = 'He worked hard'
passing more likely (Q)'   q = 'He passed his exams'

FIGURE 4.5. Mental-space configuration for *He did not pass his exams although he worked hard*

Or suppose we consider the reverse situation, with negation in the concessive clause as in (22):

(22) He passed his exams although he did not work hard.

As the content of the *although*-clause is projected to Space₂, the latter now contains an explicit negation marker. The mental-space configuration can be represented as in Figure 4.6.

The content and structure of Space₂ is the same as that of Space₁ in the analysis of negation in Chapter 2 (Sect. 2.3.3, Fig. 2.5). In this case, too, there is no need for an extra rule, nor for an additional mechanism to introduce the negative epistemic stance in Space₂, since this is done linguistically, by means

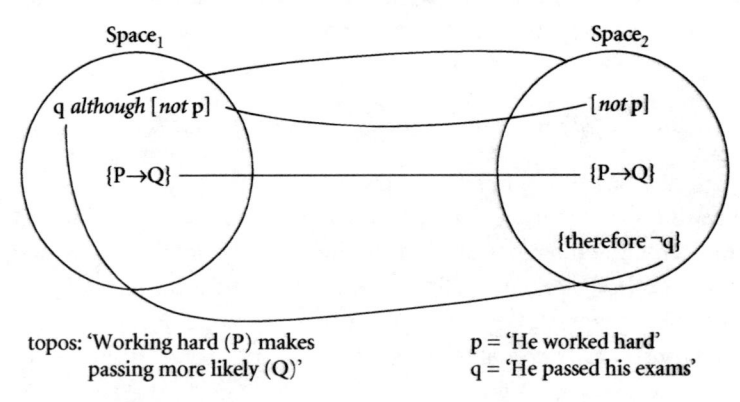

[Figure 4.6 diagram: Space₁ contains "q although [not p]", {P→Q}; Space₂ contains [not p], {P→Q}, {therefore ¬q}]

topos: 'Working hard (P) makes   p = 'He worked hard'
passing more likely (Q)'   q = 'He passed his exams'

FIGURE 4.6. Mental-space configuration for *He passed his exams although he did not work hard*

of *not*.[11] The overall structure of the content of the mental spaces in Figures 4.5 and 4.6 is the same; in particular: the assertion in Space₁ in both cases directly addresses an inference in Space₂. In Figure 4.4 (for *He failed his exams although he worked hard*) it does so only indirectly, as ¬q has to be derived from r, via the topos and an associated semantic rule.

Thus what superficially looks like a more complex utterance (because of the added sentential negation) corresponds to a more simple conceptual configuration, given the intersubjectivity analysis of concession and negation. This is not the only phenomenon of this kind. Recall that we saw in Chapter 2 (Sect. 2.4), that there are cases in which 'double' negation of the type *not impossible* produces a less complex conceptual configuration than the use of the single-word expression of the type *possible*. In view of this, it is interesting to note that a relatively high percentage of sentences with concessive clauses contain a negation operator. In the Dutch Eindhoven Corpus 18 per cent of all sentences contain at least one instance of the negation markers *niet* ('no'), *geen* ('no', as determiner), *nooit*, *nimmer* ('never'), and *niets* ('nothing'). But of the 153 concessive sentences in the corpus with *hoewel* or *ofschoon* ('although'),[12] 65 cases, that is 42 per cent, contain at least one of these elements.

In summary, I specified the general idea of a 'background assumption' in the meaning of concessive sentences in terms of the notion 'topos' and mental spaces. In that way we can avoid the basic problem that the characterization of this meaning seems to produce a contradiction. In the present framework no contradiction arises in either mental space. First, causality does play a role in the meaning of an *although*-sentence, but actually not in the mental space of the conceptualizer uttering it. It is conceptualizer 2 who is projected to make a causal inference 'p, therefore q', but she is not the one entertaining the contradictory ¬q. Conceptualizer 1 does entertain ¬q, but she does not make the causal inference. Even though conceptualizer 1 may share knowledge of the causal topos (P→Q), this is a default rule, a generalization that does not have the same kind of logical properties as the clauses connected by *although*;

---

[11] The mental space projected by *not* in Space2 can be taken to be Space1; that is, conceptualizer 1 of (22) may envisage the possibility that conceptualizer 2 thinks that 1 thinks: 'He has worked hard', a manifestation of the recursiveness of the perspective-taking capacity (see also the end of Sect. 4.2.3). But this is not strictly necessary.

[12] Only 14 of these contained *ofschoon*, which is clearly obsolete. There is another element that is listed as a concessive conjunction, namely *al*. But this has salient other possibilities of use, e.g. in counterfactuals, that are not possible for *hoewel* and *ofschoon*, and it also has some special constructional properties. The total number in the Eindhoven Corpus is 211, but it is not clear what proportion of these express a concessive relation, so they were not included in the present count. As to the negation elements included, notice that the element *niemand* ('nobody') does not occur in the concessive sentences with *hoewel*. But in the whole corpus it also occurs in only 0.3 per cent of the sentences, so it does not alter the ratio observed in the text.

the use of *although* precisely implies that conceptualizer 1 indicates that the topos does not apply to the case at hand.

The idea that the relationship between concession and causality might be an instance of duality can only arise when one does not see that the inferential processes involved are distributed over distinct conceptualizers. But, as we have seen several times now, it is not at all uncommon for an utterance produced by one speaker/writer inherently to coordinate multiple perspectives; some grammatical constructions are specifically geared to functioning in this domain, and concessive clauses are another case in point.

The approach developed in this section also provides the basis for solving the problems described in Section 4.2:

(i) How can it be explained that all concessives seem to operate in the epistemic domain, while there are nevertheless two different types of use that look like content use and epistemic use, respectively?
(ii) Why is it that a concessive reading can sometimes be produced by a causal connective under the scope of negation, while, on the other hand, a concessive connective can never occur under the scope of negation (to produce a causal reading)? This asymmetry must still be explained, even if the relation between cause and concession is not one of duality.

The next two sections are devoted to answering these questions, respectively.

4.2.3 *The double link between epistemic concessives and epistemic causals*

For an answer to the first of these two questions we have to consider the relation between the notion of 'epistemic use' as developed by Sweetser (1990) and the intersubjectivity approach adopted here. The idea that all uses of *although* (more generally: contrastive conjunctions) have an epistemic character (see Sect. 4.2.2) is implied by the intersubjectivity approach, because the contrast involved is one between mental spaces. In other words: it operates in the dimension of intersubjective coordination of the construal configuration, not in that of the objects of conceptualization. But is this just a special case of 'epistemic use', or does every kind of epistemic use involve the coordination of two different perspectives? Recall Sweetser's characterization of epistemic use of *because* for cases like (13):

(13) John worked hard, because he passed his exams.

The point was that the causal relation in (13) does not hold in the real world, but in the conceptualizer's mind; that is, the proposition that John worked hard is epistemically caused by the knowledge that he passed his exams. Formulated in this way, epistemic causality may appear to involve no more than a relation between a single subject of conceptualization and an object of conceptualization; it is construed as a case of subjectivity as opposed to objectivity (see Ch. 1, Sect. 1.2.2). Thus the intersubjectivity of concessives, involving the coordination of two perspectives, would be a special subtype of epistemic relations between clauses. However, there is in fact a good reason to consider (13) as operating in the intersubjective dimension as well, and that raises the question of which approach to its interpretation is most explanatory: the subjective or the intersubjective one.

Epistemic causality and perspectives: what concessions and arguments have in common
To see why (13) involves intersubjective coordination, notice that it is a case of reasoning from consequences to (probable) causes; that is, abductive reasoning. Given a rule of the type 'If it rains, the streets get wet' or 'Normally, if one works harder, one has a better chance of passing', and given the particular information that the streets are wet or that John has passed his exams, then the inference is licensed that is has been raining or that John has been working hard, respectively, though without settling the issue definitively.[13] But since the situation in the result clause does not *follow* from the *because*-clause, given the topos, its sole function can be to present an argument, *supporting* the assertion of the result clause. Therefore, its actual use implies that the speaker/writer views the result clause as in need of (some) support. If the result clause were already taken to represent undisputed knowledge at its being uttered, then the use of the second clause would be totally beside the point, violating the pragmatic (Gricean) maxim of relevance; one does not provide support for information that one knows will not be doubted. So *if* a speaker provides an argument for a statement, then she envisages the possibility that someone entertains a non-positive epistemic stance towards that statement. This is presented schematically in Figure 4.7.

An important respect in which this configuration differs from other ones we have been considering so far is that nothing in the utterance itself has the conventional function of opening another mental space in which the epistemic stance towards some proposition differs from the one in Space$_1$. It is not a convention of English that *because*—or an identifiable linguistic pattern of which *because* is an element—evokes this configuration (although we should perhaps allow for the possibility that it is a convention of

---

[13] See Keller (1998) on the significance of abductive reasoning in language use in general, and its ramifications.

176 Discourse connections

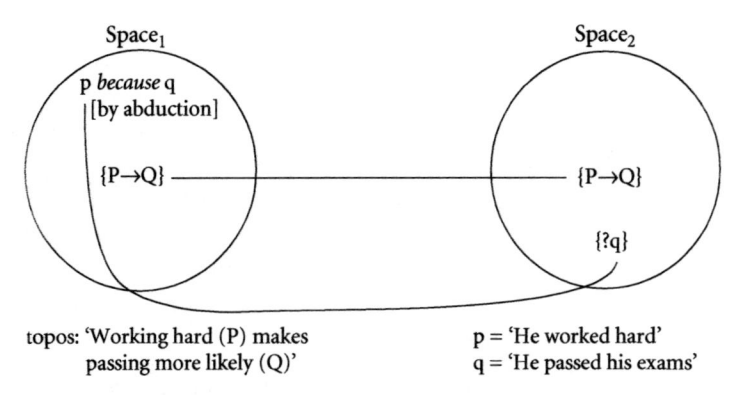

```
   Space₁                              Space₂
 ┌─────────────┐                    ┌─────────────┐
 │ p because q │                    │             │
 │ [by abduction]                   │             │
 │             │                    │             │
 │  {P→Q} ─────┼────────────────────┼──── {P→Q}   │
 │             │                    │             │
 │             │                    │    {?q}     │
 └─────────────┘                    └─────────────┘

 topos: 'Working hard (P) makes      p = 'He worked hard'
        passing more likely (Q)'     q = 'He passed his exams'
```

FIGURE 4.7. Mental-space configuration in abductive reasoning (*He worked hard, because he passed his exams*)

English, which must be learned, that the word is *compatible* with such configurations). But it is of course conceivable that the configuration is activated explicitly by the conventional meaning of some element. In written English one can still find the element *for* used for this purpose. And I will claim in Section 4.3.1 that the common Dutch conjunction *want* realizes this possibility as well.

The content reading of a causal relation in (12) (*John passed his exams because he worked hard*) does not have to involve the construction of another mental space representing another epistemic stance. Consequently, it does allow for the possibility of representing totally undisputed information. As has been observed frequently, the content reading of a *because*-sentence may provide only a single statement; for example, an answer to a question of the type 'How (did John pass his exams)?' In such a reading, the content of the first conjunct (that John passed his exams) is not asserted but presupposed; the *because*-clause contains the only news: the cause of John's success is the fact that he worked hard.

On the other hand, this is a possibility for interpreting a content causal relation, but not a necessity. That is, it is also possible for both clauses in (12) to be interpreted as asserted at the time of the utterance, with the *because*-clause construed not only as a representation of the real-world cause of the situation described in the result clause, but (simultaneously) as an argument in support of accepting it. Causes can be very good arguments for accepting the conclusion that some result has occurred, so a real-world causal link may often be used as an epistemic one as well. Pander Maat and Degand (2001: 221 ff.) call textual coherence relations of this type 'causality-based epistemic relations'. Sentences realizing such relations may contain linguistic markers indicating the way they should be interpreted, as in (23) (adapted from ibid. 222):

(23) It has rained continuously for two days, so the tennis court will probably be unplayable on.

Here the modal verb *will* and the adverb *probably* indicate that the speaker considers the issue of the condition of the tennis court something that is still to be settled. So the first clause is apparently intended as an argument to support a conclusion about the condition of the court. But both the topos used and the order of the inferential steps are the same as in (24):

(24) It has rained continuously for two days; that's why the tennis court is unplayable on.

In the reverse order, the nature of the relation may be undetermined when modal elements are not present, as the English word *because* does not conventionally limit the interpretation to one or the other (see above):

(25) The tennis court is unplayable on, because it has rained continuously for two days.

The difference here purely concerns the question of whether the result clause is considered to represent completely shared and accepted information or not. If it does, the *because*-clause simply answers the question of what caused this situation; but if the result clause is not presupposed but asserted, the *because*-clause may (also) count as an argument supporting the assertion of the result clause (a 'causality-based epistemic relation'). In either case, the order of the inferential steps (cause–consequence) matches that of the topos. If the order of the inferential steps is reversed, then the *because*-clause is *necessarily* an argument, projecting another mental space, as we have seen before; a parallel to (13) is (26):

(26) It must have been raining a lot, because the tennis court is unplayable on.

But, as the preceding discussion shows, when the order of the inferential steps matches that of the topos, the *because*-clause may both be a straightforward explanation of a cause ((25) interpreted as (24)) but also an explanation-plus-argument ((25) interpreted as (23)). Now the point is that the difference between (23) and (24), and between the two corresponding interpretations of (25), cannot be described in terms of different domains in which the causal link is located. This is obviously the real world in both cases. But it can be described in terms of the argumentative status of the causal clauses, and in particular in terms of the question whether the speaker/writer is using that clause to address a possible non-positive epistemic stance of the addressee towards the result clause.

Notice that in (23) and (24)—instances of 'forward' causality—the linguistic difference between the connectives *so* and *that's why* precisely marks the latter difference in argumentative status and assumptions about the addressee's epistemic stance towards the result clause, without changing the order of the steps in the inferential processes. This is an indication from language use that the relevant difference between 'epistemic' and 'content' causality might not be so much a matter of the relationship between a subject and an object of conceptualization, but a matter of the mutual relationship between subjects of conceptualization.[14] We will see in Section 4.3.1 that certain aspects of the use of causal connectives in Dutch corroborate this.

Now consider cases like the following:

(27) The curve is simple because the equation has only a few variables.
(28) The argument is transparent because the metaphors are appropriate.

It is hard to locate such causal relationships anywhere else than in a conceptualizer's mind. Any connection between the evaluation of the shape of a curve and the properties of an equation that describes it can only be a matter of reasoning, given the nature of the elements involved. Similarly, it makes no sense to talk about the transparency of an argument, the appropriateness of metaphors, and the relation between them, independently of a conceptualizer entertaining them. So these examples will have to be considered as epistemic according to the characterization given by Sweetser (1990) and others. But they are not necessarily argumentative (although they may be). Moreover, there are abductive counterparts to them:

(29) The equation can only have a few variables, because the curve is simple.
(30) The metaphors are undoubtedly appropriate, because the argument is transparent.

---

[14] Even for epistemic relations that are not 'causality-based', Pander Maat and Degand (2001: 224) consider it 'unfortunate' that abductive reasoning has become the prototype in the literature. However, this evaluation is at least partly due to their definition of 'epistemic' and 'cause'. For example, they consider 'He is probably tall, because his twin brother is tall, too' not as a case of causal reasoning, but reasoning based on non-causal assumptions (presumably something of the kind: 'Normally, twins look alike'). They put it in the category of 'noncausal epistemic relations', of which abductive reasoning is only a special subtype. I cannot review all of the arguments here (and the analysis is very conscientious); however, I fail to see an essential difference between reasoning with this kind of knowledge and reasoning with knowledge about the causal structure of the world, as in (I presume) 'Normally, children look like their parents'. Moreover, notice that one can reason abductively with this topos ('Your boys have the same height, eyes, and hair—they must be twins!'), which would then be just as epistemic as the 'normal' form (see the discussion in the text).

The difference between (27) and (28) on the one hand and (29) and (30) on the other cannot be adequately captured in terms of the relations existing 'in the mind' or 'in the world'—they all seem to be equally subjective. So the intersubjective features of epistemic causality may be better suited to characterize it theoretically. What (27) and (28) share with 'standard' causal reasoning is the directness of the connection between the specific case in the sentence and accepted cognitive models: we think of the shapes of curves as determined by equations rather than the other way around, and, similarly, of the rhetorical qualities of discourse as determined by the proper or improper use of figures of speech rather than the other way around. (The latter is presumably a special case of the model that properties of the whole are determined by its parts.) The activation of a topos ('the more variables in an equation, the more complex the curve', 'the better the metaphors, the better the argument') suffices to provide a basis for understanding the sentences, just as in the case of causal reasoning ('the harder you work, the better your chances of passing')

Finally, this last insight is also relevant for understanding what precisely is going on in a case like (31) (cf. Sect. 4.1, ex. (2)) and the Dutch (32), which appear to be epistemic and argumentative, but do not involve abductive reasoning:

(31) Too bad if it isn't clear, because it's late and I don't feel like explaining it.
(32) In het laatste decennium is onze kennis van het universum dramatisch uitgebreid, want dat mogen we wel stellen.
'Over the last decade, our knowledge of the universe has expanded dramatically, because we may safely assert that.'

The time of the day and the way I feel do not lead to something being unclear or a pity. But neither are the former the consequences of the latter, so there is no basis for abductive reasoning either. Similarly, a dramatic expansion of our knowledge and the possibility of safely asserting it are not linked by some rule, in such a way that the latter might provide an argument in support of the former. These are not cases of reasoning from results to probable causes, but they still represent argumentative usage: the causal clauses contain arguments supporting the other clauses. In both cases the speaker/writer acknowledges that the addressee may have reasons to question the apparent full import of what the speaker/writer has just stated or implied, and then presents something to strengthen it. In (31) and (32) this is not a concept from which, according to standard assumptions, the first assertion could directly follow, and that is one thing that these sentences share with the abductive cases already considered. As explicated in connection with example (2) in Section

4.1, a reader may normally expect clarification if something is not clear, but the writer presents 'it's late' as the cause of the reader's rights being overridden. The relation between the conjuncts is thus quite indirect, requiring the use of topoi which are not immediately connected to the content of the connected clauses. Similarly, there is no obvious topos in (32) that can directly associate the content of the two clauses, so the relation is more indirect. It may be formulated in this case as another sort of general rule concerning communication; namely, that a speaker/writer must have sufficient basis for saying what she says.[15] So here too the fact that something is presented in support of an assertion implies that the speaker/writer projects another mental space with a less-than-positive epistemic stance towards the asserted proposition.

The overall conclusion from these considerations is that concessive conjunctions and epistemically used causal conjunctions share the property that they activate a mental-space configuration with two conceptualizers, the second of which contains an epistemic stance towards some idea that is different from the one that is being entertained by conceptualizer 1.

Epistemic inferences in the background
Given this view of what concessive conjunctions and epistemically used causal ones have in common, let us now turn to the question of how the difference between apparent content and epistemic use of concessives might fit in. As a matter of fact, the answer is fairly straightforward. The phenomenon to be explained is that the difference between (33) and (34) is the same as that between (12) and (13), the first case instantiating use 'in the content domain', the second use 'in the epistemic domain'.[16]

(33) He did not pass his exams although he worked hard.
(34) He did not work hard, although he passed his exams.
(12) John passed his exams because he worked hard.
(13) John worked hard, because he passed his exams.

Recall that the conclusion from Section 4.2.2 was that the causal inference evoked by the use of *although* is to be located in the mental space *projected* by *although*, not in the mental space of conceptualizer 1 herself. The addressee is invited to cancel the conclusion from this inference. We can now see that the difference between (33) and (34) resides in a difference between the inferences

---

[15] Thus these cases may be viewed as exploiting the 'preparatory conditions' for a speech act (Searle 1969) to support the assertion, by making them explicit.

[16] Example (33) is identical to (21). I use examples with an explicit negation here, rather than (14) and (15), because the conceptual configurations associated with the former are simpler to represent and to 'read', for reasons explained in Section 4.2.3 (see Fig. 4.5).

being overridden by the *although*-construction: in the first case this is a 'content' one, in the second case it is an 'epistemic' one. Example (33) may be paraphrased as follows (cf. (18)):

(i) the speaker/writer envisages the possibility, given that John worked hard, that someone might make the inference 'therefore, John must have passed his exams' (i.e. (12)), on the basis of a mutually shared causal topos;
(ii) by uttering *John did not pass although he worked hard* she gives the instruction to override this conclusion, while acknowledging the basic validity of the inference.

And (34) may be paraphrased as follows:

(iii) the speaker/writer envisages the possibility, given that John passed his exams, that someone might make the inference 'therefore, John must have been working hard' (i.e. (13)), by abductive reasoning on the basis of a mutually shared causal topos;
(iv) by uttering *John did not work hard although he passed his exams* she gives the instruction to override this conclusion, while acknowledging the basic validity of the inference.

As demonstrated above, providing support for an assertion p implies, for pragmatic reasons, that a mental space is projected with a non-positive epistemic stance towards p. Similarly, the speaker/writer of a concessive sentence implicitly attributes to the addressee the willingness to support a conclusion with an argument, and thus the view that the question—in (34): whether John has been working hard or not—is not yet fully settled. In fact, this is completely in line with the assertion made by the speaker herself, which contradicts this conclusion.

Thus the basic mental-space configuration for (34) is not different from that of other concessive sentences (see Figs. 4.4 and 4.5), but since it is an epistemic inference that is being overridden, another mental space is projected from Space$_2$.[17] Consider Figure 4.8.

The parallel between epistemic causality and epistemic concessivity is that both involve a mental space containing argumentation, which therefore projects yet another mental space. The difference is that in the concessive

[17] Space$_3$ may be 'anchored' to the same individual as Space$_1$, which comes down to conceptualizer 1 envisaging conceptualizer 2 thinking that 1 does not believe p (which is correct), and that there is a ground for believing p. This is certainly a 'workable' interpretation, but I do not think it is strictly necessary. The speaker/writer may also 'simply' understand that conceptualizer 2 entertains the idea of presenting an argument supporting p to someone else, and proceed to correct or prevent this.

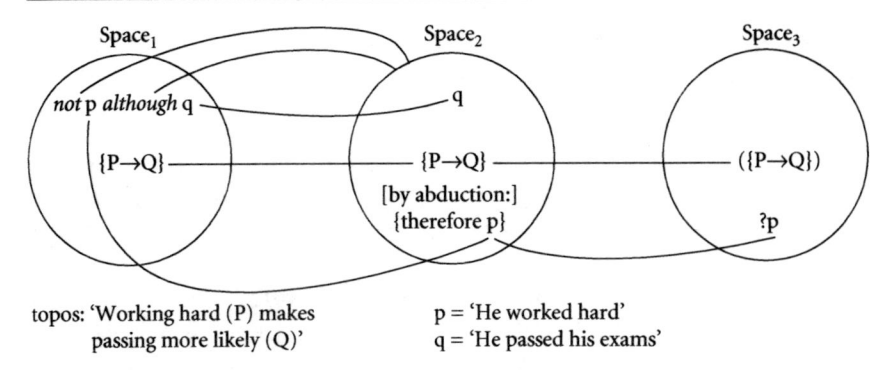

```
         Space₁              Space₂              Space₃

    ⎛ not p although q ⎞   ⎛      q       ⎞
    ⎜                  ⎟   ⎜              ⎟
    ⎜     {P→Q}        ⎟───⎜    {P→Q}     ⎟────    ({P→Q})
    ⎝                  ⎠   ⎜ [by abduction:]⎟
                           ⎜  {therefore p} ⎟         ?p
                           ⎝              ⎠
```

topos: 'Working hard (P) makes   p = 'He worked hard'
passing more likely (Q)'   q = 'He passed his exams'

FIGURE 4.8. Mental-space configuration for epistemic concessivity (*He didn't work hard, although he passed his exams*)

case this constellation is the *background* of conceptualizer 1's mental space rather than that space itself. The constellation of the two rightmost spaces in Figure 4.8 is the same as the one for epistemic causality depicted in Figure 4.7; the two leftmost spaces in Figure 4.8 correspond to the basic constellation for concessivity in Figure 4.5. The parallel between concessives in general and epistemic causality is that both kinds of relationship involve more than one space with a difference in epistemic stance towards the same proposition.

Recursion again

As observed in Chapter 3 (Sect. 3.3.1), the human cognitive ability to view others as mental, intentional agents like the self is inherently recursive; the cognitive abilities attributed to others include the ability to take another person's perspective. The complementation constructions studied in Chapter 3 distribute a perspective and what is embedded in it systematically over different parts of the construction, and these also exhibit structural recursion. The case of epistemic concessives provides an example of conceptual recursion of perspectives that is not necessarily reflected in the formal structure of the utterance. The possibility of recursion here is an automatic consequence of the fact that *although* overrides causal inferences and some of these inferences themselves involve the coordination of more than one perspective. It is the possibility of embedding spaces that allows us to simultaneously account for differences and similarities between the pairs of causal and concessive sentences that we started out with. The intersubjectivity approach thus provides a way to account for multiple levels of interpretation without multiplying levels in the theory: the same mechanism of projecting a mental space from another one is sometimes applied recursively.

Thus we now have a solution to one of the theoretical problems that we started out with. We can now, without contradiction, simultaneously account for two observations. First, all concessives share a fundamental property with epistemic causatives: they both project a second mental space with a non-positive stance towards what the speaker/writer asserts. Secondly, in standard concessives the inference to be overridden is a straightforward causal one, but in some cases it is itself an instance of epistemic, argumentative causality; so we can still distinguish between 'content' and 'epistemic' concessives, in terms of the content of the background mental spaces involved.

A note of caution is in order at this point. The main reason for undertaking this exercise was a theoretical one. We saw that attempts to formulate the connection between concessivity and causality produced some paradoxes. By assuming a causal inference in a background mental space projected by *although*, one of these problems has now been solved, I claim. But that does not necessarily mean that the difference between 'content' and 'epistemic' concessivity—the difference in the number of projected mental spaces—is a very important one for the way concessive clauses are used in discourse. In fact, I expect that the distinction is far less important in actual practice than in the case of content and epistemic causals. The reason is precisely that the 'step' from content to epistemic causality is one from interpretation at the level of an object of conceptualization and its construal, to the level of intersubjective coordination. But concessives are inherently always functioning in the latter dimension;[18] that does not change with the move from 'content' to 'epistemic' concessivity. In the course of the discussion I claimed that the function of *although* was to acknowledge the validity of a causal inference 'p, therefore q', while nevertheless inviting the addressee to adopt ¬q, implying that there must be very good reasons (overriding p) to do so. A speaker/writer has just asserted something or wants to assert something, and foresees a possible objection; *although* allows her to acknowledge and try to override that objection immediately, thereby managing her relationship with the addressee. This is certainly the primary point; whether the objection that the speaker/writer foresees involves straightforward causal reasoning or more indirect, epistemic reasoning is not the most important aspect to acknowledge. This does not mean that the result produced here is unimportant, but it is useful to keep the background of the original problem in mind.

So let us now turn to the other problem: that of the asymmetry in the behavior of *although* and *because* in their interaction with negation.

---

[18] A good illustration that this is indeed the case, also when more uses of concessive relations are taken into consideration, is Pander Maat (1999b), which is partly based on the argumentative approach of (Anscombre and) Ducrot, as well as some other literature that is at least roughly compatible with it.

4.2.4 Concessivity and negated causality

Negation of causality and the source of scope-phenomena

What I intend to show is that the intersubjectivity approach to negation and concession also accounts, in fact quite directly, for the connection between concessivity and negated causality, and the limits of this connection. The first thing to look at is the (partial) overlap between the wide-scope interpretation of (3) and the narrow-scope interpretation of (4), repeated here for convenience:

(3) The house is no less comfortable because it dispenses with air-conditioning.
(4) The house is no less comfortable, although it dispenses with air-conditioning.

What the relevant interpretations of these sentences have in common is that an alternative space is set up in which a causal inference 'the house is less comfortable' (q) is licensed on the basis of a topos of the type 'Air-conditioning normally makes a house more comfortable', and that this inference is overridden in the conceptualizer's space, while the statement that the house dispenses with air-conditioning holds in both spaces. The abstract mental-space representation (i.e. without indicating which aspects are triggered by which linguistic elements) of this interpretation is given in Figure 4.9: both spaces contain the topos, and the proposition that the house dispenses with air-conditioning; the latter is the basis for the conclusion that it is less comfortable in Space$_2$, which is overridden in Space$_1$.

It is evident from this configuration that the concessive interpretation of (3) entails that the element *because* marks a causal relationship in *another*

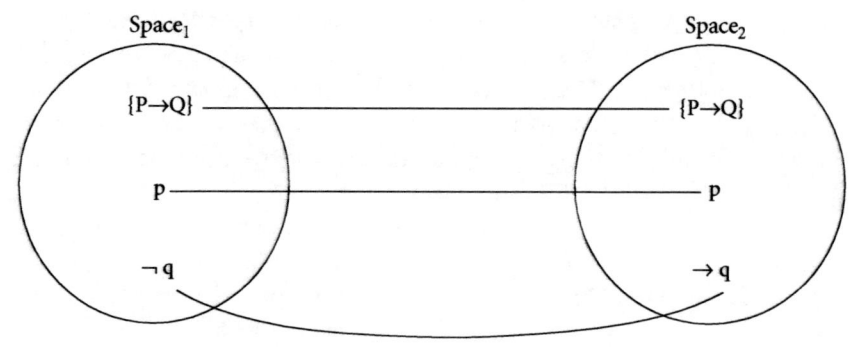

Space$_1$ \{P→Q\} \qquad Space$_2$ \{P→Q\}

P \qquad P

¬q \qquad →q

topos: 'Lack of air-conditioning (P) makes accommodation less comfortable (Q)'

p = 'The house dispenses with air-conditioning'
q = 'The house is less comfortable'

FIGURE 4.9. Common mental-space configuration for (3) and (4)

Space₁ {P→Q}   Space₂ {P→Q}

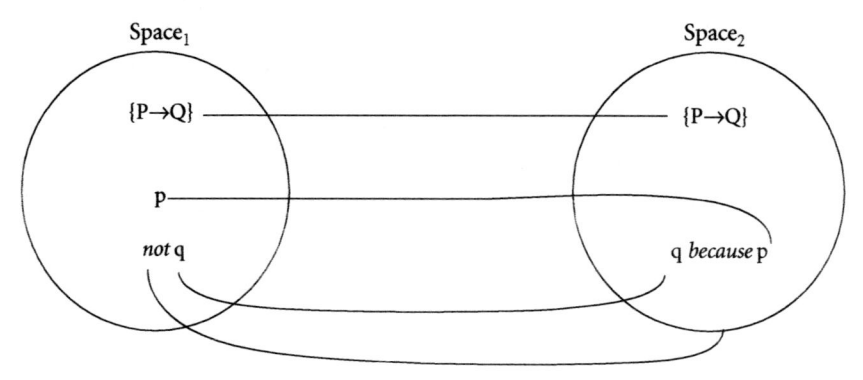

p

not q   q *because* p

topos: 'Lack of air-conditioning (P) makes accommodation less comfortable (Q)'

p = 'The house dispenses with air-conditioning'
q = 'The house is less comfortable'

FIGURE 4.10. Mental-space configuration for (3) (*The house is no less comfortable because it dispenses with air-conditioning*)

mental space than the conceptualizer's: in the concessive reading, *q because p* corresponds to the inference 'p, therefore q' in Space₂. The conceptual structure of Figure 4.9 is linked to the linguistic material in (3) as indicated in Figure 4.10.

The element *not* projects a second mental space, in the standard way. In the concessive reading of (3) the causal conjunction must mark a relation in another mental space than the conceptualizer's; the latter is the one containing the denial of q. This explains why it is the so-called wide-scope interpretation of negation that corresponds to concessivity: in this interpretation the *because*-relation cannot hold in the same space as the negation, thus it is itself negated. Note, furthermore, that Figure 4.10 actually gives a more accurate picture of the interpretation than a one-dimensional formula for wide scope negation of the type 'not (q because p)', as the latter does not explicitly indicate that 'not q' is actually asserted in the mental space of conceptualizer 1.

Note that the interpretation of the element *because* does not *have* to be assigned to another mental space when it occurs in the context of negation. But when it is interpreted as belonging to the same mental space as *not*, then the same conceptualizer takes responsibility for the negation and for the causal inference, and a so-called narrow-scope interpretation is the result.

By itself the causal connective *because* does not indicate the relevance of multiple viewpoints, but in a context of two mental spaces it may apparently be used to mark causality in either one of these, as long as the overall interpretation of the utterance does not produce internal contradictions. In other words: it is not a part of the function of *because* to impose constraints on the constellation of mental spaces associated with the utterance in which it occurs, and this can become especially manifest when more than one space is available, for independent reasons such as the use of negation. Another example of a causal connective demonstrating this possibility is the following, from a Dutch newspaper text:

(35) De nieuwe tariefstructuur is marktconform, maar daarom
 The new price-structure is market-conformable but therefore
 niet per definitie klantvriendelijk.
 not by definition customer-friendly
 'The new price structure is in accordance with market principles, but therefore not by definition customer-friendly.'

The causal connective *daarom* ('that's why', 'therefore') indicates a causal connection between being in accordance with market principles and being customer-friendly. The customer-friendliness is denied by *not* in the same clause, while the conformity to market principles is acknowledged in the first. So the causal inference must be assigned to another mental space than that of conceptualizer 1. I will return to this kind of case in section 4.3.2; here it suffices to show that the kind of configuration depicted in Figure 4.10 is not isolated to a single element, or a single language.

The conceptual structure represented in Figure 4.9 may also be marked in other ways; in particular, as in sentence (4). A concessive connective like *although* is itself an indication for projecting a mental space containing a causal inference that is overridden in Space$_1$. That is, the conceptual structure that is evoked by marking causality in a projected space—as in (3) and (35)—may also be evoked by a single element that *conventionally* indicates this structure; that is, a concessive connective. As shown in Figure 4.11, the mental-space configuration evoked by *although* in (4) shares its structure with the constellation in Figure 4.10: the same conceptual relationships (depicted in a general way in Figure 4.9) are marked in linguistically different ways.[19]

Thus the connections between causality and concessivity that lie at the basis of König's proposal (1991) appear to be produced by the mechanisms of the intersubjectivity approach automatically. But what is especially important is that it also follows from this approach that the relationship is not one of

---

[19] The elements *not* in the main clause and the conjunction *although* relate to the same mental space; cf. the discussion of (21) and Fig. 4.5 in Sect. 4.2.2.

Discourse connections 187

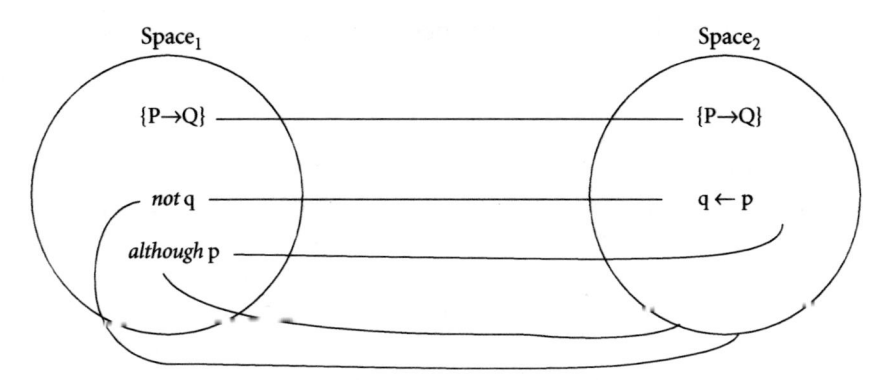

```
     Space₁                                    Space₂
   ⌒⌒⌒⌒⌒                                    ⌒⌒⌒⌒⌒
  {P→Q} ─────────────────────────────── {P→Q}

   not q  ──────────────────────────────── q ← p

  although p
```

topos: 'Lack of air-conditioning (P) makes accommodation less comfortable (Q)'

p = 'The house dispenses with air-conditioning'
q = 'The house is less comfortable'

FIGURE 4.11. Mental-space configuration for (4) (*The house is no less comfortable, although it dispenses with air-conditioning*)

complete duality, for a reason that may now appear very simple. What would it amount to, in this view, to try to negate a concessive relation? This would have to involve construing the mental space of conceptualizer 1 as opposed to both mental spaces involved in the concessive relation, but that is impossible, since one of these two is also the mental space of conceptualizer 1.

Negation only adds a mental space, it does not remove one. It is therefore impossible to construct a conceptual configuration that does not involve mental spaces with different epistemic stances from the multiplication of mental spaces. But that is what we would need in order to get a causal reading. As shown in the previous section, a basic qualitative difference between causal and concessive connectives is that the causal ones do not necessarily involve the construction of multiple spaces with different epistemic stances, while the concessive ones do. Once we have a concessive sentence, we have mental spaces with different epistemic stances, and there is no way of getting rid of them.

Negation of concession produces contradiction
On the contrary, by embedding a mental-space configuration under negation, one can only get more and more complicated constellations. Recall that a sentence such as (7)—an attempt to negate a concessive sentence—not only resists a causal interpretation, but is virtually uninterpretable:

(7) ??It is not the case that John failed his exams although he worked hard.

Interestingly, this is precisely a situation in which the intersubjectivity approach derives a contradiction. The concessive sentence *p although q* projects a mental space in which p is valid and one in which it is not (q licensing ¬p). Including *although q* in the scope of the same negation operator has the consequence that the new Space$_1$ contradicts both p and ¬p, which is inconsistent. In the case of (7): the denial of *John failed his exams* projects conceptualizer 2 as committed to 'John failed his exams', and the simultaneous denial of *(although) he worked hard* projects the same conceptualizer 2 as committed to 'John did not fail his exams', since *although* acknowledges the inference 'he worked hard, so he passed' as valid. And since the orientation in Space$_1$ is the mirror image of that in Space$_2$, conceptualizer 1 is committed to both contradictory propositions as well. The highly problematic status of (7) is precisely what is to be expected in the intersubjectivity approach, which otherwise has the virtue of avoiding a contradiction where it should (see Sect. 4.2.2).

In (7) an attempt is made to embed an *although*-sentence in a matrix clause of a negative complementation construction. The failure of this attempt, for general reasons, does not mean that an *although*-sentence could never be the complement of a negative CT-clause (in the terminology of Chapter 3). The problem with (7) is that it evokes a configuration in which conceptualizer 1 adopts a negative stance towards both conjuncts, which produces a contradiction. In complementation in general, the speaker/writer invites the addressee to entertain the content of the complement in the way marked in the CT-clause, and thus she is by default assumed to align her perspective with that of the onstage conceptualizer (see Ch. 3). And if an *although*-sentence in a complement clause can be taken to hold in the Ground as well, there should be no problem. First, consider the positive case in (36),[20] with either the CT-verb *denken* ('to think') or *beseffen* ('to realize':)

(36) De regering denkt/beseft dat, hoewel de intenties van de wet en het verdrag dezelfde zijn, de systematiek van de wet beter is.
'The government thinks/realizes that, although the intentions of the law and the treaty are the same, the structure of the law is better.'

With either verb the addressee is invited to adopt a more positive attitude towards the law than towards the treaty (as the government does), while acknowledging that they are of similar import. As we have seen in Chapter 3, Section 3.3.4, some CT-verbs give specific indications about the relation

---

[20] Modeled on an actual example of which the CT-clause was: *Wij zijn van mening dat...* ('It is our opinion that...').

between the onstage conceptualizer's mental space and the Ground; whereas *to think* simply puts the fact that a thought is being entertained on stage, *to realize* specifies that this thought is already accepted in the Ground (it is 'factive'). The combination of *think* with negation therefore invites the addressee not to adopt a positive stance towards the content of the complement—the combination functions, so to speak, holistically as a negation operator[21]—but the combination of *realize* with negation specifically dissociates the perspective of the onstage conceptualizer from the Ground, maintaining the relation between the complement and the Ground. Consider the difference between (37) and (38):

(37) ??The government does not think that, although the intentions of the law and the treaty are the same, the structure of the law is better.

(38) The government does not realize that, although the intentions of the law and the treaty are the same, the structure of the law is better.

The conceptual configuration that (37) attempts to evoke is basically the same as that in (7), which is inconsistent. And indeed (37) is hard to process, it is not clear what it should mean. On the other hand, (38) is not difficult to understand at all. The reason is that, *realize* being factive, the entire *although*-sentence is presented as valid in the Ground, where it functions just like any 'ordinary' concessive sentence: the speaker/writer invites the addressee to prefer the law over the treaty, despite that fact that the intentions of both are the same.

The explanation for the observation that wide scope of negation over concessive clauses is impossible is ultimately based in the idea that inconsistency within a single perspective is not allowed. The difference observed here confirms this analysis. A concessive sentence may certainly be embedded in a negative CT-clause, but only if that produces a configuration in the Ground without internal contradictions in one of the mental spaces involved. Conflicts *between* mental spaces are not a problem; managing those is precisely what negation and concession are instruments for. But if certain combinations of them produce a contradiction within a single perspective, the system certainly breaks down.

---

[21] In view of these elementary observations, it seems worthwhile to reconsider the phenomenon known as 'negative raising' (Horn 1978, 1989) from the present perspective. This phenomenon concerns the (near?) equivalence of 'I don't think that p' and 'I think that not p', as opposed to 'He does not know that p' vs. 'He knows that not p'. As Boye and Harder (2007) indicate, negative raising is also relevant in connection with the analysis of complementation. Interestingly, Bolinger (1968: 22–5) briefly suggests a connection between this phenomenon and that of '*Wh*-extraction', discussed in Chapter 3, Section 3.3.5, as a manifestation of more general connections between negation and interrogation.

We now also have an answer to the second question posed at the end of section 4.2.2: What is the explanation of the asymmetry in the behavior of causality and concessivity in interaction with negation? The answer is that it is also a consequence of the inherent asymmetry between negation and concession on the one hand, and causality on the other. The former always operate in the dimension of intersubjective coordination, the latter does not, at least not necessarily. The addition of a negation operator does not 'remove' any available perspective, it only serves to manage the relations between one and another.

With hindsight, the problem in previous approaches seems to lie, as before, in an implicit single-viewpoint conception of negation, as no more than the reversal of truth value. This creates the illusion that two negations, or negation and concession, should cancel each other out. Indeed, if we were to consider negation and concession as operations on the relation between a single conceptualizer and the world, we would not be able to arrive at the present result. As before, I take this as further confirmation of the crucial role of the level of intersubjective coordination in the way these linguistic elements work.

4.3 Arguing, reasoning, and construing causes

4.3.1 *Causal connectives imposing constraints on perspectives*

In the preceding discussion, a number of assumptions were made about the ways causality may be marked linguistically and how this interacts with different mental-space configurations. These deserve more explicit attention. Recall the possibility of interpreting sentence (3) in a way that resembles a concessive one:

(3) The house is no less comfortable because it dispenses with air-conditioning.

When we interpret the *because*-clause as included 'in the scope of negation', I argued in Section 4.2.4, the causal inference indicated by *because* takes place in another mental space than that of the speaker/writer (see Fig. 4.10). Apparently, this is allowed for the word *because*; it does not as such seem to impose specific constraints on the mental space configuration associated with the utterance in which it occurs. Precisely because *although* does itself impose such constraints, it is much more restricted in its possible interactions with negation.

This seems to be in line with an earlier observation; namely, that the English word *because* is compatible with both a 'content' and an 'epistemic' reading of the relationship between the conjuncts. An 'epistemic' relationship implies that the speaker/writer sets up a secondary mental space in which his assertion is (at least) not fully accepted yet (see the discussion of epistemic causality and perspectives in Section 4.2.3); the word *because* is compatible with such a mental space configuration, but also with other ones, in which different epistemic stances play no role. The question is whether causal connectives are generally neutral in the way *because* is. In fact, there are good reasons to doubt this.

Dutch want *and* omdat *(and* aangezien*)*
Dutch translations of English *because*-sentences often permit a choice between *omdat* (with 'subordinate' word order) and *want* (with 'main-clause' word order, i.e. the finite verb in second position). Not only *omdat* but also *want* is quite common (unlike *for* in English). However, it is well known that there are cases in which only *want* seems to be possible (see De Vries 1971; Van Belle 1989), and this class includes the cases of epistemically used *because* in English discussed above. First, this is true for the cases of abductive reasoning; consider the possible Dutch translations of (12) and (13):

(39) Jan is geslaagd voor zijn tentamens, $\begin{cases} \text{want hij heeft hard gewerkt.} \\ \text{omdat hij hard gewerkt heeft.} \end{cases}$

'John passed his exams because he worked hard.' (= (12))

(40) Jan heeft hard gewerkt, $\begin{cases} \text{want hij is geslaagd voor zijn tentamens.} \\ \text{*omdat hij geslaagd is voor zijn tentamens.} \end{cases}$

'John worked hard, because he passed his exams.' (= (13))

The content reading allows for marking with both *want* and *omdat* in Dutch, but the epistemic reading only allows for *want*. Secondly, this is also true for other 'indirect' argumentative uses of *because*, as in the Dutch translation of (31):

(41) Jammer als 't niet duidelijk is,
$\begin{cases} \text{want 't is laat en ik heb geen zin om 't uit te leggen.} \\ \text{*omdat 't laat is en ik geen zin heb om 't uit te leggen.} \end{cases}$
'Too bad if it isn't clear, because it's late and I don't feel like explaining it.' (= (31))

Similarly, in the original Dutch example (32), repeated below, only *want* can be used; *omdat* would be unacceptable:

(32) In het laatste decennium is onze kennis van het universum dramatisch uitgebreid, want dat mogen we wel stellen.

'Over the last decade, our knowledge of the universe has expanded dramatically, because we may safely assert that.'

Recall that I analyzed the use of a clause to support a statement as always involving the projection of a mental space with a non-positive epistemic stance towards this statement (first part of Sect. 4.2.3). Given the distribution of *want* observed above, the hypothesis suggests itself that evoking this mental space configuration is the *conventional* function of *want* in Dutch. In other words, what the construction *p want q* in Dutch marks is, in terms of the construal configuration: 'the attitude of conceptualizer 2 towards p may not be sufficiently positive, and q should strengthen it', whether the argument consists of an abductive inference or another, more or less direct, form of support. By the use of *want* in (32), for example, the speaker/writer acknowledges that the addressee may not immediately accept the import of the statement, and the explicit claim that the speaker/writer knows what she is saying is an attempt to increase the addressee's willingness to 'go along' with it. We have also seen that causes may always be used to support a claim, and we have seen that apparent content sentences such as (39) in principle allow for the use of both *want* and *omdat*; in a way, this can be seen as something to be expected: the use of a causal relation as an argument could precisely be reinforced by a marking with *want*. So suppose *want* evokes a mental-space configuration as in Figure 4.12.

Structurally, that is apart from the contents of the mental spaces, this is similar to the configuration in Figure 4.7, for abductively used *because*. There is no specific constraint on the direction of the topos used to support the inference from q to p. This may be parallel, in which case we have a 'causality-based' argument (cf. the discussion of epistemic causality in Section

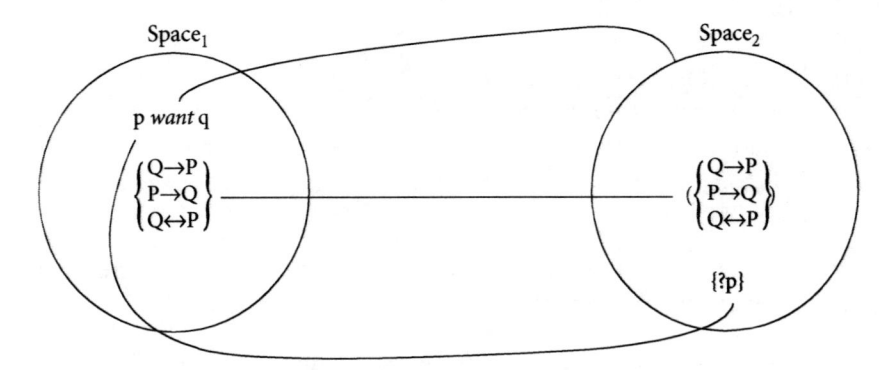

FIGURE 4.12. Mental-space configuration associated with Dutch *want*

4.2.3), or reverse, which would come down to an abductive argument; of course, the same (shared) model must be assumed to be operative in both spaces on any specific occasion of use. The difference with English *because* is that this configuration is evoked conventionally, as a consequence of the use of the linguistic element *want*; in Figure 4.12 this is indicated by the line from *want* to Space$_2$. In this respect, this element differs from *p omdat q*, which suggests that the status of p in the Ground is unproblematic.[22] Can we adduce further evidence, beyond the fact that it accounts for the distributional observations above, that *want* is indeed conventionally associated with Figure 4.12? An obvious area to look at is the way *want* interacts with negation.

First, recall from Chapter 2 (Sects. 2.2.2 and 2.4) that sentential negation differs from morphological negation (with the prefix *un-*) in that only the former evokes a constellation of mental spaces with opposite epistemic stances. So if in principle a choice exists between using one or the other (*not happy* vs. *unhappy*, *not fair* vs. *unfair*, etc.), then the above hypothesis predicts a relative preference for the use of *want* after a clause with sentential negation, and a relative preference for *omdat* after morphological negation. This prediction was tested on copular sentences with adjectival predicate nominals and followed by a *want-* or *omdat*-clause in the Eindhoven Corpus; only sentences with adjectives that allow for *un*-prefixation were included in the set. The total number of these sentences is 59. Examples of the patterns predicted to be preferred are given in (42) and (43):

(42) Bovendien was het terrein onbruikbaar omdat over de hele lengte
Moreover was the terrain unusable *omdat* over the entire length
een brede weg loopt.
a wide road runs
'Moreover, the terrain was unusable because a wide road stretches over the entire length.'

(43) Eigenlijk is dat niet fair, want het rantsoen voor beiden is toch
Actually is that not fair *want* the ration for both is yet
al karig genoeg.
already meager enough
'Actually this is not fair, because the ration for both is meager enough just as it is.'

---

[22] Leaving aside, for the time being, whether this is a conventional aspect of the meaning of *omdat*, or a consequence of the fact that it is in opposition to *want*. I will have a bit more to say about the meaning of *omdat* below.

TABLE 4.1. Correlation of morphological and sentential negation with *omdat* and *want* in Eindhoven Corpus (Dutch)

	omdat		want		Total
	N	%	N	%	
on-adjective	16	62	10	38	26
niet adjective	7	21	26	79	33

$\chi 2 = 9.94$; df = 1; $p < 0.01$.

Table 4.1 gives the relevant numbers.

The table shows that the prediction is borne out. Almost 80 per cent of the relevant clauses with the sentential negation *niet* are followed by a causal clause marked with *want*. In the clauses with the morphological negation *on-*, this happens in less than half of that percentage. This difference is considerable, and statistically significant.[23]

Second, we might look at the possibilities of interaction between the connectives and sentential negation directly. In discussing the connection between concessivity and negated causality (Sect. 4.2.4), we have already encountered a relevant example, (10):

(10) Jan is niet meteen de beste kandidaat omdat hij
John is not straight-away the best candidate *omdat* he
gepromoveerd is.
promoted is
'John is not the best candidate just because he has a Ph.D.'

Like the English connective *because*, Dutch *omdat* can be used to indicate a causal inference in the background mental space projected by negation in the

---

[23] Interestingly, the differences in Table 4.1 are even bigger than those for *en* ('and') and *maar* ('but'), for which a similar prediction was made, in view of the contrast-marking function of *maar*. The results are displayed in Table 4.2.

TABLE 4.2. Correlation of morphological and sentential negation with *en* and *maar* in Eindhoven Corpus (Dutch)

	en		maar		Total
	N	%	N	%	
on-adjective	45	63	26	37	71
niet adjective	63	48	68	52	131

$\chi 2 = 4.33$; df = 1; $p < 0.05$.

result clause, which produces a concessive-like reading for the whole sentence: John may not be the best candidate despite the fact that he has a Ph.D. In the case of *although* we could show that this connective inherently projects a background mental space with an opposite epistemic stance, and that this implies that an *although*-clause cannot itself be negated. Assuming that *want* projects a similar background mental space, what should we expect in this regard?

Answering this question is complicated by the fact that *want* may only introduce main clauses (in present-day Dutch), so that the clause could never be in the scope of a negation operator in another clause. However, the same question applies to certain subordinate clauses.[24] Present-day Dutch has a subordinating conjunction, *aangezien*, for which it has been established that its meaning resembles that of *want* much more closely than that of *omdat* (Van Belle 1989; Degand and Pander Maat 2003: 184, 195; Pit 2003);[25] it appears to correspond rather well to English *since* (in its non-temporal use; see Dancygier and Sweetser 2000: 126 ff.).

So consider a construction with a negative result clause of the general form $\neg p$ *want/aangezien* q. Could q be included in the operation of the negation? Obviously not, as it would immediately destroy the possibility of using q as support for the result clause. In a somewhat more technical way, this conclusion can also be reached by considering what the effect of including q in the negation operation in the result clause would be in the constellation of Figure 4.12. First, notice that both p and P must now everywhere be read as $\neg p$ and $\neg P$, respectively. For the sake of simplicity, assume that the topos involved is straightforward; that is, $Q \rightarrow \neg P$ (producing a causality-based argument). Negating q in Space$_1$ now implies the presence of q (the opposite of $\neg q$) in Space$_2$, where it would license the inference $\neg p$—which is precisely what the speaker/writer states in the first place. But this contradicts the assumption, incorporated in this analysis, that conceptualizer 2 has a non-positive stance towards what the speaker asserts; the whole point of the argumentative causal sentence is the presence of '?($\neg p$)' in Space$_2$. Alternatively, we may observe that in such a case Space$_1$ is supposed to contain both $\neg p$ (result clause) and

---

[24] It seems quite plausible that the increase in use of *want* for argumentation may have contributed to its developing into a coordinating conjunction in late medieval and early modern Dutch (Burridge 1993; Van Megen 2002), a development that German *weil* now seems to be undergoing in similar uses (see Keller 1995).

[25] Degand and Pander Maat (2003) also postulate some semantic difference between *aangezien* and *want*, having to do with their scalar interpretation of the meanings of the connectives (see the discussion of inferential and non-inferential causal relations in section 4.3.2 below), but they agree that *aangezien* is in any case closer in meaning to *want* than to *omdat*. See also Pit (2003: 287), who assigns them, 'tentatively', the same degree of subjectivity.

¬q (causal clause included in the scope of negation), which destroys (the relevance of) the topos (Q → ¬P). Either way, we always end up with a contradiction in a single mental space, just as in the case of including *although* in the scope of negation. The prediction must be, then, that it is impossible to get a concessive reading of a version of (10) in which *omdat* has been replaced by *want* or *aangezien*; and it is, for both cases:

(44) Jan is niet meteen   de beste kandidaat want hij is gepromoveerd
     John is not straight-away the best candidate *want* he is promoted

(45) Jan is niet meteen   de beste kandidaat aangezien hij
     John is not straight-away the best candidate since   he
     gepromoveerd is.
     promoted   is
     ('John is not the best candidate, since he has a Ph.D.')

If anything, (44) and (45) can only mean that John's having a Ph.D. is the argument for concluding that he should not be hired.

Notice that the following *omdat*-sentence is ambiguous:

(46) Omdat je   conditie beroerd is, hoef je   nog niet zo hard te
     Because your condition miserable is need you still not so hard to
     gaan trainen.
     go   train

   (a) 'Just because your condition is miserable, you don't have to start training so hard.'

   (b) 'Since your condition is miserable, you don't have to start training so hard yet.'

Interpretation (a) is a concessive one. What it suggests is that the addressee has the idea that his bad condition is a good reason to start power training; he is apparently operating with a topos of the kind: 'The worse one's condition, the more reason to seriously do something about it'. The speaker/writer acknowledges the validity of this topos and the inference it licenses, but still suggests that the addressee should not overdo things. The causal inference is particularly located in the addressee's mental space: '*You* may think that your bad condition is a reason for training so hard, but I disagree.' The relation between the mental spaces evoked by the whole sentence is the same as in the explicitly concessive clause (47):

(47) Hoewel je conditie beroerd is, hoef je nog niet zo hard
    Although your condition miserable is need you still not so hard
    te gaan trainen.
    to go train
    'Although your condition is miserable, you don't have to start training so hard yet.'

We have seen before that the abstract conceptual structure associated with the combination of a concession and a negative statement (see Fig. 4.9) can be implemented linguistically both with a causal and a concessive connective. Here we have another instantiation in Dutch.[26]

In interpretation (*b*) of (46) the primary responsibility for the causal inference is with the speaker/writer. She presents this as a reason not to start the training at too high a level. Here the topos involved is something like 'The worse one's condition, the more reason to avoid over-exertion'.

The interesting point is that replacing *omdat* with *aangezien* in (46) has the effect of reducing the number of readings to one, removing the concessive-like interpretation; see (48):

(48) Aangezien je conditie beroerd is, hoef je nog niet zo hard
    Since your condition miserable is need you still not so hard
    te gaan trainen.
    to go train
    'Since your condition is miserable, you don't have to start training so hard yet.'

Obviously, the topos that a bad condition is a good reason to start training hard cannot be applied here; only the idea that it is a good reason to avoid over-exertion can.

The conclusion is that not only negative connectives (those indicating relations of opposition and concession) project mental spaces with distinct epistemic stances, but that certain causal connectives may do so as well.

4.3.2 *Causal connectives and the structure of the construal configuration*

On the basis of the analysis in the previous section we can use the interaction with negation as a criterion for testing whether other causal connectives

---

[26] This is not to say that there may not be functional differences between (47) and (46) in its concessive reading (*a*). Intuitively, it looks as if (47) presents the addressee's bad condition more as *shared* knowledge than (46), and locates the source of the modal force of the result clause more in the speaker/writer than in the addressee. Future research will have to show whether these and possibly other factors really play a role in the actual use of the patterns involved.

impose constraints of this kind on a mental-space configuration or not. In Section 4.2.4 we have already encountered a case of a forward causal connective, namely (35), that can mark a causal link in a background mental space:

(35) De   nieuwe tariefstructuur is marktconform,   maar daarom niet
     The new   price-structure is market-conformable but   therefore not
     per definitie   klantvriendelijk.
     by definition customer-friendly
     'The new price structure is in accordance with market principles, but therefore not by definition customer-friendly.'

The conceptual structure associated with this usage is similar to a concessive relation, and it can indeed also be expressed with a concessive conjunction, with the difference that the force of the second conjunct in (35') is weaker than in (35) (cf. the discussion of (19) and (20) in Section 4.2.2):

(35') De   nieuwe tariefstructuur is marktconform,   hoewel   niet per
      The new   price-structure is market-conformable although not   by
      definitie   klantvriendelijk.
      definition customer-friendly
      'The new price structure is in accordance with market principles, although not by definition customer-friendly.'

In particular, the expression *maar daarom nog niet* (lit. 'but therefore still not') seems to have become specialized for this concessive-like use, often also with elliptic clauses as in (35). An example is (49):

(49) Je   conditie is beroerd,   maar daarom   nog niet hopeloos.
     Your condition is miserable but   therefore still not hopeless
     'Your condition is miserable, but not therefore hopeless.'

But other combinations, also with complete sentences, can be found as well; (50) is an example:

(50) Wie   zou   het geloven?—Niemand. Toch was het daarom   niet
     Who would it   believe   Nobody   Yet was it therefore not
     minder waar.
     less   true
     'Who would believe it?—Nobody. Yet this did not make it less true.'

Two other common, one-word forward causal connectives in Dutch are *dus* and *daardoor*. How do these interact with negation? Can they also indicate causal reasoning in other mental spaces than that of conceptualizer 1? Let us look at *dus* first. This is generally recognized as the marker that is most appropriate for introducing conclusions (and translated accordingly as *so* in English). In view of what we have seen above, we may therefore expect that it cannot be included in the scope of a negation operator in its own clause. Indeed, replacing *daarom* with *dus* in (35), (49), and (50) leads to strange sentences, witness (51), (52), and (53), respectively:[27]

(51) De nieuwe tariefstructuur is marktconform, maar dus niet
 The new price-structure is market-conformable but so not
 per definitie klantvriendelijk.
 by definition customer-friendly

(52) ? Je conditie is beroerd, maar dus nog niet hopeloos.
 Your condition is miserable but so still not hopeless

(53) ? Wie zou het geloven?—Niemand. Toch was het dus niet minder waar.
 Who would it believe Nobody Yet was it so not less true

These versions produce an impression of something contradictory. The reader tries to construct the second conjunct as something both that contrasts with the first and that follows from it. That is: the addressee apparently understands that the link indicated by *dus* is one that the speaker/writer takes responsibility for, and that is not to be attributed to conceptualizer 2. The addressee is invited to somehow find something in the first conjunct that serves as a basis for accepting the force of the second; that is, the argumentative orientation of the second conjunct must somehow be construed as *parallel* to the first, which is not necessary in (35), (49), and (50). The only difference between these and (51), (52), and (53) is that the latter have *dus* instead of *daarom*; so apparently the connective *daarom* in a negative clause is compatible with a non-parallel orientation of the connected clauses, while *dus* is not. This can be explained in a straightforward manner by assuming that the structure of the mental-space configuration associated with *dus* is analogous to that for *want* (see Fig. 4.12), with the order of argument and conclusion reversed, as in Figure 4.13.

With the use of *p dus q* the speaker/writer acknowledges that the addressee's epistemic stance towards q may be insufficiently positive, and tries to strengthen it by claiming that it is licensed by p, in view of some topos that she assumes can at least be activated by the addressee.[28] Given this

---

[27] Notice that it is not possible in this case to attribute the exclusion of *dus* from the scope of negation to its syntactic position (cf. the discussion of *want* and *aangezien* in Sect. 4.3.1).

[28] As before, I want to stress that this is not meant as a comprehensive semantic analysis of *dus*, only as the claim that, whatever other aspects may be relevant, it operates in the configuration of Figure 4.13. In fact, I believe there may be two *dus*-constructions in Dutch that are not entirely equivalent (a

200   *Discourse connections*

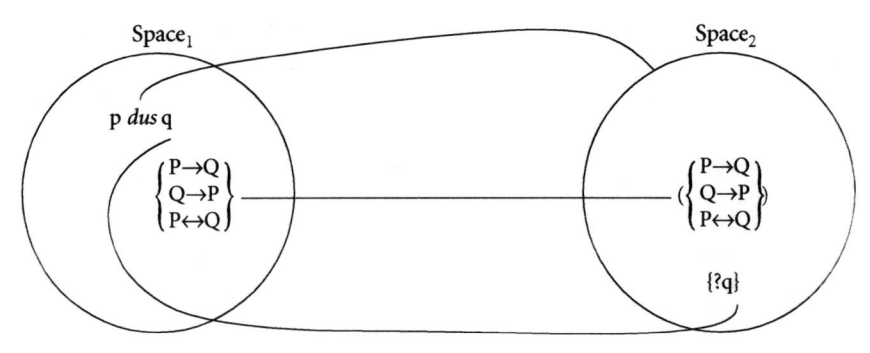

FIGURE 4.13. Mental-space configuration associated with Dutch *dus*

configuration, the facts above follow in the same way as those for *want*: the *dus*-conjunct cannot be included in the scope of negation without producing a contradiction in at least one mental space.

Notice that it is not inherently impossible to interpret the same situation as licensed by one inference and as opposing another. Indeed, the following (attested) examples show that it is, in principle and in practice, perfectly possible for the same conjunct to be marked by *maar* ('but') and by *dus* ('so') (in example (54) the percentage figure refers to the quality of grapes used to produced champagne):

(54) Wat onder de 90% zit, is aardig maar dus niet super.
     What under the 90% sits is nice   but   so not super
     'Everything below 90% is nice, but not superb then.'

(55) [We hebben nog geen webwinkel.]
     In principe kunnen er   wel modellen vanaf de foto's
     In principle can   there PRT models from the photographs
     besteld worden, maar dus niet via internet.
     ordered become but so not via internet

distinction not present in English). One is *dus* used as a conjunction of complete clauses, the other is *dus* used as a constituent of the second conjunct (and traditionally labeled 'adverb'). It seems to me that the former marks less distance between the speaker/writer and the onstage conceptualizer than the latter, in view of the fact that the first of the following two sentences is considerably more natural than the second.

(i) Het is weer droog, dus ik denk dat ik naar huis ga.
    It is again dry,   so I think that I to   home go
    'It has stopped raining, so I think I'll go home.'
(ii) ?Het is weer droog, dus denk ik dat ik naar huis ga.
     It   is again dry,   so think I that I to   home go

But further research is required, taking findings like those from Pander Maat and Degand (2001) into account, before any firm conclusions can be drawn here.

'[We do not have a webstore yet.] In principle it is possible to order models from the pictures, but not through the Internet then.'

In (54) it is the qualification in the free relative clause meaning 'Everything below 90%' that provides the basis for the conclusion 'not superb'. This is marked by *dus*, projecting conceptualizer 2 as possibly not yet convinced of this conclusion. And it is the positively oriented qualification 'nice' that provides the basis for a contrast with the same negatively oriented conclusion 'not superb'. Thus the mental spaces projected by *maar* and *dus* are the same: conceptualizer 2 may, mistakenly, think as positively about the products from places scoring 89 per cent as about champagne from a 100 per cent vineyard. This is the only possible reading for (54); there is no way to read *dus* as indicating a possible inference of conceptualizer 2 (e.g. 'It is below 90%, so it is superb' is not a sensible inference). This is exactly the configuration to be expected according to the above analysis.

Example (55) is similar, except that it shows that the basis for the conclusion marked with *dus* need not be contained in the first conjunct of the *dus*-sentence itself. Here it is to be found in the previous sentence: the absence of the webstore is the basis for the conclusion 'no orders through the Internet', while the first conjunct of the *dus*-sentence itself (one can order a dress without visiting the shop in person) provides the basis for the contrast with the same conclusion. The structure of the mental-space configuration associated with this case is the same as the previous one.

Thus there is a difference between *dus* and *daarom* in the way they conventionally relate to the construal configuration. Whereas *daarom* marks an inference as accessible to the conceptualizers in the Ground, it imposes no specific constraints on the relationship between the two. It will often serve to get the addressee to adopt the inference and the conclusion, but its validity may be restricted to one mental space, and contradicted in the other (thus allowing it to appear 'in the scope of' negation). An instance of *dus*, on the other hand, indicates an attempt to manage the intersubjective coordination relation as part of its conventional function; it evokes a conceptual configuration with distinct epistemic stances towards some thought. In view of the discussion in Section 4.3.1, a parallel characterization may be given of *omdat* and *want*, respectively. And the conclusion from Section 4.2 (esp. 4.2.4) was that concessive connectives cannot but evoke such a configuration, since they acknowledge the validity of an inference while overriding its conclusion. We may therefore view concessive connectives (English *although*, Dutch *hoewel*), Dutch *dus*, *want*, and *aangezien*, and presumably English *so* and *since*, as sharing the function, because of their conventional meanings, to 'profile' the

O: *Object of conceptualization:*

S: *Subject of conceptualization (Ground):*

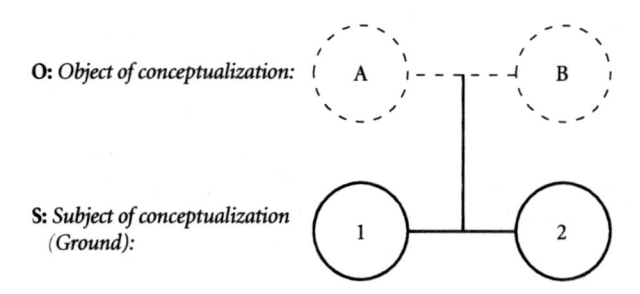

FIGURE 4.14. Conventional function of concession and of argumentative causal connectives: includes operation on intersubjective coordination

elements of the construal configuration that are marked with bold lines in Figure 4.14.

By evoking a difference between the epistemic stances of conceptualizers 1 and 2, these elements of the Ground are considered to be profiled, in the same way as is the case with negation (see Ch. 2, Sect. 2.3.3, Fig. 2.4). As connectives evoking causal inferences relating two situations A and B, they also impose constraints on the construal of these situations and the relation between them; in this additional respect, they differ from negation.

Inferential and non-inferential causal relations

As for Dutch *daarom* and *omdat*, the assumption is that it is not part of their conventional meaning to impose constraints on the intersubjective coordination relationship; this can be represented in terms of the construal configuration as indicated in Figure 4.15.

Unlike Dutch *omdat*, English *because*[29] can be used to mark argumentation, but it is not restricted to that kind of relation. So it is not a part of its conventional meaning to impose particular constraints on the relationship at level S, nor to impose such constraints at level O. While Dutch *omdat* construes the A–B relation as directly following from some topos, English *because* may also be used in abductive and other indirect inferences, where in Dutch only *want* fits. Thus it seems that the English word conventionally only profiles the part of the construal configuration that the representations of Figures 4.14 and 4.15 have in common, namely the construal relationship itself; it indicates *some* causal inference, no matter how it is supported by the object of conceptualization (see Fig. 4.16):

---

[29] I am uncertain about the possible ranges of use for the most widely used translations of *daarom* into English, namely *that's why* and *therefore*, which is why I leave them out here.

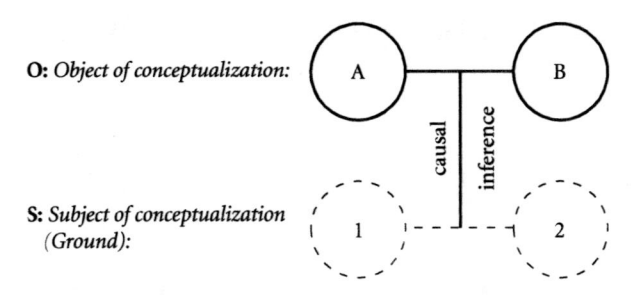

FIGURE 4.15. Conventional function of (some) non-argumentative causal connectives: no constraints on structure at level S

One might wonder whether the Dutch elements *daarom* and *omdat* should not be assumed to *only* impose constraints on the connection between A and B in the dimension of the object of conceptualization. However, there is a good reason to consider the representation in Figure 4.15 more adequate. This has to do with a difference between these and another class of causal connectives, of which *daardoor* (± 'as a result') is a prototypical instance. There are some contexts in which *dus* and *daarom*, as well as *daardoor*, can be used; an example is (56):[30]

(56) Ze   hadden flink   geoefend. Daardoor / Daarom   / Dus
     They had   soundly practiced As a result / That's why / So
     leverden de vragen   geen problemen op.
     produced the questions no   problems PRT
     'They had been practicing well. As a result,/That's why/So the questions did not pose any problems.'

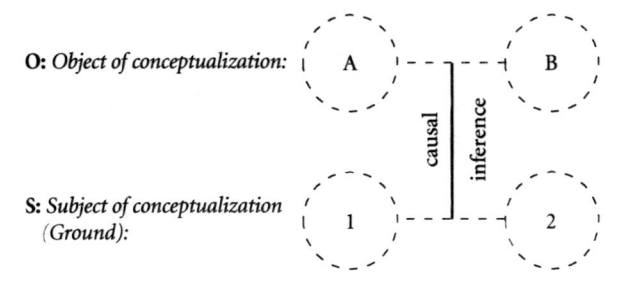

FIGURE 4.16. Conventional function of *because* not specifically tied to one level

[30] The original version (from *de Volkskrant* 1995) on which this example is modeled had *Daarom* ('That's why').

However, Pander Maat and Degand (2001) observe some interesting differences in certain specific kinds of context. First, with a precisely quantified result clause only *daardoor* appears to fit:

(57) Er   stond een harde wind. Daardoor / #Daarom   / #Dus
     There stood a   strong wind As a result / That's why / So
     zijn er   drie   pannen van   het dak   gevallen.
     are there three tiles   from the roof fallen
     'There was a strong wind. As a result,/#That's why/#So three tiles fell off the roof.'

All three connectives suggest a causal connection between the strong wind and the damage to the roof. But *daarom* and *dus*[31] additionally 'suggest that the consequence is entirely predictable from the cause' (ibid. 213); that is, as if there were some general rule licensing the inference that a strong wind leads to the fall of a specific number of tiles.

Secondly, when the result-clause specifies something that is obviously not acceptable for the addressee, *daarom* may be the only appropriate connective:

(58) Ik had haast, ?daardoor / daarom   / ?dus hield ik me niet aan
     I had haste as a result / that's why / so kept I me not to
     het inrijverbod.
     the no-entry-sign
     'I was in a hurry, ?as a result/that's why/?so I ignored the no-entry sign.'

But when the result-clause describes something that is in accordance with a generally accepted rule, *dus* is also appropriate (ibid. 234):

(59) Ik had haast, ?daardoor / daarom   / dus nam ik een taxi.
     I had haste as a result / that's why / so took I a   taxi
     'I was in a hurry, ?as a result/that's why/so I took a taxi.'

Pander Maat and Degand comment as follows:

In the first case, the hearer is addressed indirectly as a potential member of the community sharing the assumption that the argument increases the acceptability of the claim [...] a certain reason may be sufficient for the speaker, but not necessarily for the hearer. This [...] seems to be expressed by *daarom* in Dutch [...]

---

[31] Pander Maat and Degand (2001) only contrast *daardoor* with *dus* in this context. In my experience, informants generally agree that *daarom* is much worse than *daardoor*, and that *daarom* tends to get more acceptable, but there is disagreement about the question of whether it is as bad as *dus* in (57); so far I have not found sufficient actual usage data exemplifying this specific issue to be able to clarify the matter further.

If one wants to introduce stronger assumptions, i.e. force the hearer to accept the protagonist's/speaker's reasoning, then *dus* [...] should be used. (ibid. 234–5)

Pander Maat and Degand interpret these differences in terms of their proposal of a one-dimensional scale of 'speaker involvement'; the more the relation between clauses is constituted by assumptions of the speaker, the higher the degree of speaker involvement.[32] *Daardoor* is supposed to indicate the lowest degree, *daarom* an intermediate degree, and *dus* a high degree of speaker involvement. However, I find the formulation in the quotation above more revealing than the idea of different points on a one-dimensional scale of speaker involvement. Moreover, this formulation comes close to what is captured in Figures 4.14 and 4.15. In the present framework, the cited characterization follows straightforwardly from the assumption that *dus*, like Dutch *want*, operates in the dimension of intersubjective coordination, while *daarom* only marks an inference assumed to be accessible in the Ground, but not imposing specific constraints on the relationship between the conceptualizers. And, as we have seen, inferences marked by *daarom* ('therefore') or *omdat* ('because', not used to mark an argument) may also be restricted to the perspective of conceptualizer 2, unlike inferences marked by *dus* or *want*—in which case it is not the speaker but another conceptualizer who is involved in the causal relationship. The interaction of the connectives with negation, which requires the intersubjectivity approach anyway, finds an immediate explanation in the present framework, whereas it is not clear how the sharp differences involved could be accommodated in a one-dimensional scalar framework. Notice also that an observation from Pander Maat (1999*b*) can be explained as well: there is no concessive counterpart of the causal connection marked with *daardoor* in (57), as the strangeness of (60) indicates:

(60) ?? Hoewel er   een harde wind stond, zijn er   niet drie pannen
     Although there a strong wind stood are there not three tiles
     van   het dak   gevallen.
     from the roof fallen
     'Although there was a strong wind, it is not the case that three tiles fell off the roof.'

Assuming that a concessive connective inherently operates in the dimension of intersubjective coordination, it is always inferential processes of conceptualizers that it operates on. In other words, a concessive sentence like (60)

---

[32] Pit (2003) is another study elaborating this approach, applying it to forward causal connectives in Dutch, German, and French.

must be associated with a causal link that can be seen as licensed by an inference (in the background mental space), and, as we have seen in (57), this is impossible for such exactly quantified results. Although the difference may be mainly terminological, it is for these reasons that I assume that the difference between *dus* and *want* on the one hand and *daarom* and *omdat* on the other is not just a matter of degree along a one-dimensional cline; rather, it involves a basic distinction in the construal configuration as indicated in Figures 4.14 and 4.15, respectively. *Dus* and *want* are not just 'more subjective' than *daarom* and *omdat*; the former conventionally profile intersubjectivity, the latter do not.

At the same time, these differences indicate that *daardoor* ('as a result')[33] is compatible with causal links that are not licensed by inferential processes. Consequently, it is not a feature of the conventional meaning of this element to profile a subject of conceptualization, or even to activate the notion of such a subject as involved in establishing the link between the clauses. Its own meaning must therefore be assumed to involve no more than the imposition of a causal interpretation on the connection between the objects of conceptualization evoked by the clauses involved. Precisely in this respect it differs from *daarom*, which, as these observations indicate, must indeed be assumed to mark the link as licensed by an inference, based on a rule: the situation described in the result clause is (to some extent) the outcome of some subject of conceptualization following a rule, which is cognitively accessible to the conceptualizers in the Ground.[34] That is, the part of the construal configuration involved in the conventional meaning of *daarom* does indeed include the construal relation *between* levels O and S, as indicated in Figure 4.15. Structurally, this conceptual configuration is similar to that for impersonal complementation constructions of the type 'it is clear/a problem/etc. that' discussed in Chapter 3, Section 3.3.6, which also invoke the notion of a subject of conceptualization entertaining something as clear, a problem, etc., but without necessarily attributing it to a specific conceptualizer. On the other hand, the part of the construal configuration conventionally marked by *daardoor* is indeed restricted to level O, as depicted in Figure 4.17.

Notice that this does not mean that *daardoor* is incompatible with relations that do involve some inferential process. The point is that its *conventional*

---

[33] The same presumably holds for the backward causal conjunction *doordat* ('due to/as a result of the fact that').

[34] Notice that the subject of conceptualization can be viewed as a kind of mediating factor in the connection between the segments. This view is elaborated, tested, and compared to the meaning of verbal causative constructions in Stukker (2005), which also contains more detailed analyses of the three forward causal connectives discussed here.

Discourse connections 207

O: *Object of conceptualization:*

S: *Subject of conceptualization (Ground):*

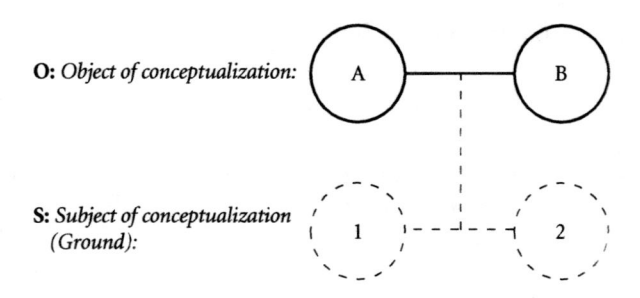

FIGURE 4.17. Conventional function of *daardoor* ('as a result') in dimension of object of conceptualization

function does not activate the notion of a subject of conceptualization, unlike most other common causal connectives. So the harder it is, in view of the content of A and B and cultural models associated with them (see example (57)), to construe the connection between A and B as inferential, the more the use of *daardoor* will appear to be required, or even obligatory. But in cases where an inferential construal is in principle possible, *daardoor* can be used to indicate the 'objective' aspect of the causal link, its independence of some subject conceptualizing it (see Stukker, 2005). In principle, then, it should be possible to include such a case in the scope of negation, and in that way construct a concessive-like relation. An example is the following:

(61) De Pentium 4 heeft een hogere kloksnelheid dan de Athlon, maar
 The Pentium 4 has a higher clock-speed than the Athlon but
 daardoor niet automatisch een hoger prestatieniveau.
 as-a-result not automatically a higher performance-level
 'The Pentium 4 has a higher clock speed than the Athlon, but not therefore automatically a higher performance level.'

Notice that this sentence does not express the idea that the higher clock speed is the reason why the Pentium 4 does not automatically have a higher performance level. Rather, the higher clock speed does not automatically lead to better performance. So this is indeed a concessive-like reading of the type we encountered at the beginning of this section and in Section 4.2.4. At the same time, it is clear that this type of use is even less common for *daardoor* than it is for *daarom*. In newspaper texts, for example, the frequencies of *daarom* and *daardoor* are of the same order of magnitude (roughly, the ratio is 1.7 : 1). On the Internet (Google) the ratio seems even to be 1 : 1. But *de Volkskrant* of 1995 contained only one instance of 'concessive' *daardoor*, as opposed to some fifty cases of *daarom*; and the ratio of *maar daarom (nog) niet* to *maar daardoor (nog) niet* (the most common forms of these concessive expressions) on the Internet is roughly 14 : 1. This is a clear indication that the use of *daardoor* in this kind of inferential context is marginal as compared to *daarom*, which is as we should expect in view of the above analysis.

In summary, several causal connectives are adequately distinguished from others in terms of the difference between the levels of subjects and objects of conceptualization in the basic construal configuration; this phenomenon is not limited to a single element, or to only one direction of causality marking. At the same time, it has become clear that the domain of causality marking is richer in conventionally marked distinctions than that of concessivity. But basic differences between common causal connectives appear to conform closely to intrinsic distinctions in the conceptual structure of the construal configuration.

4.4 Conclusion

In Chapter 1 I argued that from the perspective of language use there is a fundamental asymmetry in the construal configuration. There are both expressions with a conventional meaning that only relates to the dimension of the object of conceptualization, and expressions with a conventional meaning that only operates in the dimension of the relationship between subjects of conceptualization. This may not seen asymmetrical at first sight. However, when used in actual utterances, elements with an 'objective' conventional meaning always participate in an attempt by the speaker/writer to manage the addressee's cognitive state, and they are evaluated by addressees for their contribution to what the utterance is supposed to establish intersubjectively. But elements with a conventional intersubjective meaning simply do not lose that aspect of their interpretation when actually put to use.

It is this basic asymmetry that underlies one of the linguistic asymmetries discussed in this chapter. A causal conjunction may sometimes be included in the scope of negation, and then it yields a concessive-like interpretation. But a concessive conjunction cannot be denied by natural language negation, and such a combination certainly never gives rise to a causal interpretation. The point is that both concessive conjunctions and negation are instruments for managing intersubjective coordination. The use of both in the same utterance either means a double marking of the same configuration of perspectives, or it simply introduces more perspectives. But perspectives do not remove one another to yield a non-perspectivized picture; that is just not the kind of thing perspectives can do. Any attempt to include a concessive constellation in a perspective introduced by negation results in a contradiction within one or more mental spaces, and is therefore excluded.

While it is not a matter of conceptual necessity, it is not at all unusual for causal connectives to fall into one of two classes: one type profiles a difference in epistemic stances between two mental spaces, and the other does not impose specific constraints on the configuration of mental spaces and their relationship. The latter type is compatible with different mental-space configurations, including those in which it is not the speaker/writer who is entertaining a causal inference but another conceptualizer whose perspective is introduced by a negation element. Those causal connectives that conventionally evoke another perspective themselves do not allow for such flexibility of construal, just as concessive connectives do not allow it.

These considerations certainly do not produce an exhaustive analysis of concessive and causal connectives, and we have not taken such relations as are marked by conditional connectives into account. Still, they do suffice to strengthen the basis for this conclusion: the linguistic behavior of discourse connectives shows that the management of inferences across different perspectives is a fundamental feature of human cognition in general. If intersubjective coordination were not so important, it is unlikely that it would play the role in grammar that it does.

5

Concluding Remarks

5.1 Not everything is intersubjectivity (though intersubjectivity is widespread)

In this book I have been operating as a linguist, using linguistic theories and standard linguistic methods of investigation to produce analyses of linguistic phenomena and to draw theoretical conclusions related to them. I have also been using language as a window on the mind, taking results from the linguistic case studies as evidence for or against particular conceptions of human nature and human cognition. Each of the domains of negation, complementation, and connectives constitutes a common part of grammar, and each of them provides evidence for two very general insights. The first is that there is a strong 'dialectics' between specific, sometimes minute problems of linguistic analysis and very general views of the function and structure of language. A particular view of language may help or hinder the solution of a specific problem of grammatical description, and specific linguistic analyses may support or contradict very general conceptions of language.

The second insight concerns the *content* of the general conception of language supported by specific linguistic analyses. I argued that identifying the nature of language with its capacity to provide information about the world is an obstacle to seeing the solution to some problems, such as the nature of the difference between sentential and morphological negation; this identification may even be the source of certain problems, such as inconsistencies in assigning syntactic roles in complementation sentences. In contrast, specific details in the linguistic behavior of a number of constructions strongly suggest that the linguistic system is tightly integrated with the specific human ability to coordinate cognitively with others.

At this point it may be useful, in order to avoid possible misunderstandings, explicitly to indicate what is *not* being claimed here. What is being claimed is that the grammatical phenomena discussed in the previous chapters require a view of language according to which it is completely *normal* that the function of grammatical elements and constructions relates to the dimension of intersubjective coordination. It is not being claimed that *all* linguistic meaning is related to this dimension, nor that intersubjectivity must be a part of the function of any grammatical element or grammatical construction.

For example, the difference between the functions of two elements may consist in one being related to intersubjectivity and the other one not, which presupposes that intersubjectivity is not a necessary component of conventional linguistic meaning. I have in fact already been using this idea at a number of points in the preceding discussions; recall, for example, the difference between sentential and morphological negation in Chapter 2, or the difference between Dutch *want* and other causal connectives (in particular *doordat* and *daardoor*) in Chapter 4. Another illustration was Anscombre and Ducrot's proposal (1989) to consider numerical expressions as operators removing the argumentative orientation of predicates they are combined with. The intrinsic argumentative nature of everyday linguistic utterances does not preclude the possibility of talking about the world without immediately suggesting some conclusion or course of action, but it requires continuous special efforts.

For the study of linguistic meaning this situation implies that it is always an open question whether some element or construction has a specific conventional function in the dimension of intersubjectivity or not. Consider the situation of wanting to determine the extent to which elements in different languages are similar in meaning. When the hypothetical meanings include some component of contrast or negation (coordinating opposite epistemic stances) there may still be differences, but the involvement of the level of intersubjectivity will necessarily be a point of similarity. In other cases, however, an element in one language may precisely have the distinct function of invoking intersubjectivity while an apparently corresponding element in another language need not; for example, the Dutch causal connective *want* and English *because* frequently translate each other, but Dutch *want* conventionally imposes a specific constraint on the interpretation of the intersubjective-coordination relation, while English *because* does not (see Ch. 4, Sect. 4.3.2).

On the other hand, this does not mean that the intersubjectivity dimension is completely irrelevant to the study of words and constructions that are not conventionally linked to it. Causative constructions, for example, do not operate in any *specific* way on the coordination relation between the subjects of conceptualization in the construal configuration. In many languages a few types of causative events can be distinguished by means of different causative constructions, and these often involve some kind of difference between direct and indirect causation (see Kemmer and Verhagen 1994; Verhagen and Kemmer 1997, and refs. cited there). The boundaries between the kinds of events that typically count as direct causation and those that typically count as indirect, vary between languages, and they also change over time. It can be shown that the mechanisms driving the maintenance of as well as changes in such boundaries involve the argumentative character of the utterances containing causative constructions (see Verhagen 2000b, 2004). In present-day Dutch the use of the causative construction for direct causation (marked by *doen*) for intentional human actions is definitely marked, but it is still maintained as an option and may be employed for attributing different degrees of responsibility and guilt to agents. And the process by which this kind of use changed from normal to marked (over the eighteenth and nineteenth centuries) itself also involved the inferences it gave rise to when it was used in describing human interaction; depicting a human agent as a direct cause of a result in another person's mind characterizes the latter person as not fully autonomous, as it suppresses the idea of intermediate causes such as this person's interpretive role, and his freedom to decide how to react. This became less and less socially acceptable, because of general changes in the cultural images of individual human beings and relations between them during this period, which resulted in such a sharp decline of the use of *doen* for this kind of event that this construction is now typical for non-intentional causes. As far as we know, the conventional function of the two Dutch causative constructions has never related directly to the level of intersubjectivity, and the process of semantic change briefly described here is not one of subjectification. Still, in the development of the meaning of these constructions, inferences induced by speakers in addressees play a crucial role. The impact of what language users achieve in the dimension of intersubjective coordination extends far beyond those parts of language that are conventionally related to this dimension. Three of those have been discussed in the previous chapters, and I will now, once again, return to them.

5.2 Grammar provides systematic instruments for mutual management—of a special kind

5.2.1 *Looking ahead*

The analyses and theoretical conclusions from these chapters give rise to several further questions, of various kinds. Some questions of linguistic analysis are, for example:

(i) What are the differences between languages in the kinds of functions conventionally performed by constructions in the dimension of intersubjectivity, and are there any regularities in or limits to this variation?
(ii) How precisely do special complementation constructions, such as those with interrogative or non-finite complements (see Ch. 1, Sect. 1.3.2), fit into the intersubjectivity approach?
(iii) How do different negation elements, different complementation constructions, and different discourse connectives interact?

Some questions concerning dynamic processes related to intersubjectivity are:

(iv) How does the capacity to coordinate different perspectives develop in children, and what are the relations between linguistic and conceptual development in this domain?
(v) What role do narratives and literacy play in the development of the capacity for linguistic and conceptual management of perspectives?
(vi) How did words and constructions expressing complex mental-space configurations (e.g. special complement-taking predicates and concessive connectives) develop over time, and what role did the cultural evolution of such systems as writing and institutional education play in this development?

Naturally, these are only a few illustrative examples of relevant and interesting issues that might be addressed. Answers to these and other questions will be important for linguistics, and also for cognitive science in general. For example, it is conceivable that the 'full' capacity for managing perspectives that we observe in modern adult human beings is completely the result of genetic evolution, but it may also be the product of some combination of genetic evolution and cultural evolution, or of co-evolution of genes and culture. Developing further insights into the structure of those parts of grammars that specifically relate to the dimension of intersubjective coordination, and into the way they develop in individuals and in communities, is in my view a promising avenue for deepening our understanding in this area.

There is an important guideline emerging from the analyses in the preceding pages for the way linguistics may contribute optimally to this enterprise. Structure and function, conventional meaning and context-bound usage should be studied in parallel, keeping all options for systematic relations between them open. Even though what is communicated normally encompasses much more than what is explicitly said, linguistic elements and constructions do provide systematic cues for the interpretation of utterances. But the character of this systematicity may remain obscure—possibly giving rise to the idea that the relation between form and meaning is far from systematic after all—if one does not look in the right place. A prime example is provided by complementation constructions. Looking at isolated instances of these with first- and third-person matrix clauses, it is practically impossible to see the parallelism in their argumentative character, and this may then, erroneously, be taken as confirming the independence of the common structure of complementation sentences from their function(s); but, in fact, the latter only appear to be completely different because of the limitations of the phenomena one looks at.

5.2.2 Looking back

Looking at connected discourse as a source of evidence for the systematic meaning of grammatical elements and constructions is part of a conceptual shift that I have proposed at several points in the preceding chapters; namely, the shift from considering the elements under discussion as operating at the level of objects of conceptualization, to considering them as operating at the level of the mutual coordination between subjects of conceptualization. This was especially relevant for linguistic practice when such a shift contributed to a solution of one or more problems of analysis. At the same time, however, it has important consequences of a much more general nature and at a much more general level, for the cognitive sciences and for our view of the place of humans in the evolutionary process.

The recognition of the importance of intersubjective coordination for understanding some core parts of grammar comes down to a claim about parallels and differences between language as the human communication system 'par excellence' and animal communication. Human languages provide instruments for managing and assessing conspecifics, just as animal communication systems do—not just in the relatively superficial sense that information about the world may secondarily be used to exert influence on and learn about others, but in the more interesting sense that the conventional function of several grammatical devices is *directly* and *primarily* related to such mutual management and assessment. At the same time, what is managed and assessed by means of these conventional grammatical devices relates to a typically human ability: the capacity to recognize others as mental agents like oneself and thus to understand things from another person's point of view and to coordinate these distinct perspectives.

The grammatical system of negation—a set of operators (*not, barely,* etc.) and connectors (*but, let alone,* etc.) interacting with each other in systematic ways—is used to coordinate perspectives characterized by opposite epistemic stances, not so much with respect to the descriptive contents of the utterances involved but with respect to their argumentative, rhetorical orientation. This is what underlies the fundamental asymmetry between linguistically positive and negative statements. While utterances lacking any negative element do not have to invoke the dimension of intersubjective coordination explicitly, utterances containing such an element always do. Despite the logical equivalence of expressions like *not impossible* and *possible*, the cognitive constellations associated with them remain different, and thus so do their conditions of use.

Complementation constructions are not structural devices to present one objectively construed event as subordinate to another, but devices to invite an addressee to consider an object of conceptualization (presented in a complement clause) from a particular perspective in a particular way (as specified in the matrix clause). The standard syntactic relations of subject and object have no role to play in the grammatical characterization of complementation constructions. On the contrary, they may sometimes even be a source of confusion and unnecessary complications. The reason is that they derive from the analysis of simplex clauses which do present a situation as an object of conceptualization. Applying them to complementation constructions thus suggests that the latter also evoke an objective event (be it a complex one). It has turned out that this complicates rather than simplifies our understanding of complementation, and that the idea that this consists of an independent network of constructional templates offers much better prospects.

In prototypical cases, including those that are typically acquired early, the distance between the explicit perspective (the 'onstage conceptualizer') of a matrix clause and the participants in the Ground is small, or even minimal. But as far as the ultimate (adult) schematic complementation construction is concerned, the relation between the explicit perspective presented in the matrix clause and that of the speaker/writer and the addressee is variable. It is the function of the lexical content of the matrix clause to specify the nature of this connection, with the default situation still being that the speaker/writer aligns herself with the onstage conceptualizer; third-person and/or non-present-tense matrix clauses have the same argumentative orientation (though not the same force) as the first-person, present-tense ones that constitute so-called performative utterances marking speech acts. The notion of minimal distinctness of the onstage conceptualizer from the Ground is also crucial for understanding the apparent occurrence of a question phrase 'outside' the clause that seems to determine its roles as participant in an event (what is known as 'long distance *Wh*-movement' or '*Wh*-extraction', see Ch. 3, Sect. 3.3.5).

In the domain of discourse connectives, finally, it is crucial to distinguish connections between the situations represented in text segments from connections at the inferential and argumentative level. Just a few, apparently specialized, connectives such as Dutch *daardoor* ('as a consequence') operate *only* at the level of the objects of conceptualization. The distinction involved has been recognized, in different forms, in several studies in discourse analysis (see Sanders et al. 1993 for discussion), but it is only when reconstructed in terms of the coordination of multiple perspectives that it becomes possible to understand asymmetrical interactions between such connectives and negation; these concern both causal and contrastive (particularly, concessive) connectives.

The system of negation is not properly understood as long as it is viewed as a relation between a thought and an object of thought. Complementation constructions are not properly understood as long as they are viewed as a way of subordinating the representation of one situation to another. The system of discourse connectives is not properly understood as long as they are viewed as connecting states of affairs. In each case, the recognition that the construction relates to the dimension of intersubjective coordination contributes to a better understanding of its linguistic behavior. In each case, such a move also makes the phenomenon at hand more natural from an evolutionary perspective, given what is known about animal communication as mutual management and assessment. Still, in each case, it also illustrates the capacity to manipulate and organize multiple points of view as something that humans are especially good at.

Further Reading

Conceptual foundations

The insight that intersubjectivity is crucial for understanding human language and cognition in a very basic way was apparently 'in the air' when *Constructions of Intersubjectivity* (henceforth: *CoI*) first came out. Zlatev, Racine, Sinha, and Itkonen were preparing an interdisciplinary volume that has now entered the editorial process; two theme session proposals were submitted for the 10th International Cognitive Linguistics Conference in Cracow, Poland (July, 2007), which the conference organisers urged to be merged into one. All contributions to the volume and the conference theme session are relevant to the conceptual foundations of *CoI*; the chapters by Itkonen and by Zlatev deserve special mention. A slightly older paper by Sinha (2004) is also directly relevant here, especially in connection with the comparative evolutionary perspective of chapter 1 of *CoI* (more on evolution below, in relation to complementation and recursion).

The goal of my chapter in the Zlatev et al. volume (Verhagen, forthcoming, a) is to demonstrate how the analysis of linguistic structure discussed in *CoI* provides a 'window' on human intersubjectivity. Precisely this link is challenged in an interesting way by Hinzen & Van Lambalgen (forthcoming), from the perspective of what they call the 'traditional' views of logical semantics and generative syntax. My response, focusing on the question what may count as evidence and as explanation, will be published in the same issue of *Cognitive Linguistics* (Verhagen, forthcoming, b).

Mental spaces

A ground-breaking addition to the study of mental spaces in the domain of grammar is the book on conditional constructions by Dancygier and Sweetser (2005). It contains a number of discussions that are directly relevant to *CoI*, especially negation (chapter 2 of *CoI*) and concessivity (chapter 4), and offers a perspective for an even more comprehensive treatment of the semantics and pragmatics of grammatical constructions in terms of operations on mental spaces. Another theme session at ICLC 10 in Cracow, which will no doubt produce a number of new publications, will be devoted to 'mental spaces and viewpoint in grammar and discourse' (i.a. Verhagen, in prep., b).

Complementation

Chapter 3 of *CoI* develops the idea that complementation constructions constitute a relatively autonomous part of the grammar of a language, which specifically provides users of the language with instruments to perspectivize the content of the complement clause, with the content of the matrix clause providing details of the manner of perspectivisation. Hyland and Tse (2005) give an analysis of the use of this construction in a specific type of discourse, which can be straightforwardly incorporated into the general approach of *CoI*. Although couched in the terminology of a different framework, the same holds for Delahunty's (2006) analysis of a specific subtype of complementation constructions: *not that* sentences. Verhagen (in prep., b) elaborates the analysis of differences between impersonal (*It is well known that...*) and personal (*We all know that...*) complementation constructions in terms of their rhetorical uses.

CoI proposes to view the complementation construction as a linguistic device for explicitly indicating perspectives. Thus it is seen as directly connected to the human capacity for taking another person's perspective, i.e. the capacity that goes under the label 'Theory of Mind' among philosophers and psychologists. Several properties of complementation constructions are explained on this basis, e.g. the relative ease of recursion (since perspective taking is intrinsically recursive; see also below). From this perspective, the discussion by De Villiers and De Villiers (2003) of the possible connections between the command of complementation constructions and the development of 'Theory of Mind' in children is extremely interesting. What they are specifically concerned with is the cognitive control of 'false beliefs': my understanding that another person's view of the world, given the evidence available to this person, is false, i.e. different from my own given the evidence available to me. This is considered the culmination of the capacity to 'take another's perspective'. In general, this capacity allows us to adequately predict another person's actions, but it clearly comes at different levels: seeing something from another perspective in itself does not have to involve a simultaneous active comparison with yet another perspective, which *is* required to adequately predict what someone else will do in the case of a false belief. De Villiers and De Villiers argue that this highest level of 'Theory of Mind' may very well be dependent on a sufficient development of the command of the complementation construction, providing children with the representational means necessary for cognitively manipulating beliefs. From the perspective of *CoI* it is especially intriguing that this top level of 'Theory of Mind' –understanding the *false* beliefs of others– involves the *combination* of negation and complementation, the prototypical way of expressing it being "X does *not know that* Y". So while initial complementation constructs in children's language serve to mark subjective perspectives (Diessel and Tomasello 2001), this linguistic development itself possibly functions as a stepping stone for advancing cognitive capacities.

Another special subtype of complementation constructs discussed in *CoI* is that of so-called '*Wh*-extraction' or 'long-distance *Wh*-movement'. A separate discussion of this phenomenon can be found in Verhagen (2006). The conclusion that this phenomenon involves a highly idiomatic template, and not a general rule for displacing question words to positions outside their own clause (*CoI*, 119–131), has profound consequences for syntactic theory in general, but especially for the view that what is really unique to human language is recursion (as suggested in Hauser, Chomsky, and Fitch 2002). *Wh*-extraction would be one of the few cases of so-called 'true' recursion in human language, but if even this is shown to be better accounted for in terms of a kind of constructional idiom with a specific function, this actually provides partial support for the alternative view on what is special about language among animal communication systems put forward by Jackendoff and Pinker (2005), in response to Fitch, Hauser, and Chomsky (2005), with the additional hypothesis that recursion in human language may be a consequence of cultural rather than strictly genetic evolution. These consequences are explored and linked to other aspects of syntactic theory and evolution in Verhagen (in press) and (in prep., a) (see Parker 2006 for a more general discussion of conceptual constraints on syntactic theorizing provided by evolution). A number of different approaches to these issues have been presented and discussed at the conference "Recursion in Human Languages" held in Normal, Illinois (27–29 April, 2007); a selection of the papers is likely to appear as a journal special issue, edited by Daniel Everett.

References

Akmajian, Adrian (1970), 'Aspects of the grammar of focus in English', Ph.D. diss. (MIT).
Anscombre, Jean-Claude, and Ducrot, Oswald (1983), *L'argumentation dans la langue*. Liège/Bruxelles: Mardaga.
—— (1989), 'Argumentativity and informativity', in Michel Meyer (ed.), *From Metaphysics to Rhetoric*. Dordrecht: Kluwer, 71–87.
Ariel, Mira (1990), *Accessing NP Antecedents*. London: Routledge.
Austin, John L. (1962), *How To Do Things With Words*. Oxford: Oxford University Press.
Banfield, Ann (1982), *Unspeakable Sentences: Narration and Representation in the Language of Fiction*. Boston: Routledge & Kegan Paul.
Barlow, Michael, and Kemmer, Suzanne (2000) (eds.), *Usage-Based Models of Language*. Stanford, Calif.: CSLI.
Barth, Dagmar (2000), ' "that's true, although not really, but still": expressing concession in spoken English', in Couper-Kuhlen and Kortmann (eds.), 411–37.
Benveniste, Émile (1958), 'De la subjectivité dans le langage', *Journal de psychologie*, 55 (juillet-septembre), repr. in *Problèmes de linguistique générale*. Paris: Éditions Gallimard, 1966.
—— (1971), *Problems in General Linguistics*, trans. Mary Elizabeth Meek. Coral Gables, Fla.: University of Miami Press.
Blom, Alied, and Daalder, Saskia (1977), *Syntaktische theorie en taalbeschrijving*. Muiderberg: Coutinho.
Bolinger, Dwight (1968), 'Postposed main phrases: an English rule for the Romance subjunctive', *Canadian Journal of Linguistics/La Revue canadienne de Linguistique*, 14: 3–30.
Boogaart, Ronny (1991), 'Temporele relaties en tekstcoherentie', *Voortgang. Jaarboek voor de Neerlandistiek*, 12: 241–64.
—— (1999), *Aspect and Temporal Ordering: A Contrastive Analysis of Dutch and English*. The Hague: Holland.
Boye, Kasper, and Harder, Peter (2007), 'Complement-taking predicates: usage and linguistic structure'. *Studies in Language* 31: 569–606.
Bradbury, Jack W., and Vehrencamp, Sandra L. (2000), 'Economic models of animal communication', *Animal Behaviour*, 59: 259–68.
Bühler, Karl (1934), *Sprachtheorie. Die Darstellungsfunktion der Sprache*. Jena: Fischer.

Burridge, Kate (1993), *Syntactic Change in Germanic: Aspects of Language Change in Germanic with particular reference to Middle Dutch.* Amsterdam/Phila.: Benjamins.

Bybee, Joan (1995), 'Regular morphology and the lexicon', *Language and Cognitive Processes*, 10: 425–55.

—— (2003), 'Cognitive processes in grammaticalization', in Tomasello (ed.), 145–67.

—— and Hopper, Paul (2001) (eds.), *Frequency and the Emergence of Linguistic Structure.* Amsterdam/Phila.: Benjamins.

Byrne, Richard W., Barnard, Philip J., Davidson, Iain, Janik, Vincent M., McGrew, William C., Miklósi, Ádam and Wiessner Polly (2004), 'Understanding culture across species', *Trends in Cognitive Sciences*, 8: 341–6.

Chomsky, Noam (1977), 'On wh-movement', in Peter W. Culicover, Thomas Wasow, and Adrian Akmajian (eds.), *Formal Syntax.* New York: Academic, 71–132.

Clark, Herbert H. (1996), *Using Language.* Cambridge: Cambridge University Press.

Comrie, Bernard (2003), 'On explaining language universals', in Tomasello (ed.), 195–209.

Cornelis, Louise H. (1997), *Passive and Perspective.* Amsterdam/Atlanta, Ga.: Rodopi.

Cornillie, Bert (2004), 'The shift from lexical to subjective readings of Spanish *prometer* "to promise" and *amenazar* "to threaten": a corpus-based account', *Pragmatics*, 14: 1–30.

Coulson, Seana, and Oakley, Todd (2000) (eds.), *Conceptual Blending*, special issue, *Cognitive Linguistics*, 11/3,4.

Couper-Kuhlen, Elizabeth, and Kortmann, Bernd (2000), (eds.) *Cause—Condition—Concession—Contrast: cognitive and discourse perspectives.* Berlin: de Gruyter.

Croft, William (2000), *Explaining Language Change: An Evolutionary Approach.* Harlow: Longman.

—— (2001), *Radical Construction Grammar: Syntactic Theory in Typological Perspective.* Oxford: Oxford University Press.

—— (2003), 'Lexical rules vs. constructions: a false dichotomy' in Hubert Cuyckens, Thomas Berg, René Dirven, and Klaus-Uwe Panther (eds.), *Motivation in Language: Studies in Honour of Günter Radden.* Amsterdam/Phila.: Benjamins, 49–68.

—— and Cruse, D. Alan (2004), *Cognitive Linguistics.* Cambridge: Cambridge University Press.

Dąbrowska, Ewa (2004), *Language, Mind, and Brain: Some Psychological and Neurological Constraints on Theories of Grammar.* Edinburgh: Edinburgh University Press.

Dancygier, Barbara, and Sweetser, Eve (2000), 'Constructions with *if*, *since*, and *because*: causality, epistemic stance and clause order', in Couper-Kuhlen and Kortmann (eds.), 111–42.

—— (2005), *Mental Spaces in Grammar: Conditional Constructions.* Cambridge: Cambridge University Press.

Dawkins, Richard, and Krebs, John R. (1978), 'Animal signals: information or manipulation?', in J. R. Krebs and N. B. Davies (eds.), *Behavioural Ecology: An Evolutionary Approach*. Oxford: Blackwell, 282–309.

Degand, Liesbeth, and Pander Maat, Henk (2003), 'A contrastive study of Dutch and French causal connectives on the speaker-involvement scale', in Verhagen and Van de Weijer (eds.), 175–99.

Delahunty, Gerald P. (2006), 'A relevance theoretic account of *not that* sentences'. *Pragmatics* 16: 213–246.

Den Hertog, Cornelis H. (1973) (ed. Hulshof), *Nederlandse Spraakkunst. Tweede stuk: de leer van de samengestelde zin*. Amsterdam: Versluys (2nd edn. 1904).

De Villiers, Jill G., and De Villiers, Peter A. (2003), 'Language for thought: coming to understand false beliefs', in Dedre Gentner and Susan Goldin-Meadow (eds.), *Language in Mind: Advances in the Study of Language and Thought*. Cambridge, MA/London: The MIT Press, 335–384.

De Vries, Jan W. (1971), 'Want en omdat', *De Nieuwe Taalgids*, 64: 421–7.

De Vries, Matthias, Winkel, Lammert A. te, et al. (1864–1998) (eds.), *Woordenboek der Nederlandsche taal.* 's-Gravenhage: Martinus Nijhoff.

Diessel, Holger, and Tomasello, Michael (2001), 'The acquisition of finite complement clauses in English: a corpus-based analysis', *Cognitive Linguistics*, 12: 97–141.

Du Bois, John W. (1985), 'Competing motivations', in John Haiman (ed.), *Iconicity in Syntax*. Amsterdam/Phila.: Benjamins, 343–65.

Ducrot, Oswald (1980), *Les échelles argumentatives*. Paris: Minuit.

—— (1996), *Slovenian Lectures: Argumentative Semantics/Conférences Slovènes: Sémantiques argumentatives*, ed. Igor Ž. Žagar. Ljubljana: ISH Inštitut za humanistične študije Ljubljana.

Elffers, Els (1979), 'De semantiek van de koppelwerkwoordzin en haar plaats in de taalbeschrijving', *Spektator*, 9: 97–143.

Erteschik-Shir, Nomi (1973), 'On the nature of island constraints', Ph.D. diss. (MIT), repr. by the Indiana University Linguistics Club, Bloomington, Ind.

—— (1997), *The Dynamics of Focus Structure*. Cambridge: Cambridge University Press.

Fauconnier, Gilles (1994), *Mental Spaces: Aspects of Meaning Construction in Natural Language*. Cambridge: Cambridge University Press (1st edn., Cambridge, Mass.: MIT Press 1985).

—— (1997), *Mappings in Thought and Language*. Cambridge: Cambridge University Press.

—— and Turner, Mark (2000), 'Compression and global insight', *Cognitive Linguistics*, 11: 283–304.

Fillmore, Charles J., Kay, Paul, and O'Connor, Mary Catherine (1988), 'Regularity and idiomaticity in grammatical constructions: the case of *let alone*', *Language*, 64: 501–38.

Fitch, W. Tecumseh, Hauser, Marc D., and Chomsky, Noam (2005), 'The evolution of the language faculty: Clarifications and implications'. *Cognition* 97, 179–210.

Foolen, Ad P. (1993), *De betekenis van partikels: een dokumentatie van de stand van het onderzoek, met bijzondere aandacht voor 'maar'.* Wageningen: Ponsen and Looijen.

Geeraerts, Dirk, and Cuyckens Hubert (forthcoming) (eds.), *Handbook of Cognitive Linguistics.* Oxford: Oxford University Press.

Goldberg, Adele E. (1995), *Constructions: A Construction Grammar Approach to Argument Structure.* Chicago, Ill./London: University of Chicago Press.

—— (2002), 'Surface generalizations: an alternative to alternations', *Cognitive Linguistics,* 13: 327–56.

—— (2003), 'Constructions: a new theoretical approach to language', *Trends in Cognitive Sciences,* 7: 219–24.

Grice, H. Paul (1957), 'Meaning', *Philosophical Review,* 66: 377–88, repr. in Danny D. Steinberg and Leon A. Jakobovits (eds.), *Semantics.* Cambridge: Cambridge University Press, 1971, 53–9.

—— (1975), 'Logic and conversation', in P. Cole and J. Morgan (eds.), *Syntax and Semantics, iii: Speech Acts.* New York: Academic, 41–58.

Günthner, Susanne (2000), 'From concessive connector to discourse marker: the use of *obwohl* in everyday German interaction', in Couper-Kuhlen and Kortmann (eds.), 439–68.

Haeseryn, Walter, Romijn, Kirstin, Geerts, Guido, De Rooij, Jaap and Van den Toorn, Maarten C. (1997), *Algemene Nederlandse Spraakkunst,* 2nd rev. edn. Groningen/Deurne: Martinus Nijhoff/Wolters Plantyn.

Haiman, John, and Thompson, Sandra A. (1988) (eds.), *Clause Combining in Grammar and Discourse.* Amsterdam/Phila.: Benjamins.

Halliday, Michael A. K. (1978), *Language as Social Semiotic: The Social Interpretation of Language and Meaning.* London: Edward Arnold.

—— (1985), *An Introduction to Functional Grammar.* London: Edward Arnold.

Hauser, Marc D., Chomsky, Noam, and Fitch, W. Tecumseh (2002), 'The faculty of language: what is it, who has it, and how did it evolve?', *Science,* 298: 1569–79.

Heine, Bernd (1995), 'Agent-oriented vs. epistemic modality, some observations on German modals', in Joan Bybee and Suzanne Fleischman (eds.), *Modality in Grammar and Discourse.* Amsterdam/Phila.: Benjamins, 17–53.

Hinzen, Wolfram, and Van Lambalgen, Michiel (forthcoming), 'Review Essay of Verhagen, *Constructions of Intersubjectivity*'. *Cognitive Linguistics.*

Horn, Laurence R. (1978), 'Remarks on neg-raising', in Peter Cole (ed.), *Syntax and Semantics ix. Pragmatics.* New York: Academic, 129–220.

—— (1989), *A Natural History of Negation.* Chicago, Ill.: Chicago University Press (repr. Stanford, Calif.: CSLI, 2001).

—— (1996), 'Exclusive company: *only* and the dynamics of vertical inference', *Journal of Semantics,* 13: 1–40.

—— (2002), 'Assertoric inertia and NPI licensing'; paper presented at the 38th Meeting of the Chicago Linguistic Society, 27 April 2002, University of Chicago.

Hyland, Ken, and Tse, Polly (2005), 'Evaluative *that* constructions: signalling stance in research abstracts'. *Functions of Language* 12, 39–63.

Israel, Michael (1996), 'Polarity sensitivity as lexical semantics', *Linguistics and Philosophy*, 19: 619–66.
—— (1998), 'The rhetoric of grammar: scalar reasoning and polarity sensitivity', Ph.D. diss. (University of California, San Diego).
Iten, Corinne (1998), '*Because* and *although*: a case of duality?', in Villy Rouchota and Andreas H. Jucker (eds.), *Current Issues in Relevance Theory*. Amsterdam/Phila.: Benjamins, 59–80.
Itkonen, Esa (forthcoming). 'The central role of normativity in language and linguistics', in Zlatev et al. (eds.).
Jackendoff, Ray (1972), *Semantic Interpretation in Generative Grammar*. Cambridge, Mass.: MIT Press.
—— (2002), *Foundations of Language: Brain, Meaning, Grammar, Evolution*. Oxford: Oxford University Press.
—— and Pinker, Steven (2005), 'The nature of the language faculty and its implications for evolution of language (Reply to Fitch, Hauser, and Chomsky)'. *Cognition* 97, 211–225.
Jakobson, Roman (1957), 'Shifters, verbal categories and the Russian verb', Russian language project, Dept. of Slavic Languages and Literature, Harvard; repr. in R. Jakobson, *Selected Writings, ii. Word and Language*. The Hague: Mouton, 1971, 130–47.
Kay, Paul (1997), *Words and the Grammar of Context*. Stanford, Calif.: CSLI.
Keller, Rudi (1994), *On Language Change: The Invisible Hand in Language*. London: Routledge.
—— (1995), 'The epistemic *weil*', in Stein and Wright (eds.), 103–28.
—— (1998), *A Theory of Linguistic Signs*. Oxford: Oxford University Press.
Kemmer, Suzanne, and Verhagen, Arie (1994), 'The grammar of causatives and the conceptual structure of events', *Cognitive Linguistics*, 5, 115–56.
Klima, Edward S. (1964), 'Negation in English', in J. Fodor and J. Katz (eds.), *The Structure of Language: Readings in the Philosophy of Language*. Englewood Cliffs, NJ: Prentice-Hall, 246–323.
Koenig, Jean-Pierre (1998) (ed.), *Discourse and Cognition. Bridging the Gap*. Stanford, Calif.: CSLI.
König, Ekkehard (1991), 'Concessive relations as the dual of causal relations', in D. Zaefferer (ed.), *Semantic Universals and Universal Semantics*. Dordrecht: Foris, 190–209.
—— (1994), 'Concessive clauses', in R. E. Asher (ed.), *The Encyclopedia of Language and Linguistics*, ii. Oxford: Pergamon, 679–81.
—— and Siemund, Peter (2000), 'Causal and concessive clauses: formal and semantic relations', in Couper-Kuhlen and Kortmann (eds.), 341–60.
Koster, Jan (1978), 'Why subject sentences don't exist', in Samuel J. Keyser (ed.), *Recent Transformational Studies in European Languages*. Cambridge, Mass.: MIT Press, 53–64.
Lagerwerf, Luuk (1998), *Causal Connectives Have Presuppositions: Effects on Coherence and Discourse Structure*. The Hague: Holland.

Lakoff, George (1987), *Women, Fire, and Dangerous Things: What Categories Reveal about the Mind*. Chicago, Ill: University of Chicago Press.

Langacker, Ronald W. (1987), *Foundations of Cognitive Grammar*, i. *Theoretical Prerequisites*. Stanford, Calif.: Stanford University Press.

—— (1990), 'Subjectification', *Cognitive Linguistics*, 1: 5–38.

—— (1991), *Foundations of Cognitive Grammar*, ii. *Descriptive Application*. Stanford, Calif.: Stanford University Press.

—— (1993), 'Universals of construal', in *Proceedings of the Annual Meeting of the Berkeley Linguistic Society*, 19: 447–63.

—— (1998), 'On subjectification and grammaticalization', in Koenig (ed.), 71–89.

—— (2000), 'A dynamic usage-based model', in Barlow and Kemmer (eds.) 1–63.

—— (2005), 'Construction grammars: cognitive, radical, and less so', in: Francisco J. Ruiz de Mendoza Ibáñez and M. Sandra Peña Cervel (eds.), *Cognitive Linguistics: Internal Dynamics and Interdisciplinary Interaction*. Berlin and New York: Mouton de Gruyter, 101–159.

Lewis, David K. (1969), *Convention: A Philosophical Study*. Cambridge, Mass.: Harvard University Press.

Lundquist, Lita, and Jarvella, Robert J. (1994), 'Ups and downs in scalar inferences', *Journal of Semantics*, 11: 33–53.

Lyons, John (1982), 'Deixis and subjectivity: *Loquor, ergo sum?*', in Robert J. Jarvella and Wolfgang Klein (eds.), *Speech, Place, and Action: Studies in Deixis and Related Topics*. New York: Wiley, 101–24.

Majid, Asifa, Bowerman, Melissa, Kita, Sotaro, Haun, Daniel B. M. and Levinson, Stephen C. (2004), 'Can language restructure cognition? The case for space', *Trends in Cognitive Sciences*, 8: 108–14.

Matthiessen, Christian, and Thompson, Sandra A. (1988), 'The structure of discourse and "subordination" ', in Haiman and Thompson (eds.), 275–329.

Nuyts, Jan (2001a), 'Subjectivity as an evidential dimension in epistemic modal expressions', *Journal of Pragmatics*, 33: 383–400.

—— (2001b), *Epistemic Modality, Language and Conceptualization: A Cognitive-Pragmatic Perspective*. Amsterdam/Phila.: Benjamins.

OED (1989), *The Oxford English Dictionary*, 2nd edn. Oxford: Clarendon.

Onrust, Margreet, Verhagen, Arie, and Doeve, Rob (1993), *Formuleren*. Houten/Zaventem: Bohn Stafleu Van Loghum.

Oversteegen, Leonoor E. (1997), 'On the pragmatic nature of causal and contrastive connectives', *Discourse Processes*, 24: 51–85.

Owings, Donald H., and Morton, Eugene S. (1998), *Animal Vocal Communication: A New Approach*. Cambridge: Cambridge University Press.

Pander Maat, Henk L. W. (1999a), 'The differential linguistic realization of comparative and additive coherence relations', *Cognitive Linguistics*, 10: 147–84.

—— (1999b), 'Two kinds of concessives and their inferential complexities', in Alistair Knott, Jon Oberlander, Johanna D. Moore, and Ted J. M. Sanders (eds.), *Levels of*

Representation in Discourse: Working Notes of the International Workshop on Text Representation. Edinburgh: Human Communication Research Centre, 45–54.

—— (2006), 'Subjectification in gradable adjectives', in Angeliki Athanasiadou, Costas Canakis, and Bert Cornillie (eds.), *Subjectification: Various Paths to Subjectivity*. Berlin/New York: de Gruyter, 279–320.

—— and Degand, Liesbeth (2001), 'Scaling causal relations and connectives in terms of speaker involvement', *Cognitive Linguistics*, 12: 211–45.

Parker, Anna R. (2006), 'Evolution as a constraint on theories of syntax: the case against minimalism', Ph.D. diss. (University of Edinburgh).

Pasch, Renate (1992*a*), *Sind kausale und konzessive Konstruktionen Duale voneinander? (Arbeiten des Sonderforschungsbereich 282,* 31). Wuppertal.

—— (1992*b*), 'Kausale, konzessive und adversative Konnektive: Konnektive als Mittel des Ausdrucks von Diskurspräsuppositionen', *Münstersches Logbuch zur Linguistik* 1: 33–48.

—— (1994), *Konzessivität von* wenn-*Konstruktionen*. Tübingen: Gunter Narr.

—— (2000), 'Zur Bedeutung von deutsch *geschweige (denn)*', *Linguistik online*, 6, 2/00 <http://www.linguistik-online.de/2_00/pasch.html>, accessed Oct. 2004.

Pinker, Steven, and Jackendoff, Ray (2005), 'The faculty of language: what's special about it?', Cognition, 95: 201–236.

Pit, Mirna (2003), *How to Express Yourself with a Causal Connective: Subjectivity and Causal Connectives in Dutch, German and French*. Amsterdam/Atlanta, Ga.: Rodopi.

Popper, Karl R. (1972), *The Logic of Scientific Discovery*. London: Hutchinson (1st Eng. edn. 1959).

Raccah, Pierre-Yves (1995) (ed.), *Argumentation within Language*. Amsterdam: Elsevier (special issue, *Journal of Pragmatics*, 24).

Rendell, Luke, and Whitehead, Hal (2001), 'Culture in whales and dolphins', *Behavioral and Brain Sciences*, 24: 309–82.

Renkema, Jan (1981), *De taal van 'Den Haag': een kwantitatief-stilistisch onderzoek naar aanleiding van oordelen over taalgebruik*. 's-Gravenhage: Staatsuitgeverij.

Sanders, José (1994), 'Perspective in Narrative Discourse', Ph.D. diss. (Tilburg University).

—— and Spooren, Wilbert (1996), 'Subjectivity and certainty in epistemic modality: a study of Dutch epistemic modifiers', *Cognitive Linguistics*, 7: 241–64.

Sanders, Ted J. M., Spooren, Wilbert P. M., and Noordman, Leo G. M. (1993), 'Coherence relations in a cognitive theory of discourse representation', *Cognitive Linguistics*, 4: 93–133.

Schilperoord, Joost (1996), *It's About Time: Temporal Aspects of Cognitive Processes in Text Production*. Amsterdam/Atlanta, Ga: Rodopi.

—— (1997), 'Temporele modificatie in clauses: een pauze-analytische studie naar tekstproductie', in H. van den Bergh, D. Janssen, N. Bertens, and M. Damen (eds.), *Taalgebruik ontrafeld: Bijdragen van het zevende VIOT-taalbeheersingscongres gehouden op 18, 19 en 20 december 1996 aan de Universiteit van Utrecht*. Dordrecht: ICG, 263–74.

—— and Verhagen, Arie (1998), 'Conceptual dependency and the clausal structure of discourse', in Koenig (ed.), 141–63.

Searle, John R. (1969), *Speech Acts: An Essay in the Philosophy of Language*. Cambridge: Cambridge University Press.

—— (1976), 'A classification of illocutionary acts', *Language in Society*, 5: 1–23.

Sinha, Chris (1999), 'Situated selves', in Joan Bliss, R. Säljö, and P. Light (eds.), *Learning Sites: Social and Technological Resources for Learning*. Oxford: Pergamon, 32–46.

—— (2004), 'The evolution of language: from signals to symbols to system', in D. Kimbrough Oller and Ulrike Griebel (eds.), *Evolution of Communication Systems. A Comparative Approach*. Cambridge, MA/London: The MIT Press, 217–235.

—— (forthcoming), 'Cognitive Linguistics, Psychology and Cognitive Science', in Geeraerts and Cuyckens (eds.).

Spooren, Wilbert P. M. S. (1989), 'Some aspects of the form and interpretation of global contrastive coherence relations', Ph.D. diss. (Katholieke Universiteit Nijmegen).

Steels, Luc (2003), 'The evolution of communication systems by adaptive agents', in Eduardo Alonso, Daniel Kudenko, and Dimitar Kazakov (eds.), *Adaptive Agents and Multi-agent Systems: Adaptation and Multi-agent Learning*. Heidelberg: Springer-Verlag (*Lecture Notes in Artificial Intelligence* 2636), 125–40.

Stein, Dieter, and Wright, Susan (1995) (eds.), *Subjectivity and Subjectivisation: Linguistic Perspectives*. Cambridge: Cambridge University Press.

Stukker, Ninke, Sanders, Ted, and Verhagen, Arie (1999), 'Waar een wil is, is geen wet. De categorisering van causale relaties binnen en tussen zinnen', *Gramma/TTT*, 7: 66–86.

Stukker, Ninke (2005), *Causality Marking across Levels of Language Structure*. Utrecht: LOT.

Sweetser, Eve E. (1990), *From Etymology to Pragmatics: Metaphorical and Cultural Aspects of Semantic Structure*. Cambridge: Cambridge University Press.

Talmy, Leonard (1988), 'Force dynamics in language and cognition', *Cognitive Science*, 12: 49–100.

Thompson, Sandra A. (2002), ' "Object complements" and conversation: towards a realistic account', *Studies in Language*, 26: 125–64.

Tomasello, Michael (1999), *The Cultural Origins of Human Cognition*. Cambridge, Mass./London: Harvard University Press.

—— (2003a), *Constructing a Language: A Usage-based Theory of Language Acquisition*. Cambridge, Mass./London: Harvard University Press.

—— (2003b) (ed.) *The New Psychology of Language: Cognitive and Functional Approaches to Language Structure*, ii. Mahwah, NJ/London: Lawrence Erlbaum.

—— and Abbot-Smith, Kirsten (2002), 'A tale of two theories: response to Fisher', *Cognition*, 83: 207–14.

Tomasello, Michael, Call, Josep, and Hare, Brian (2003a), 'Chimpanzees understand psychological states—the question is which ones and to what extent', *Trends in Cognitive Sciences*, 7: 153–6.

—— (2003b), 'Chimpanzees versus humans: it's not that simple', *Trends in Cognitive Sciences*, 7: 239–40.

Traugott, Elizabeth Closs (1989), 'On the rise of epistemic meanings in English: an example of subjectification in semantic change', *Language*, 65: 31–55.

—— (1995), 'Subjectification in grammaticalisation', in Stein and Wright (eds.), 31–54.

—— (1997), 'Subjectification and the development of epistemic meaning: the case of *promise* and *threaten*', in Toril Swan and Olav Jansen Westvik (eds.), *Modality in Germanic Languages: Historical and Comparative Perspectives*. Berlin: de Gruyter, 185–210.

—— (2006), 'The semantic development of scalar focus modifiers', in Bettelou Los and Ans van Kemenade (eds.), *The Handbook of the History of English*. Oxford: Blackwell, 335–359.

—— and Dasher, Richard B. (2002), *Regularity in Semantic Change*. Cambridge: Cambridge University Press.

Uit den Boogaart, Pieter C. (1975), *Woordfrequenties in geschreven en gesproken Nederlands*. Utrecht: Oosthoek, Scheltema & Holkema.

Van Belle, William (1989), 'Want, omdat en aangezien. Een argumentatieve analyse', *Leuvense Bijdragen*, 78: 435–56.

Van der Horst, Joop, and Van der Horst, Kees (1999), *Geschiedenis van het Nederlands in de twintigste eeuw*. The Hague/Antwerp: Sdu Uitgevers/Standaard Uitgeverij.

Van der Mast, Niels, Janssen, Daniël, and Verhagen, Arie (1994), 'Interactionele schrijfprocessen en tekstkenmerken', in A. Maes, P. van Hauwermeiren, and L. van Waes (eds.), *Perspectieven in taalbeheersingsonderzoek*. Dordrecht: ICG, 412–20.

Van der Wouden, Ton (1996), 'Litotes and downward monotonicity', in Heinrich Wansing (ed.), *Negation: A Notion in Focus*. Berlin: de Gruyter, 145–67.

—— (1997), *Negative Contexts: Collocation, Polarity and Multiple Negation*. London/ New York: Routledge.

Van Hoek, Karen (2003), 'Pronouns and point of view: cognitive principles of co-reference', in Tomasello (ed.), 169–94.

Van Megen, Netty (2002), '*Dan* en *want*: hun functie en betekenis in zeventiende-eeuws taalgebruik', *Neerlandistiek.nl* 02.02 <http://www.neerlandistiek.nl>, accessed Oct. 2004.

Verhagen, Arie (1986), *Linguistic Theory and the Function of Word Order in Dutch: A study on Interpretive Aspects of the Order of Adverbials and Noun Phrases*. Dordrecht: Foris/Berlin: de Gruyter.

—— (1995), 'Subjectification, syntax, and communication', in Stein and Wright (eds.), 103–28.

—— (1997), 'Context, meaning, and interpretation, in a practical approach to linguistics', in L. Lentz and H. L. W. Pander Maat (eds.), *Discourse Analysis and Discourse Evaluation*. Amsterdam: Rodopi, 7–39.

—— (2000a), ' "The girl that promised to become something": an exploration into diachronic subjectification in Dutch', in Thomas F. Shannon and Johan P. Snapper (eds.), *The Berkeley Conference on Dutch Linguistics 1997: The Dutch Language at the Millennium*, Lanham. Md.: University Press of America, 197–208.

—— (2000b), 'Interpreting usage: construing the history of Dutch causal verbs', in Barlow and Kemmer (eds.), 261–86.

—— (2000c), 'Concession implies causality, though in some other space', in Couper-Kuhlen and Kortmann (eds.), 361–80.

—— (2001a), 'Terug naar *want* en *omdat*', in Berry Dongelmans, Josien Lalleman, and Olf Praamstra, (eds.), *Kerven in een rots: Opstellen over Nederlandse taalkunde, letterkunde en cultuur, aangeboden aan Jan W. de Vries bij zijn afscheid als hoogleraar Dutch Studies aan de Universiteit Leiden*. Leiden: Stichting Neerlandistiek Leiden, 107–19.

—— (2001b), 'Subordination and discourse segmentation revisited, or: why matrix clauses may be more dependent than complements', in Ted Sanders, Joost Schilperoord, and Wilbert Spooren (eds.), *Text Representation: Linguistic and Psychological Aspects*. Amsterdam/Phila.: Benjamins, 337–57.

—— (2002), 'From parts to wholes and back again', *Cognitive Linguistics*, 13: 403–39.

—— (2003a), 'Semantics, inferential cognition, and understanding text', in Ellen van Wolde (ed.), *Job 28: Cognition in Context*. Leiden: Brill, 231–52.

—— (2003b), 'The Dutch *way*', in Verhagen and Van de Weijer (eds.), 27–57.

—— (2004), 'Language, culture, nature: exploring new perspectives', in Augusto Soares da Silva, Amadeu Torres, and Miguel Gonçalves (eds.), *Linguagem, Cultura e Cognição: Estudos de Linguística Cognitiva*. Coimbra: Editora Almedina, 165–87.

—— (2006), 'On subjectivity and 'long distance *Wh*-movement''. In: Angeliki Athanasiadou, Costas Canakis & Bert Cornillie (eds.), *Subjectification: Various Paths to Subjectivity*. Berlin/New York: Mouton de Gruyter, 323-346.

—— (in press), 'Syntax, recursion, productivity – a usage-based perspective on the evolution of grammar'. In: A. Lubotsky, J. Schaeken, J. Wiedenhof (eds.), *Evidence and Counter-evidence, Festschrift F. Kortlandt, Volume I (SSGL 32 & 33)*. Amsterdam/New York: Rodopi, 2007.

—— (forthcoming), 'Construal and perspectivisation', in Geeraerts and Cuyckens (eds.).

—— (forthcoming, a), 'Intersubjectivity and the architecture of the language system', in Zlatev et al. (eds.).

—— (forthcoming, b), 'Intersubjectivity and explanation in linguistics – a reply to Hinzen and Van Lambalgen'. *Cognitive Linguistics*.

—— (in prep.), 'General syntactic patterns and constructions: finite verb positions in Dutch and German'.

Verhagen, Arie (in prep., a), 'What do you think is the proper location of recursion? An empirical exploration'.

—— (in prep., b), 'Impersonal complementation constructions and the management of viewpoints in different types of discourse'.

—— and Foolen, Ad (2003), 'Hoe kan een woord zijn negatieve lading nou verliezen, laat staan integendeel? Over betekenisverschuiving bij ontkennende woorden', in Jan Stroop (ed.), *Waar gaat het Nederlands naar toe? Panorama van een taal.* Amsterdam: Bakker, 308–18.

—— and Kemmer, Suzanne (1997), 'Interaction and causation: Causative constructions in modern standard Dutch', *Journal of Pragmatics*, 27: 61–82.

—— and van de Weijer, Jeroen (2003) (eds.), *Usage-based Approaches to Dutch.* Utrecht: LOT.

Wierzbicka, Anna (1988), *The Semantics of Grammar.* Amsterdam/Phila.: Benjamins.

Zlatev, Jordan. (forthcoming), 'The co-evolution of intersubjectivity and bodily mimesis', in Zlatev et al. (eds.).

——, Racine, Timothy P., Sinha, Chris, and Itkonen, Esa (eds.) (forthcoming), *The Shared Mind: Perspectives on Intersubjectivity.* Amsterdam/Philadelphia: John Benjamins Publishing Company.

Index

Words and phrases analysed in the text are indexed in italics., e.g. *let alone*. Figures, notes and tables are indicated by f, n and t.

aanwezig 90
Abbot-Smith, Kirsten 3n
abductive arguments 193
abductive inferences 202
abductive reasoning 175, 178, 178n, 179–180, 191;
    see also reasoning
    mental space configurations 175, 175f
abstract constituents 83
abstractness, in grammar 82
accessibility 29n, 76
acquisition 90–92, 128
    language 76
active clauses 133; *see also* clauses
additive connectives 12
adjectives 88, 90
    predicative 13
adjuncts 18, 82, 96n, 134–135
    as conceptualizers 132
    clauses 149, 151
        complements 91, 93, 97; matrix clauses 91, 138n
    phrases 90
adverbs 134–135
    speaker-oriented 136
    traditional 158
adverbial clauses *see* clauses, adverbial
adversative conjunctions 165–166
adversative markers 51
affixal negation 33; *see also* negation
Afrikaans 31n
agents 4, 22, 98; *see also* intentional agents; mental agents
    orientation 22n
Akmajian, Adrian 88
Algemene Nederlandse Spraakkunst (ANS) 100
almost 38, 45, 46, 46n, 48f, 49, 50–52, 56, 59, 69, 70, 76–77, 107
already 56
alternations 87

although 162–163, 166, 169–170, 170n, 171–174, 181–187, 187n, 188–189, 190, 195, 196
anaphors 29, 153
    antecedents 81
    discourse 29n, 77, 152, 154
    relations 152
and 54, 107
animal communication 8–16, 214, 216
    and cognition 14
animals 8
Anscombre, Jean-Claude 9, 9n, 10, 12, 13, 15, 42, 183n, 211
antecedents 81
antonyms 56
argument, position of verbs 83
argumentation:
    analysis 60–69, 87–88
    auxiliary syntax 23–24
    information 9
    marking 202
    orientation 13
    virtual, and negation 28–77
argumentative causal connectives, and concession 202f
argumentative causality, epistemic 183
argumentative connectors 58, 214
argumentative discourse 128, 143, 144n
argumentative force 21–22, 47, 110n, 170
argumentative operators 30, 44, 45, 50, 50f, 51, 53, 77
    conventional function of 50f
    differences in 48, 109
    linguistic meanings of 49
argumentative orientation 41, 56, 80, 105, 106, 107, 110
a-chance 45t
a-passed 46t
conjuncts 199
complement clauses 114
constraining coreference 50

232 Index

argumentative orientations (*cont.*)
  expressions and their 110
  matrix clauses 215
  negation 53n
  role 161
  scalar operators 107
  speaker-oriented markers 109n
argumentative strength 44–45, 45f, 47–50, 59, 105, 107, 109, 109n, 110
argumentativity:
  and complementation 105
  in language system 10, 11, 22
  theory of 8–16, 23, 28, 41, 80
arguments 82
  abductive 193
  clausal 84
  nominal 84
    and predicates 104; without CT-predicates 138
  noun phrases 83n
  position of verb 83
Ariel, Mira 29n
Aristotle 59n
as well as 91
assessment 8, 9, 28, 47, 92, 214, 216
assumptions:
  background 167–168
  concessive sentences 167–174
  propositions 167
asymmetry:
  of expressions 23
  syntactic 24
Austin, John L. 14, 107, 108, 110
autonomous adaptive agents 4; *see also* agents
auxiliary syntax *see* syntax, auxiliary

Banfield, Ann 104, 130
bang zijn dat 86
barely 38–39, 45, 46, 46n, 48f, 49, 50n, 51–53, 53n, 56, 57, 59, 60, 61, 69, 70, 72, 107, 109
Barth, Dagmar 170n
be afraid 104, 138
because 91, 162–163, 165, 175–177, 183–184, 185–186, 190–191, 193, 202, 203f, 211
behavior 14
  of negation 42; *see also* negation
behavioural biology 2, 8, 10, 14, 35, 36
beloven 19–20, 23–24
Benveniste, Émile 4, 110, 110n
binary distinction 3n, 44

blending 114n, 127
Blom, Alied, 87, 88
Bolinger, Dwight 101n, 189n
Boogaart, Ronny 128, 145, 146
bottom-up syntactic analysis 82
Bowerman, Melissa 4
Boye, Kasper 94n, 189n
Bradbury, Jack W. 8, 9
Brown Corpus (English), *Wh*-extraction in 122
Bühler, Karl 6
Burridge, Kate 195n
but 53, 54, 55n, 64, 107, 109, 166
Bybee, Joan 101n, 102
Byrne, Richard W. et al 3n

cancelling of inferences 166
causal clauses *see* clauses, causal
  causal conjunctions 180
causal connectives *see* connectives, causal
causal CT-predicates *see* CT-predicates, causal
causal inferences 180–181, 183, 186–187, 190, 196–197, 202–203, 209;
  see also inferences
causal reasoning 179; *see also* reasoning
causal relations 176, 202
causals, epistemic 183
causality 160
  concession 174
  concessivity 163–165, 183, 187
  discourse coherence 149
  epistemic 175, 179, 181, 182
    argumentative 183; perspective 175, 191
  expressions 149
  forward 178
  marking 147–149, 185–187, 190, 208
    mental space configurations and 190
  negated 163–164, 190
    concessivity 184–187, 194
causality-based:
  arguments 192–193
  epistemic relations 176–177
causation 15, 91, 142, 143, 146, 212
  clauses 145
  conditional 113
  connections 141
  connectives, and concessive relations 59n

complement-taking predicates *see*
  complement-taking predicates,
    causal
  expressions 103n
  perspectivization 147
  properties 50
  recursive 148–149
  relations 27, 81, 141, 144, 145
  verbs 143
causative constructions 144, 145, 145n, 207, 207n, 211–212
causatives, epistemic and concessives 183
chaining patterns 151, 152, 153
children:
  development 2, 35n, 113
    complementation constructions 92
  language of young 110
  perspective 213
  speech 128
  utterances 92
Chomsky, Noam 3n, 99n, 119, 119n, 219
Clark, Herbert H. 7
clause combining 82–83, 98, 157;
clause integration, matrix 151
clauses;
  see also adjuncts, clauses;
      complementation clauses;
      CT-clauses;
  matrix clauses
  active 133
  adverbial 82, 98
  boundaries 81, 121n
  causal 177–178, 179
    negation 196
  constituents 81–83
    hypotactics 94
  complement 215
  complementation in written
    languages 93–94
  concessive 170, 174, 189, 196–197
    in discourse 183
  connected 180
  discourse segments 149–154
  embedding of 1, 78, 79, 91, 93
  finite 95n
  grammatical arguments 83n
  object 82
    direct, and verbs 100
  simplex 27, 82, 90, 143, 149, 215
    in complementation
      constructions 154; transitive 78–79

subject 81, 82, 139n
subordinate 82, 90, 95, 96, 96n, 119, 121
syntactic structure 81
transitive 100
cognition 59, 60
  animals 2
    and communication 14
  cultural origins of 3, 3n
  human 2–3, 4, 50, 210
  social 2n
  spatial 4
  verbs of 110
cognitive accessibility 29, 29n
cognitive capacities 14, 98–99
cognitive constellations 29, 57
cognitive coordination 7, 7n, 8, 10, 17, 22, 28, 35, 51, 60, 97, 99, 104–106, 107, 108, 113, 133, 135, 156, 210
  complement-taking clauses 128, 150
  complementation constructions 98, 131
  conceptualization, between subjects 67, 76, 101, 151
  conceptualizers 107
cognitive grammar 4
  construction-based approaches to 24
cognitive linguistics 15n
cognitive models 12, 13, 17, 42, 43, 44, 47, 50, 52, 53, 56, 57, 59, 60, 142, 167–174, 175, 177, 179, 180, 184, 193, 195, 196, 197, 199, 202
  as default rule 58, 58n, 168, 173–174
cognitive operations 57, 72, 75, 76
cognitive systems 76
  influencing 26
  intersubjective coordination 97
  mutual coordination 28
coherence relations 91
  grammaticalization of 97
  textual 176
  with discourse segments 112–113
coherent continuations *see* continuations, coherent
coherent discourse 25; *see also* discourse
cohesion patterns, and object
  dimension 153
common ground 4–8, 117; *see also* ground
communication; *see also* animal
  communication
  acts of 104, 114
  between beings 7, 59
  human 8–16, 29, 214, 216

Index

communication; *see also* animal communication (*cont.*)
  languages and 42
  verbal 35n
complement clauses 80, 82, 83, 85–87, 93, 100, 112–114, 119–120, 135, 145; *see also* clauses
  as nominal predicates 90
  conceptualization:
    objects 215; subjects 141
  content 115, 117, 142, 151
  conversation 92
  complement-taking clauses 138, 151, 151n
  complement-taking predicates 138
  deictic elements 104
  extraposed 90
  ground 115, 116
  interpretation 138
  matrix clauses 92, 93
  object 132
  subject 132
  '*Wh*-word' 122n
complement-taking clauses 99, 100–101, 105, 113, 113n, 114n, 119, 120, 123, 134–137, 138, 138n, 149–151, 151n, 152–153, 154;
  see also clauses
  as extension of epistemic stance 135
  cognitive coordination 128
  coherence relations in discourse 112–113
  conceptualization, object of 149
  conceptualizers 133
  content 107, 114, 119
  copular epistemic 133
  impersonal complementation structures 135
  in causation 145
  intersubjective coordination 147
  marking epistemic stance 131
  negative 188, 189
  onstage conceptualizers 104, 118
  personal complementation structures 135
  perspectival 145
  second person 104, 112
  third person 134
  verbs 84, 100
complement-taking predicates 99, 101n, 102, 110, 115, 116, 136, 141–143, 149;
  see also predicates
  causal 141–142, 142t, 143, 143t, 147
  in impersonal complementation sentences 136, 137t
  indicating mental states 115
  mental-space building 147
  object complementation constructions 136n
  object complements 103, 103t
  perspectival 143t
  verbs 84, 100
  with '*Wh*-extraction' in *de Volkskrant* 124t
complementation 4, 93, 218; *see also* complementation constructions; sentences, complementation
  analysis 79, 149, 156, 189n
  argumentativity 105
  complementizers and 101n
  constructional templates 215
  discourse structure 97, 149
  domain 210
  patterns 111
  properties 126
  questions, in construal configuration 120
  recursiveness 99
  structure 79, 93
  subjectivity 80
  syntactic relations 137–141
  syntax 119, 155
complementation constructions 15, 25, 26–27, 64n, 80, 81, 93–94, 97, 100, 112, 114, 114n, 115, 118, 120, 129, 144, 150;
  analysis 139, 214
  use of simplex clauses 154
  child development 92
  cognitive coordination 98
  construal configuration 154
  direct speech 113–114
  Dutch 101, 111, 111f, 144n
    partial general network 138f
  functions 67, 104
  impersonal 132, 133, 137
    conceptual configurations 207;
    construal configuration 134f;
    complement-taking clauses 133;
    predicates 132–133
  intersubjective coordination 98, 112
    construal configuration 132
  intersubjectivity 213
  matrix clauses 26, 80–81, 97, 109–110, 149, 155, 214

negative clauses 188
network of 81, 94n, 110–113, 128–129, 131, 137, 141, 149, 155
    causation in 147–149
object 136, 136n, 137–138
    complement-taking-predicates of 136n
personal 132, 133
    predicates 132–133
perspective 182
polyphony 114
predicates 143
syntax 154
syntactic roles 113n
Wh-extraction 124, 129
    network 126f
complementizers 152
complements:
    adjunct clauses 90
    analyzed as subjects 97
        constituents 90, 119, 131
    clausal 100–101
        constituents 83; predicates 104
    conceptualization 91–92
    contents 105, 118–119, 188
    embedding 127
    finite 78–155
    ground, relation to 107
    matrix clauses *see* clauses, matrix
    matrix predicates 85
    object 97, 97, 103, 103t, 131, 136, 139n, 141t
        complement-taking predicates 103
    predicates used with 110
    sentences 132
    status 94
    subject 97
complex expressions 87; *see also* expressions
complex sentences *see* sentences, complex
compression 114n
computation 152, 152n
Comrie, Bernard 99n
conceptual configurations 34, 173, 207
    complementation constructions 105
    impersonal
conceptual relationships 91, 93
conceptualization 4–5, 6, 6n, 7, 9, 12–13, 16, 146
    complements 91–92
    construal configuration 208
    Ground 160

objects 18, 23, 24, 26, 41, 42, 49–51, 53, 53n, 56, 59, 60, 61, 69, 72, 76, 79, 97, 101, 105, 112, 113, 128, 132, 133, 149, 154–156, 159, 161, 175, 178, 183, 202–203, 206, 208, 214, 215, 216
subjects 24, 41, 42, 60, 61, 97, 112, 113, 128, 132, 133, 135, 142, 151, 154, 156, 160, 175, 178, 206–207, 208
    cognitive coordination 67, 76, 151;
    complement clauses 141;
    construal configuration 211–212;
    mutual coordination 214
conceptualizers 30, 59, 133
    construal configuration 98, 134
    in world 97
    complementation constructions 80–81
    impersonal 207
    complement-taking clauses 133
    epistemic stance 202
    explicit 120
    inferences 205–206
    finite complements 78–155
    in the Ground 132, 147, 158, 201, 206–207
    mental spaces and 169
    negation 209
    onstage 97–98, 105, 106, 113–115, 115n, 1116–118, 120, 131, 132
        complement clauses and 105; and complement-taking clauses 104;
        matrix clauses 215; Ground 113, 115n, 117, 120, 129–131;
        mental space 115, 116, 118, 128, 130;
        minimal distinctness 215–216
    third-person 104–107, 109, 215
    onstage 11, 107, 114, 214
concession; *see also* negation, concession
causality 174
concessive clauses *see* clauses concessive
concessive conjunctions 180, 198
    intersubjective coordination 208
concessive connectives *see* connectives, concession in
concessive constructions *see* constructions, concessive
concessive relations 27
    and causal connectives 59n, 161
concessive sentences *see* sentences, concessive
concessives 167
    content 183
    epistemic 182, 183

concessives (*cont.*)
    causals 174; causatives in 183;
        domain 174; use of 180–182
    intersubjectivity of 175
concessivity:
    causality 163–165, 183, 187
        negated 184–187, 194
    distinctions 208
    epistemic 181–182
        mental space configurations 182f
    negation 163, 164, 185, 190
conditional constructions 217
conjunctions;
    see also concessive conjunctions;
        connectives
    adversative 165–166
    causal 185, 208
        epistemic 180
    contrastive 12, 65, 66, 109, 174
    coordinating 157
    interpretation 157n, 158
    subordinating 96n, 157
    traditional 158
conjuncts 37, 38, 38n, 39, 60–65, 69, 88, 190–191, 199–201
connective expressions *see* expressions, connective
connectives 76, 77, 107, 158, 158n; *see also* discourse, connectives
    asymmetrical interactions 216
    causal 161, 162, 164, 174, 187, 191, 197, 202, 207, 208, 209, 211
        argumentative 202f; in Dutch 178; forward 198, 206n;
        constraints on perspective 190–197;
        construal configuration 197;
        negation 198; non-argumentative 203f
    conceptualization, objects of 159
    concessive 162, 187, 197, 201, 209
        inferences 201
        construal configuration 162
        domain 210
        intersubjective dimension 159, 205–206
        negation 205, 216
conspecifics 2, 3, 4, 14, 98
constant pattern 151
constituents 80, 88
    abstract 83
    clausal 81, 82, 119
        manifestions 82
    clauses 81–83, 119

complements 90, 119
    displaced 126
    embedded 131
    'movement' 81
    nominal 82, 100
    structure 84
    view of complement clauses 81
construal configuration 4–5, 6n, 8, 10, 11, 13, 15n, 16, 22, 23, 30, 50n, 57, 59, 60, 75–76, 79, 97, 98n, 105, 120, 133, 136, 150, 158f, 202
    basic 161, 206
    causal connectives 197–202
    complementation constructions 154
    complementation questions 120
    conceptual structure 208
    conceptualization, subjects of 211–212
    conceptualizers 98, 134
    first-person perspective 106f
    for impersonal complementation constructions 134f
    for second-person perspective in questions 121f
    intersubjective dimension 119, 129, 132, 155
    third-person perspective 106f
construals:
    argumentative character 21
    asymmetry 24
    basic elements 7f, 31f, 41f, 55, 183
    grammar 79
    meaning 44n
    'objective' expressions 17f
    relations 5–6, 6n, 136
        of reasoning 166; vertical 59
    subjective, semantics 142–143
    subjective expressions 18f
construction grammar 24, 35, 35n, 38, 79
constructional syntax 25; *see also* syntax
constructions; *see also* complementation constructions
    analysis 67
    argumentative character 80
    causative 211–213, 212
        Dutch 212
    complement 105
    complementation 213, 215
    concessive 168–169
    copular 90
    hypotactic 157
    intersubjective coordination 67
    intersubjectivity 213

network of 93
paratactic 157
pseudo-cleft 88, 89
content domain 164–167, 177
content sentences 192; *see also* sentences
context:
  effects 77
  propositions 63
  sentences 61
context-dependence 43–44, 46
  meanings 44n
context-independence 49
continuations:
  coherent 66
contradiction 56, 71, 75, 80, 84n, 167, 168, 173, 182, 186, 187–190
  mental spaces 33, 96, 200, 209
contrary 29, 31, 33
  concepts 70
  Dutch 34, 35
  English 70
  mental spaces 32, 32f, 33
contrast, components of 211
contrast markers *see* markers, contrast
contrastive conjunctions *see* conjunctions, contrastive
contrastive connectives 64, 107; *see also* connectives
conventions/conventional 4, 8, 13, 22–24, 136
  because 203f
  causality 208
  Dutch:
    daardor 206–207, *daarom* 206; *want* 192
  English 176
  functions 9–10, 12, 26, 42, 59, 59f, 73, 75, 169 175, 201, 215
    concessions 202, 202f
  human languages 3
  implicatures 167
  linguistics 4
    constraints 35–39, 69
  meaning 10, 16–18, 22, 42, 44, 50, 50n, 60–61, 69, 76, 176, 201–202, 206, 208, 211, 214
  non-argumentative causal connectives 203, 209
conversation 6, 91, 120, 129
  complement clauses in 92
coordinating conjunctions 36
copulas 90
  constructions 87, 90

expressions 86; *see also* expressions
predicates 138; *see also* predicates
sentences 88; *see also* sentences
coreference 50–55, 150n
Cornelis, Louise H. 115, 118
Cornillie, Bert 22
corpus data 25, 81, 129
Corpus of Spoken Dutch 66n, 69
correspondence lines 30
Coulson, Seana 114n
counterparts, mental spaces 31
Croft, William 24, 40, 100, 102, 102n, 139, 157n
Cruse, D. Alan 24, 100, 102n
CT-clause/predicates 99
CT-clauses *see* complement-taking clauses
CT-predicates *see* complement-taking predicates
CT-verbs 115, 115n, 118; *see also* verbs
  in *Wh*-extraction 125t
  mental space in 188–189
cultural models 12, 13, 17, 42, 43, 44, 47, 50, 52, 53, 56, 57, 59, 60, 142, 167–174, 175, 177, 179, 180, 184, 193, 195, 196, 197, 199, 202
  as default rule 58, 58n, 168, 173–174
cultural origins of cognition 3, 3n
culture:
  human 3n, 4, 12, 213
  linguistic conventions 4
  rules 12

Daalder, Saskia, 87, 88
daardoor 198, 203, 205, 206, 206f, 207–208, 211, 216
daarom 199–201, 202–204, 206–208
Dabrowska, Ewa 128, 129, 129n
Dancygier, Barbara 195, 217
Dasher, Richard B. 6
dat 152–153, 205
Dawkins, Richard 8
De Rooij, Jaap 86n, 100
De Villiers, Jill G. & Peter A. 218, 219
De Vries, Jan W. 191
Degand, Liesbeth 176, 178n, 195, 195n, 200n, 204, 204n, 205
deictic elements:
  center 130
  complement clauses 104
  first-person 114
deixis 26
Delahunty, Gerald P. 218

Den Hertog, Cornelis H. 84, 87
denken 84, 111, 122, 123–124
   Wh-extraction 126
deontic interpretation 164
denotation 44n
   descriptive uses, of speech act verbs 110
determiners 140
dialectics 210
dialogue 35n
Diessel, Holger 91, 92, 93, 99, 110, 111, 128, 131, 219
direct objects 83, 83n, 85–86, 138
   Dutch 86n
direct speech 113–114
discourse:
   advanced 110
   analysis 34, 39, 49, 61–62, 65, 90–92, 104, 152, 216
   anaphors 29n, 152, 154
   causal 161
   coherence 24, 45, 54, 91, 105, 110, 145, 146
      causality 149; complement clauses 114;
      relations 159n; relations with complement-taking clauses 112–113
   cohesion 152
   concessive clauses 183
   connected 40–41, 53, 214
      segments 146
   connectives 4, 12, 26, 53, 216
      concession 161; linguistic behavior 209;
      negation in 161
   interpersonal 6n
   interpretation 30n, 150
   narrative 35n
   perspective 97
   pragmatics 77
   relations 53, 90–91, 146, 160–161
   segments 149–154, 156
   speech 179
   structure 77, 80, 90, 95, 97, 151, 154–155
      clauses 91; complementation 97, 98, 149–150;
   units 90–91, 155
   written 93
Doeve, Rob 151, 152, 153
double negation 28, 32, 34, 35, 70, 72, 173
dreigen 116
Du Bois, John W. 4
duality 162–163, 163n, 174, 187

Ducrot, Oswald 9, 9n, 10, 11, 28, 35n, 42, 46n, 55n, 58n, 76, 114, 168
dummy phrases 85, 86
dummy prepositional objects 104
dus 198–199, 199n, 200f, 200n, 201, 203–206
Dutch 10, 19–24, 25, 26, 33
   analysis 101n, 138, 139, 163–164, 191
   causal connectives 178
   causative constructions 212
   complementation constructions 101, 111, 111f, 135, 136, 140n
      partial general network 138f
   direct objects 86n
   epistemic stance 133
   grammarians 87
   grammatical subject 86
   language 102
   newspaper fragments 103, 136–137
   nouns 140
   sentences 151
   subordinate clauses 23
   syntactics 19n
   Wh-extraction 121, 122–123, 129

Eindhoven Corpus 63, 66n, 99, 103, 103n, 112, 121, 123, 124, 125, 125n, 137t, 147, 152, 170, 173, 173n, 193
Elffers, Els 87
embedding:
   causality 27
   clauses 1, 27, 78, 79, 91, 93
   complements 127
   infinite 99n,
   mental space 148
   perspective 27, 148
   recursive 128
   spaces 182, 188
empty 47–48
English:
   analysis 101n, 138, 141n, 163–164, 191
   complementation constructions 136
   data 25
   epistemic stance 133
   semantics 19n
   Wh-extraction 121, 122–123, 129
      with verbs 123
entailments 31, 37
   relations 41
      presuppositions 167
entrenchment 25, 102, 111
epistemic causality *see* causality, epistemic
epistemic causals 183

epistemic concessivity *see* concessivity, epistemic
epistemic domain 165, 174, 180
epistemic inferences 180–182
epistemic interpretations 22n, 164
epistemic reasoning 183; *see also* reasoning
epistemic relations 175, 178, 178n
  between conjuncts 190–191
  causality-based 176–177
  non-causal 178n
epistemic stance 18, 19, 31, 34, 72, 73, 92, 133
  conceptualizers 202
  complement-taking clauses marking 131
    extensions 135
  Dutch 133
  English 133
  Ground 120
  mental spaces 72, 176, 180, 209
    background 195
  opposite 211, 215
  speakers 129
  use 174
Erteschik-Shir, Nomi 131n
events, descriptions of 26–27, 80, 82, 87
Everett, Daniel 219
evolution 2n, 3n, 8, 35n, 213, 214, 216, 219
exceptions 18, 58n, 59n, 104, 161
expressions 9, 10, 24; *see also* construals, configuration
  argumentative 16
  causality 103n, 149
  coherent 46
  complex 87
  copular 86
  evaluative 133
  incoherent 46
  linguistic 156
  mental state 117
  modal 108n
  negative 10n, 31, 72
  numerical 13, 48, 211
  objective 16, 19
  quantitative 48
  subjective 18, 19
  third person:
    descriptive 110n; objective 110n
extensions, from prototypes 126, 132, 137, 141, 147
extraction utterances 128–129; *see also* utterances

factive verbs 117
factivity 117
fail to notice 117
false belief 218–219
Fauconnier, Gilles 22, 29, 31, 58, 100, 108n, 114n
figure/ground 6n
Fillmore, Charles J. 28, 35, 36, 37, 37n, 38, 38n, 39, 39n, 40, 41, 60, 61, 62, 63, 66, 67, 68n, 70n
finite clauses 95n; *see also* clauses
finite complements *see* complements, finite
finite verbs 137, 138; *see also* verbs
first-person:
  complement-taking predicates 110
  deictic elements 104, 114
  expressions 67, 98, 120
  for predicate slots 103
  markers 67
  matrix clauses 108n, 109, 216
  of mental states 110
  onstage conceptualizers 130
  perspective 196f
  pronouns 131
  usage 116
  utterances 108, 109
Fitch, W. Tecumseh 3n, 99n, 219
Foolen, Ad P. 55n, 68
forget 117
forward causality 178; *see also* causality; connectives, causal
free indirect speech 130
French 55n, 205
frequency 103, 110, 129, 131
  causality expressions 149
  data 24, 80
  high 102, 110, 125–126
  low 147
  token 102–104, 111
    high 111, 124
  type 125–129
fronting 88
full 47–48
functions, derived 42

Geerts, Guido 86n, 100
general rules 79, 129
generalizations 15, 24, 25, 84
generative grammar 119, 139n, 217
generative linguistics 3, 87
generative theory 83n
German 40, 67, 158, 170, 195, 205
gevaar 90

Goldberg, Adele E. 24, 25, 79, 87, 100, 102n
grammar:
  analysis 1, 83–90, 94
    abstractness 82
  constructions 24, 26, 76
  discourse structure 90
  elements 9, 16, 26
  encoding 4
  formation 101n
  intersubjective coordination 214
  management 212–214
  phenomena 26
  predicates 1
  structure 42
    construals 79
  subsystem 59
  syntactic relations 139
  traditions 81
grammatical categories 119–120
grammatical dependencies over infinite distances 99n
grammatical objects 81
grammatical subjects 22, 27, 79, 81, 86, 86n, 132
grammaticalization 97, 157
Grice, H. Paul 7n
Gricean implicatures 48
Gricean maxims/principles 63, 71, 176
ground 6, 6n, 7, 16, 17–18, 97, 128
  and onstage conceptualizers *see* conceptualizers, onstage
  and onstage perspective 81
  complement clauses 115, 116
  complement-taking clauses 150
  complements, relation to 107
  conceptualization and the 160
  conceptualizers 132, 147, 201
  epistemic stance 120, 202
  intersubjective coordination 132
  onstage mental space from 120
  status of the 193
  whether/if-clause 117n
Günthner, Susanne 170n

Haeseryn, Walter 86n, 100
Haiman, John 82
Halliday, Michael A. K. 6n, 82, 91, 157
happy 70
Harder, Peter 94n, 189n
Haun, Daniel B. M. 4
Hauser, Marc D. 3n, 99n, 219
Heine, Bernd 22n

here 104–105
het echte gevaar 89
het gevaar 88, 89
Hinzen, Wolfram 217
Horn, Laurence R. 32, 33, 34, 46n, 47, 70, 71, 73, 75, 189n
Hopper, Paul 129
human cognition *see* cognition, human
human culture 3n, 4
human languages 9, 15, 16
Hyland, Ken 218
hypotaxis:
  connected clauses 95; *see also* clauses
  grammatical relationships 91, 93
  matrix clauses 98

I think 110, 128, 129
impersonal constructions 132, 218
impersonal intersubjectivity 131–132
impersonal perspectivization 81
implicatures: 71
  Gricean 48
indirect speech 114; *see also* speech
incoherent linguistic context 16; *see also* coherent linguistic context
inferences 22, 49, 50, 52, 53, 54, 55, 58, 61, 64, 66, 68, 75, 109, 200; *see also* causal inferences; negation
  abductive 202
  background mental space 206
  cancelling of 166
  concessive connectives 201–202, 205–206
  epistemic 180–182
  linguistic constraints on 52
  perspective 209
inferential reasoning 9, 41, 42, 50; *see also* reasoning
infinite embedding 99n
influencing 10, 35
  cognitive system 26
  mutual 16
information:
  argumentation 9
  content 97
  exchange 9, 10, 14, 16
  linguistic communication 22–23, 37, 37n
  persuasion 15
  structure 131n
  validity 105
  value 13
  view 15
informativeness 37, 37n, 39

inheritance networks 25
instantiations:
  clausal 83
  complementation sentences 100
integendeel 31n, 34, 35, 70
intentions 188, 189
interjections 181
intentional agents 2, 182; *see also* agents
interpersonal function of language 6n
interpersonal interactions 35n, 129, 212
intersubjective 81
  and objective dimensions 155
  dimension 121, 150
    of discourse interpretation 152; of construal configuration 129, 155
intersubjective coordination 16, 24, 41–42, 49, 79, 97, 104, 111, 132, 156, 190, 201
  analysis 68n
  argumentative operators 50, 58f
  complement-taking clauses 147
  dimension 50, 50f, 52, 53, 56, 57, 69, 76, 79–80, 147, 190, 205, 210–213
    complementation 79–80; constructions 216; of construal configuration 50, 119–120, 174–175; sentential negation 75; third-person matrix clauses 80
  grammar 214
  horizontal relations 30, 42, 5
  linguistic constraints 35–41, 211
  marking 148–149
  negation 46, 56–57, 57f
  primary function of 42–43
intersubjectivity 210–212
  analysis of 79, 94n, 155
    with discourse perspective 149
  and objectivity 16–19
  approach 187
  basis 28
  complementation constructions 80
  concessives 175
  constructions 212–213
  definition 5n; *see also* subjectivity
  grammar 25, 211
  impersonal 131–132
  negation 97
intuitions 25, 152, 154
Israel, Michael 55n, 59n
Itkonen, Esa 217

Jackendoff, Ray 3n, 9, 9n, 10n, 15n, 84, 99n, 219
Jakobson, Roman 6, 9
Janssen, Daniël 170
Jarvella, Robert J. 46, 51, 51n

Kay, Paul 28, 35, 35n, 36, 37, 37n, 38, 38n, 39, 39n, 40, 41, 60, 61, 62, 63, 66, 67, 68n, 70n
Keller, Rudi 3, 7n, 175n, 195n
Kemmer, Suzanne 212
Kita, Sotaro 4
Klima, Edward S. 55n
König, Ekkehard 162, 163, 163n, 167, 168n
Koster, Jan 139n
Krebs, John R. 8

laat staan 28, 40, 67
Lagerwerf, Luuk 10n, 58n
Lakoff, George 9n
Langacker, Ronald, 4, 5, 6, 6n, 17, 24, 31, 67, 92, 93, 96n, 100, 102n
language 76
  acquisition 90–92, 128
  and world 28, 41, 76
    secondary function 42–43
  conceptual space in 136
  culture 3n
  human 1, 3n, 4
    conventions in 3
  metafunctions of 6n
  meaning of 1–2
  natural 13, 27
    negation 28
  spoken 93, 94
  structure, theory of 161, 210
  units, frequency 129
  use 8, 9, 14, 18, 24–25, 50, 52, 53n, 76, 161, 208
    patterns 155
  written 93–94
leave out 117
let alone 26, 28, 35–41, 60–64, 64n, 65–69, 71n, 76–77, 80
  argumentation and 60; pragmatics 37; schema 36;
  semantics 36–37; syntactics 36
Levinson, S. C. 4
lexical verbs 86; *see also* verbs
linear cohesion 81

linguistic communication:
  information 22–23
  use 35n
linguistic expressions *see* expressions, linguistic
linguistic knowledge 24, 61
  units 104, 138
    conventional meanings 17;
    distinctions between 19
linguistic negation *see* linguistics, negation
linguistics 2, 3n
  analysis 25, 210
  communication 7n
  competence, rules 93
    writing 93
  conventions 4
    constraints 35–41, 69
  elements 213–214
  functions 213–214
  expressions 9; *see also* expressions
  generalizations 15, 25, 56, 72
  meanings in 9, 10, 15n, 41, 48, 69, 76
  modern 82
  negation 31–32, 72
  paradigms 76
  practice 79
  structural 6
  symbols 4
  usage 6, 8, 25
    events 16, 60; generalizations 24
  utterances 30
litotes 28, 32, 34, 35, 70, 72, 173
little 50
little chance 43–44, 46
Lodge, David 72
long-distance dependencies 99n
long-distance *Wh*-movement *see* *Wh*-extraction
long-term validators 16
Lundquist, Lita 46, 51, 51n
Lyons, John 6

maar 55n
main clauses *see* clauses, simplex
Majid, Asifa, 4
management 53n, 160, 209
  of cognitive states 1–27, 35n, 212–214
markers; *see also* epistemic markers
  concession 161
  contrast 55, 64, 72, 161
  first-person 67
  stance 112

matrix clauses 26, 78, 79, 90, 92, 93, 97, 98, 119, 128, 131;
  see also clauses
  adjunct clauses 151
  argumentative orientations 215
  clause/predicates 99
  complementation constructions 26, 80–81, 97, 109–110, 149, 155
    negative 188
  complex sentences 82
  content 113–114, 129
  descriptions of events 87
  first person 108n, 109, 216
  hypotactics 98
  intersubjective dimension 79–80
    complements 82
  perspective 215
  subject of 132
  third-person 80, 98
matrix predicates 97
  complements 85
matrix subjects, and *Wh*-extraction 126t
Matthiessen, Christian 82, 91, 95, 98, 157
Maxim of Quantity *see* Gricean maxims
mental agents 4, 98, 214; *see also* agents
Mental-Space Builder 101n
mental spaces 28, 29, 32f, 59, 107, 217–218
  analysis 34, 57, 70
  approach 35n
  background 167–174, 183, 198
    assumptions 167–174; epistemic stance 195; inferences 205–206
  background 167–174, 183, 198
    epistemic stance 195;
    inferences 205–206
  building 133
    complement-taking predicates 147
  conceptualizers 169, 185
  configurations 30, 57, 169f, 171f, 172f, 180, 181, 184f, 185f, 186f, 191–192, 198, 201, 209
    complex 213; for epistemic concessivity 182f;
    in abductive reasoning 175, 175f;
    causal connectives 190; under negation 187
  constellations 34, 186
    with opposite epistemic stance 193
  content 173
  contrast 174
  CT-verbs 189
  embedding 148

epistemic stance 72, 176, 180, 209
identifying 114
interpretation of 30n
negation 187, 200
onstage conceptualizers 115, 116, 118, 128
    Ground 118, 131, 189
    recursion 182
    representation 184
    sentential negation 30f
    terminology 114
    theory 30, 30n, 58, 114n
    third person 117
mental states:
    be afraid as 104
    complement-taking predicates 115
    expressions 16, 117
    first-person indications 110
    influencing 14
    predicates 100, 108n
metafunctions 6n
metonymy 21
minimal distinctness 129
    onstage conceptualizer from
        Ground 215–216
modal verbs 22; *see also* verbs
    analysis 177
    epistemic interpretation 22n, 164–165
models, cognitive 12, 13, 17, 42, 43, 44, 47, 50, 52, 53, 56, 57, 59, 60, 142, 167–174, 175, 177, 179, 180, 184, 193, 195, 196, 197, 199, 202
    as default rule 58, 58n, 168, 173–174
models, cultural 12, 13, 17, 42, 43, 44, 47, 50, 52, 53, 56, 57, 59, 60, 142, 167–174, 175, 177, 179, 180, 184, 193, 195, 196, 197, 199, 202
    as default rule 58, 58n, 168, 173–174
mono-clausal structures 131
morphological negation *see* negation, morphological
Morton, Eugene S. 8, 9, 14, 15
mutually-shared knowledge 58n, 68

narrative discourse 35n
natural language negation 208
negated causality *see* causality, negated
negation 4, 10n, 26, 68n, 97, 214–215; *see also* concessivity, negation
    affixal 33
    analysis 41, 44, 49, 52, 57, 58, 59, 60, 70, 76, 155

argumentative orientation 53n
causality 163, 190
conceptualizers 209
components 211
concession 187–190, 197
connectives 205, 216
    causal 198
complement-taking clauses 188, 189
double 28, 32, 34, 35, 70, 72, 173
expressions 31
function 56
intersubjective coordination 208
languages:
    human 97; natural 28, 42–43
linguistics 31–32
mental space 187, 200
morphological 28, 32–35, 75, 76–77, 193, 194t, 194n(t), 210, 211
natural language 208
operators 199
perspective 29–35, 208–209
scope 174, 207, 208
sentential 28, 29, 32–35, 70, 72, 76–77, 163, 173, 193, 194t, 210, 211
    conditions of use for 72;
    intersubjective coordination 75;
    and mental spaces 30n; semantics 57
system 58
thought 216
truth value 190
virtual argumentation 28–77
negation-related constructions 4, 64; *see also* constructions
negation-related expressions 30, 105; *see also* expressions
negative deficit 10, 13
negative epistemic stance 117; *see also* stances
negative expressions *see* expressions, negative
negative polarity 38, 55n, 59n, 60
    licensors 58n, 59n
negative raising 189
negotiation 44, 59
network of subconstructions 80; *see also* constructions
no chance 44, 46
nominal arguments 84, 138n; *see also* arguments
    predicates 104; without complement-taking predicates 138

nominal objects 84, 113; *see also* objects
nominal predicates 88, 133
　complement clauses 90
　preposed 90
non-natural meaning 7n
non-performative, use of speech act
　　verbs 109
not 59, 72, 76–77, 107, 185
not impossible 34, 70, 75, 173
not to mention 67
not happy 71–72
not unhappy 70–71, 73
noun phrases *see* phrases, noun
nouns 17
　Dutch, without determiners 140
numerical expressions 13, 48, 211
numerical specifications 14
Nuyts, Jan 5n, 108n, 110, 110n

Oakley, Todd 114n
object dimensions 152
　anaphors in 153; and intersubjective 155;
　　cohesion patterns and 153
object complements 97, 103, 103t, 131, 136,
　　139n, 141t
objective connection, between
　　segments 159f
objective expressions 16, 19; *see also*
　　expressions
objective levels 81
objectivist semantics 9n
objectivity 5, 28
　intersubjectivity 16–19
objects:
　complement clauses and 86
　direct 83, 83n, 85–86, 138
　　Dutch 86n
　nominal 84, 113
　oblique 83
　prepositional 85
　　dummy 104
　pronominal 84
oblique objects 83
O'Connor, Mary Catherine 28, 35, 36, 37,
　　37n, 38, 38n, 39, 39n, 40, 41, 60, 61,
　　62, 63, 66, 67, 68n, 70n
of 152–153
omdat 193–194, 194t, 197, 201–203,
　　206
on the contrary 30–35, 70
one-dimensional scale of speaker
　　involvement 205

ongelukkig 73
Onrust, Margreet 151, 152, 153
onstage conceptualizers *see* conceptualizers,
　　onstage
onstage mental space, from Ground 120
onstage perspective, from Ground 81
ontogeny 2, 7n
ontological development 113
operators 76
orthogonal structures 97, 155
Oversteegen, Leonoor E. 58n
Owings, Donald H. 8, 9, 14, 15
Oxford English Dictionary, The (OED, 22nd
　　ed) 40n, 67, 68n

Pander Maat, Henk, L. W. 13, 161, 176, 178n,
　　183n, 195, 195n, 200n, 204, 204n, 205
paratactic relations 91, 157
parataxis 158n
Parker, Anna R. 219
participants:
　nominal 86
　roles 23, 24
　third person 128
parts of speech 157n
Pasch, Renate 40, 68n, 163n, 167
passive 86, 86n, 113, 118, 133
patterns; *see also* chaining patterns
　abstract 112
　cohesion 153
　complementation 129
　constant 151, 152
　entrenched 104
　extensions 155
　memory 111
　prototypical 129
　specific 112, 126
　thematic cohesion 151f
　thematic continuity 152
　transitive-event 112
performance factors 93
performative use, of speech act
　　verbs 109–110
performativity 107–108, 109n
personal constructions 132, 218; *see also*
　　complementation
　　constructions
personification 21
perspectival complement-taking
　　clauses 145;
　see also complement-taking clauses
perspectival connections 141

perspective 26, 98–99, 106; see negation, and perspective
   causal connectives and constraints on 190–197
   children 213
   complement clauses 108
   complementation constructions 182
   concessive constellation 208–209
   coordination of 214
      epistemic stance 215; of multiple 216
   epistemic causality 175, 191
   first-person 105n, 106n
   inferences across 209
   management 213
   matrix clauses 215
   onstage 81, 131
      conceptualizers 107
   reality 107
   recursion 182, 218
      applications 27
   third-person 106f
perspectivization 8, 146
   causation 147
   impersonal 81
phenomenon, in syntactic theory 126
phrases:
   dummy prepositional 84
   adjective 89
   adjuncts 90
   noun 79, 82, 83, 119
      argument 83n; complement-taking verbs 84;
      predicates 89; subjects 88, 90
   predicates 89
Pinker, Steven 99n, 219
Pit, Mirna 105n, 195, 195n, 205n
point-of-view 5
   human 216
polyphony 35n, 114
polysemy 164, 165
Popper, Karl R. 58, 168
positive polarity 55n
positive stance 72; see also epistemic stance
possible 70, 75, 173
possible worlds 57
pragmatics 9n, 16, 28, 39, 40, 61, 66, 77
predicatehood 89
predicates 33, 37, 56, 87, 89, 90, 141–143; see also complement-taking predicates
   complementation constructions 143
      impersonal 132–133

copular 138
   sentences 88
   evoking mental states 100
   main 96n
   matrix 97–98
   nominals 89, 133
      adjectival 193; arguments 104
   non-copular 133
   noun phrases as 89
   passives 133
   speech acts 108n
   types 101n
      frequency 103
   used with complements 110
      causal 104
prepositional objects 85; see also objects
prepositional phrases, dummy 86
presupposition float 108n, 109n
presuppositions 34, 88n
   background assumptions 167–168
   entailment relations 167
primates 2
productivity 102, 102n
promise 109n, 116, 116n
pronominal objects 84; see also objects
pronouns 110–111, 123, 128
   first-person 131
   personal 103
   second-person 110, 123, 124t, 125, 126, 126t, 129
   third person 123, 124t, 126t
propositions 92, 93, 117
   assumptions 167
prototypes 126, 127, 132, 137, 141, 178n
pseudo-cleft constructions 88, 89
pseudo-cleft sentences 88

quantitative expressions 48; see also expressions
questions:
   construal configuration:
      complementation 120; second-person perspective 121f
   rhetorical 130

Raccah, Pierre-Yves 9n
Racine, Timothy P. 217
reasoning:
   argumentative usage 179
   causal 179, 183
   epistemic reasoning 183

recursion 98–99, 99n, 148, 182–183, 219
  mental spaces 182
  perspective 182
recursive causation 147–149
reëel 88
relative clauses *see* clauses, relative
relevance 37, 63, 161, 175, 185
Rendell, Luke 3n
Renkema, Jan 33n, 103n
rhetorical relations 91, 98
robots 4
Romijn, Kirstin 86n, 100
rules 3, 12, 18, 49, 58, 58n, 59n, 79, 83, 86, 93, 102, 126, 128, 155, 160n, 167–168, 168n, 169, 171–173, 173n, 175 179, 180, 204, 206

Sanders, José 104, 105, 130, 133
Sanders, Ted 144, 145n, 159n, 216
say 84
scalar operators, argumentative orientations of 107
scales 13, 32, 33, 36, 44, 45, 49, 64, 65, 161, 205
schema 36, 93, 100, 102, 104, 111, 137, 139, 151, 160n, 175, 215
schematicity 25
Schilperoord, Joost 96n, 151n
scope of negation 174, 207, 208
Searle, John R. 108, 116, 180n
second person 111, 114, 115n, 120, 122, 123, 126, 130, 131n
  complement-taking clauses 104, 112
  implicit 67
  perspective 121f
  pronouns 110, 123, 124t, 125, 126, 126t, 129
  questions 130
  subjects 124
semantic change 4, 212
semantics 77
  analysis 24, 28, 33, 41, 60
  definition 15n
  extensions 143
  elements 55n
  linguistic 1, 4, 8
    change 4;
    parallels 90
  logical 217
  objectivist 9n
  pragmatics 61
  subjective construals 142–143

sentence-internal grammar 76–77; *see also* grammar
sentences:
  analysis 62, 81–82, 90, 138–139, 152
  complementation 79, 80, 100, 106, 126, 131, 155, 156, 214
    complement-taking predicates 137t; impersonal 136; syntactic roles 210
  complements 132
  complex 82, 87, 90, 135–136, 139
    grammatical structure of 90; matrix clauses of 82; matrix verbs 82
  concessive 181, 187, 188–189, 190, 205–206
    background assumptions 167–174; causal links 205–206
  content 192
  copulas 88, 88n, 193
  Dutch 151
  pseudo-cleft 88
  simplex 78–79, 90, 135–136, 155
    transitive clauses 78–79
  specifying 88
  structures 81–82
  with *Wh*-word 121, 121n
sentential negation *see* negation, sentential
shared models 12, 44, 68, 193
Siemund, Peter 163n, 167, 168n
simplex clauses *see* clauses, simplex
simplex sentences 78–79, 90, 135–136, 155; transitive clauses 78–79
single verbs 103–104; *see also* verbs
Sinha, Chris 7, 35n, 42, 217
small chance 43–44
so 53, 107, 199
social cognition 2n
social learning 3
somberen 102
space building 114n
Spanish 22
spatial cognition *see* cognition, spatial
speaker involvement, one dimensional scale of 205
speech:
  acts 15, 15n, 26, 104, 112,115, 116n, 120, 215
    theory of 14, 15; verbs of 107–108, 109–110, 161
  direct 113–114
  discourse 179
  indirect 114
    free 130
  parts of 157n

Index

spoken language *see* conversation
Spooren, Wilbert P. M. S. 55n, 133, 166
statements 15, 120, 129
Steels, Luc 4
Stein, Dieter 6
structural linguistics 6; *see also* linguistics
Stukker, Ninke 144, 145n, 206n, 207
subconstructions, network of 80; *see also* constructions
subject clauses *see* clauses, subject
subjectification 67, 212
   process of 6, 22, 40
subjective expressions 18, 19
subjectivity 4–5, 5n, 15n, 22, 23, 133
   complementation 80
   conceptualization 175
   frequency 129–131
   senses 28
subjects 87, 125
   complements, clauses 90
   noun phrases 88, 90
   second-person 124
subordinate clauses 82, 90, 95, 96, 96n, 119, 121; *see also* clauses
subordinating conjunctions 96n
subordination 90, 131
   complementation as 93
   complements 93
   matrix clauses 92
surface structure similarity 87, 89
Sweetser, Eve E. 164, 165. 166, 174, 178, 217
symbolic communication 4
symbolic units 102
synomyms 56
syntactic properties 36
syntactic relations:
   complementation 137–141
   construction-independent 139
   impersonal intersubjectivity 131
   sentences 138–139, 140–141
syntactic structure:
   abstract structures 82
   analysis 24, 87–88
   complementation constructions 113n
   complementation sentences, roles 210
   constructions 9, 82
   negative polarity 38, 60
   recursion 99
   theory 126
syntax 3n, 4, 26, 77, 102n
   auxillary, argumentation and 23–24
   complementation 119, 155

complementation constructions 154
constructional 25
history 87
semantics 38

Talmy, Leonard 146n
templates 120, 128, 129, 131, 158, 215
textual coherence relations 176–177
thematic cohesion, patterns of 151f
thematic continuity 151, 152
   patterns of 152
theory of mind 2n, 218–219
Therapy (Lodge) 72
think 84, 123
third person 106, 111, 115n, 116, 118
   complement-taking clauses 134
   expressions 108n, 110n
   matrix clauses 104–107, 109, 215
      onstage 11, 107, 114, 214
   mental spaces 117
   participants 128
   perspective 106f
   pronouns 123, 124t, 126t,
   subjects 128
Thompson, Sandra A. 82, 91, 92, 93, 95, 98, 99, 105, 110, 129, 131, 157
threaten 116, 116n, 117
thought, and negation 216
token frequency 102, 111
Tomasello, Michael 2, 2n, 3, 3n, 28, 35n, 42, 91, 92, 93, 99, 110, 111, 128, 131, 219
top-down syntactic analysis 82
topic continuity 62, 63–67, 89, 93, 119, 151–154
topos 12, 13, 17, 42, 43, 44, 47, 50, 52, 53, 56, 57, 59, 60, 142, 167–174, 175, 177, 179, 180, 184, 193, 195, 196, 197, 199, 202
   as default rule 58, 58n, 168, 173–174
traditional grammar 81; *see also* grammar
transfer 83n
transitive clauses 100; *see also* clauses
transitive verbs 86; *see also* verbs
   prototypical 100
Traugott, Elizabeth Closs 4, 6, 40, 50n, 66
truth conditions 13, 41, 44n, 48
   functions 15
   sentences 108
truth values 190
Tse, Polly 218
Turner, Mark 114n
type frequency 103, 110, 111, 125

Uit den Boogaart, Pieter C. 33n, 103n
usage events 6, 8, 16, 24, 26, 60, 111, 150
usage-based approach 24–25, 91
utterances:
   children 92
   connected 150
   extraction 128–129
   interpretation 8, 11–13, 14–16, 17, 18, 26, 35n, 46, 49, 76, 214
   linguistic 7, 42
   performative 110
   subjective 110

Van Belle, William 191, 195
Van den Toon, Maarten C. 86n, 100
Van der Horst, Joop 139, 140
Van der Horst, Kees 139, 140
Van der Mast, Niels 170
Van der Wouden, Ton 32, 55n
Van Hoek, Karen 6n, 128
Van Lambalgen, Michiel 217
Van Megen, Netty 195n
Vehrencamp, Sandra L. 8, 9
verbal communication 35n
verbs; *see also* CT-verbs; speech, acts
   argument position 81, 83
   causation 143
   clusters 23
   complement-taking 84
   copulas 133
   direct object clauses 100
   factive 117
   finite 137, 138
   independent 23
   main 90, 116
   matrix 80, 82
   modal 22
   phrases, non-finite 95n
   relationships between 102n
   single 103–104
   Wh-extraction with 123, 124
Verhagen, Arie 8, 23, 25, 35, 39, 44n, 67, 68n, 96n, 109n, 116, 116n, 126n, 128, 144, 145n, 151, 151n, 152, 153, 158n, 170, 212
viewing arrangements 5, 5f
viewpoints 26

   management of 35n
virtual argumentation *see* argumentation, virtual
vocal communication in animals 8
voices 35n
   in single utterances 114

waarschuwen 86
want (Dutch) 192, 192f, 193, 193, 194t, 195, 199, 200, 201, 202, 205, 206, 211
warn 86, 104, 116
Wh-elements 119
Wh-extraction 81, 119, 120–121, 121n, 125, 126, 129, 130, 131, 131n, 148n, 155, 189n, 216, 219
   Brown Corpus (English) 122
   complementation 128
   complementation constructions 124, 129
   network 127f
   complement-taking predicates in *de Volkskrant* 124t
   CT-verbs 125t
   examples 127
   long-distance *Wh*-movement 81, 119, 216
   matrix subjects 126t
   templates 129
   use by children 128
   verbs 123, 124
Wh-questions 128
Wh-word 121
   in complement clauses 122n
whether/if-clause 117n
Whitehead, Hal 3n
who 119
Wierzbicka, Anna 101n
Wittgenstein, Ludwig 9n
words 24
   argumentative character 80
   order 39
Wright, Susan 6
written language 93

zeggen 84
   with *Wh*-extraction 125
Zlatev, Jordan 217
zone of indifference 71